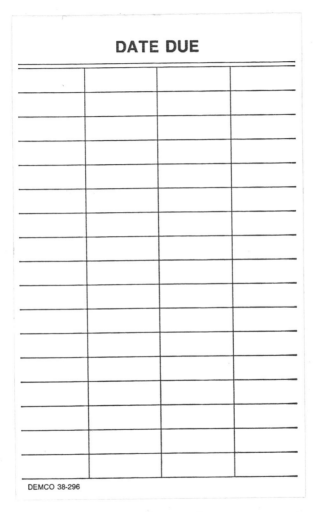

DATE DUE

The
United States,
Japan, and Asia

CONTRIBUTORS

C. MICHAEL AHO, Prudential Securities, Inc.

GERALD L. CURTIS, Columbia University

AKIRA IRIYE, Harvard University

MERIT E. JANOW, Columbia University

THOMAS L. MCNAUGHER, Brookings Institution

CHARLES E. MORRISON, East-West Center

MICHEL OKSENBERG, East-West Center

BRUCE STOKES, *National Journal*

EZRA F. VOGEL, National Intelligence Agency

R

THE AMERICAN ASSEMBLY
Columbia University

The
United States,
Japan, and Asia

GERALD L. CURTIS
Editor

W. W. NORTON & COMPANY
New York   London

First Edition

The text of this book is composed in Baskerville.
Composition and Manufacturing by the Haddon Craftsmen, Inc.

Library of Congress Cataloging-in-Publication Data

The United States, Japan, and Asia / Gerald L. Curtis, editor.
    p.   cm.
    "Prepared as background reading for an American Assembly program at Arden
House from November 11-14, 1993"—P. 2.
    Includes the Final report of the Eighty-fourth American Assembly.
    Includes bibliographical references and index.
    Contents: The United States and Japan in Asia / Akira Iriye—Trading with an
ally / Merit E. Janow—China and the Japanese-American alliance / Michel Oksenberg—Asian regionalism and U.S. interests / Bruce Stokes, C. Michael Aho—
Southeast Asia and U.S.-Japan relations / Charles E. Morrison—Japan as number
one in Asia / Ezra F. Vogel—U.S. military forces in East Asia / Gerald L. Curtis.
    1. United States—Relations—Japan. 2. Japan—Relations—United States.
3. United States—Relations—Asia. 4. Asia—Relations—United States.
5. Japan—Relations—Asia. 6. Asia—Relations—Japan. I. Curtis, Gerald L.
II. American Assembly.
E183.8.J3U735 1994
327.7305—dc20   94-15868

ISBN 0-393-03633-2
ISBN 0-393-96583-X (pbk)

W.W. Norton & Company, Inc., 500 Fifth Avenue, New York, N.Y. 10110
W.W. Norton & Company Ltd., 10 Coptic Street, London WC1A 1PU

1 2 3 4 5 6 7 8 9 0

Contents

The
United States,
Japan, and Asia

Preface

When President Clinton visited Tokyo in July 1993 for the annual G-7 summit meeting, he gave a speech at Waseda University in which he stressed the importance for the United States of building a Pacific community. In November 1993 he hosted in Seattle the first meeting ever of leaders of the major countries in the Asian-Pacific region organized in the Asia Pacific Economic Cooperation (APEC) forum. These events not only demonstrate an awareness on the part of the U.S. government of the importance of the Asian-Pacific. They also reflect the growing recognition among the American public that our relations with this region, the fastest area of economic growth in the world, are critical to the future well-being of our country.

The chapters in this volume are intended to provide Americans interested in U.S. relations with Asia with the data and analysis needed to understand why this region is so important to the United States and what choices we face in developing policies to deal with its dynamic economic developments and security concerns. The volume is unique, not only in being a comprehensive analysis of challenges to U.S. policy in the Asian-Pacific in the post–cold war era, but in its focus on U.S.–Japan relations in their regional context. Our relationship with Japan is now the most extensive and the most crucial one in Asia. How we relate to each other has an enormous impact on our policies toward the rest of the region. Similarly, how we approach regional issues and challenges can either strengthen or cause tensions in our bilateral relationship. Helping Americans understand the U.S.–Japan relationship in its regional Asian-Pacific context and the challenges posed to U.S. policy makers is a central purpose of this book. It also places the U.S.–Japan relationship in perspective of the rapidly growing importance of other Asian powers, especially China.

This volume, with its emphasis on U.S. policy, is the first of three that are planned for publication. The second will focus on Japanese policy in the Asian-Pacific and is being prepared in conjunction with an international conference to be held in Tokyo on that subject. The third is being prepared for a conference to be held in Singapore that will focus on the perspectives of countries other than the United States and Japan on the region's future.

This volume was prepared as background reading for an American Assembly program at Arden House from November 11–14, 1993, convened with joint sponsorship of The American Assembly and the Japan Center for International Exchange, under the leadership of its president, Tadashi Yamamoto. The meeting's report is included as an appendix, as is a list of participants, who came from eleven countries around the Pacific. The American Assembly and the JCIE have a long history of working together, going back to the first Shimoda conference on U.S.–Japan relations held in 1967.

The editor of this volume, Gerald L. Curtis, professor of political science at Columbia University, served as director of the Assembly program. He is among the most prominent American scholars of the region.

The American Assembly gratefully acknowledges the support of the following organizations in this undertaking.

Center for Global Partnership, Japan Foundation

The Henry Luce Foundation, Inc.

Rockefeller Brothers Fund

The Asia Foundation

United States–Japan Foundation

James D. Wolfensohn, Inc.

These organizations, as well as The American Assembly, take no positions on subjects presented in this book.

It is our belief and intention that this book fulfills the mandate of The Assembly's founder Dwight D. Eisenhower "to illuminate public policy," and will help citizens understand more fully the growing importance of Japan and the Asian-Pacific region to the United States. It is also the expectation of The Assembly in initiating this project that these papers would be of considerable usefulness in university and college courses, for research and public affairs institutions, and as background for the media as it undertakes its role of educating the public on the growing importance of Pacific Asia.

Daniel A. Sharp
President
The American Assembly

Introduction

GERALD L. CURTIS

T he chapters of this volume are all concerned with exploring various dimensions of U.S. interactions with Japan in Asia. They analyze what is arguably the most important bilateral relationship in the contemporary world in a region that is indisputably the world's most dynamic economic area. There are many studies of U.S.–Japan bilateral relations and growing numbers of studies

GERALD L. CURTIS is professor of political science at Columbia University. He served as director of Columbia's East Asian Institute for a total of twelve years between 1973 and 1990. Professor Curtis has written extensively both in English and Japanese on Japanese society and politics, foreign policy, and U.S. relations with Japan and Asia. His book *The Japanese Way of Politics* received the Masayoshi Ohira Memorial Prize for 1989. Professor Curtis is special adviser to *Newsweek* for *Newsweek Japan* and *Newsweek Korea*. He also is adviser and monthly columnist for the *Chunichi/Tokyo Shinbun* and was honored with the *Chunichi Shinbun* Special Merit Award in 1990. Professor Curtis is a member of the Advisory Council to the Center for Global Partnership of the Japan Foundation and the Board of Directors of the U.S.–Japan Foundation and the American Academy of Political Science. He is also a member of the Trilateral Commission, the Council on Foreign Relations, and the International

of U.S. and Japanese relations in the global economy. This volume fills an important lacuna in focusing its attention on the Asian region and asking questions about the future of U.S. policy there.

This volume gives equal weight to economic and political/security issues. Doing so is especially important now that the cold war has ended and economic competition has taken on new importance. In Asia as elsewhere there is an ongoing search for new approaches to deal with security issues and to foster economic cooperation. This effort to create a post–cold war structure is still in its early stages; the chapters in this book take up this theme, especially in the context of U.S.–Japan relations.

Akira Iriye goes back to the turn of the century to trace the roots of U.S.–Japan relations in Asia. He notes the commonality in U.S. and Japanese foreign policy early in the century as both sought to enter the ranks of the great powers. He then describes their growing antagonism over the issue of how to relate to the nationalism of the Third World, most especially nationalism in China.

Japanese views of China in narrow terms of military strategy and economic interests increasingly conflicted with American efforts to aid China's modernization. After the First World War there was a period when support for internationalism and for accommodating Third World countries within the new international order alleviated U.S.–Japanese animosity over China. But this did not last long. The Wall Street crash and subsequent Depression made it impossible for the United States to continue to aid China's nation building. The Japanese, for their part, goaded on by a military establishment growing ever stronger in political power, reasserted Japanese imperialism on the Asian continent.

The Japanese put their own twist on support for the Third World by advocating a pan-Asianism that argued that Japan would lead Asia to independence and prosperity by driving out Western imperialists. Iriye points out that some Japanese continued to hold this romantic notion of Japan's role in freeing Asia from Western colonialism despite the fact that Japan never in-

Institute for Strategic Studies. He is adviser and former director of the U.S.–Japan Parliamentary Exchange Program.

tended for Asia to become a region of independent nation states. Japan's objective, he argues, was to do away with independent states and put all of Asia under Japanese leadership. He points out that nationalist leaders in Asia understood this, and believed the defeat of Japanese imperialism was necessary to obtain independence. Thus they cooperated with the United States, Britain, and their allies in the war.

Iriye then goes on to analyze the shift in U.S. priorities in the context of the cold war, which essentially had the effect of freezing relations with China, producing large-scale military and economic assistance to non-Communist regimes in Asia, and fostering close cooperation between the United States and Japan. This was the context for the successful U.S.–Japan relationship of the cold war years.

Iriye concludes by asking whether the United States and Japan can cooperate in the post–cold war era in steering Asia's transformation in a desirable direction, or whether they will once again pursue divergent strategies and end up on a collision course. In Iriye's view, the answer to this question involves fundamental cultural issues. It is a question of whether Japan and the United States can pursue policies that would help transform Asia, and in the process obliterate the odious distinction between West and non-West, North and South, or the great powers and the Third World. That is both the challenge and the opportunity the two countries face in Asia.

Merit Janow focuses her attention on the bilateral U.S.–Japan economic relationship and especially on the issue of market access in Japan, a matter of concern not only to the United States but to other countries as well, especially to Asian countries that depend heavily on exports in their development strategies. Janow reviews the trade policy initiatives undertaken by the Bush and Clinton administrations to improve access to the Japanese market. She assesses the Bush administration's three-pronged approach to Japan on trade matters, involving multilateral, sectoral, and structural initiatives. She also stresses the growing support for a "results oriented" trade strategy during the Bush years, advocated in particular by American business leaders involved in the United States trade representative's (USTR) Advisory Committee on Trade Policy and Negotiations (ACTPN). In this regard, she reviews the semiconductor agreement and its provision for a 20 percent market share "target," and notes the controversy this approach provoked among senior officials in the Bush administration.

In Janow's view, the Uruguay Round, as important as it was for strengthening the General Agreement on Tariffs and Trade (GATT) system, did not address the particular problems of market access to Japan. Sectoral negotiations, on the other hand, are aimed at resolving specific problems of access to Japan and, in her view, were the most successful part of the Bush administration's Japan trade agenda, resulting in substantial increases in U.S. exports in the thirteen sectors covered by agreements concluded during the tenure of President Bush. She also refers to continuing issues of implementation of existing agreements, and points out the difficulty of measuring precisely the impact of government agreements on trade flows when there are so many other factors that affect market conditions.

Janow offers a positive assessment of the Structural Impediments Initiative (SII), arguing that it started a process of change in Japan that continues to this day. She notes the growing opposition to SII within the Japanese government and the gradual loss of enthusiasm for pressing forward with this approach on the part of the political leadership in both countries. In her view, the results of SII talks were significant, and might have become even more substantial if the level of political commitment to SII had been maintained in both the United States and Japan.

In regard to the Clinton administration, Janow reviews the president's tough rhetoric on Japanese trade policies, the emphasis on improving access for "strategic" sectors seen to be especially important for the future competitiveness of the nation, and the administration's support for new "super 301" legislation. She also notes, however, that the Clinton administration, as was the case with the Bush administration, opposes specific mandatory reductions in Japan's bilateral trade surplus with the United States. She also reviews the Clinton administration's positive assessment of the semiconductor accord as a successful example of a target-specific agreement, and the subsequent concerns that this provoked in Japan and elsewhere that the United States was embarking on a new trade strategy toward Japan that included the negotiation of specific market outcomes, irrespective of market forces.

Janow then turns to an analysis of the U.S.–Japan Framework for a New Economic Partnership (the "Framework" agreement) that President Clinton and Prime Minister Miyazawa concluded in July 1993. She reviews the various issues that are to be negotiated under the Framework and points out the rather large variety of approaches that might be available to policy makers in both the United States and Japan under the broad guidelines laid down in the Framework agreement.

Janow concludes with some observations about the challenges that face the United States and Japan as they seek to manage their trade relationship. This includes the successful conclusion of the Uruguay Round, coming to some agreement on how to measure "results" in market access, defining appropriate negotiating tactics and strategies, and distinguishing what can be accomplished in the short term from what can result only from longer-term macroeconomic adjustments. Finally, she warns that growing pressures in the United States to adopt tougher policies toward countries that do not provide access to their markets comparable to the access they enjoy in the United States can lead to shifts in U.S. trade policy that would further strain U.S.–Japan relations.

One of the most important challenges in Asia both to U.S. and to Japanese policy makers in the coming years is to devise approaches and policies toward China that strengthen, or at least do not jeopardize relations between Japan and the United States and that contribute to strengthening relations between China and both the U.S. and Japan. In his chapter on China and the Japanese-American alliance, Michel Oksenberg discusses what the United States and Japan have to do to meet successfully this challenge.

Developments subsequent to the June 1989 Tiananmen incident reflect the difficulties involved in keeping differences in U.S. and Japanese approaches to China from adversely affecting the U.S.–Japan relationship. The U.S. has pursued a confrontational approach in its dealings with China while at the same time rapidly increasing its trade and investment relationships there. The U.S. approach, Oksenberg emphasizes, has lacked coherence and consistency. The Japanese, for their part, have adopted a nonconfron-

tational stance, and they were in the forefront in restoring economic ties after Tiananmen. These differences have been kept
within manageable bounds, but opinion in Tokyo, as Oksenberg
points out, has become increasingly critical of the American approach. If the U.S. were to turn its harsh rhetoric toward China
into concrete sanctions, Japan in all likelihood would move away
from the U.S. to adopt a more independent stance toward China.

The possibility that the U.S. and Japan would go separate ways
in dealing with China in the post–cold war era draws an extra
measure of credibility for those familiar with the pre–World War
II history of East Asia that was characterized by fundamental differences over China policy between the United States and Japan.
That is to say from the late nineteenth century until 1945, Japan
and the U.S. adopted fundamentally different approaches toward
China, differences that were crucial factors leading up to the Japanese attack on Pearl Harbor, as described by Oksenberg.

After the Second World War, China became more a source of
cooperation between the U.S. and Japan as both countries developed their China policies to contain the threat of Soviet expansionism. Some Japanese were unhappy with the virtually complete
closing off of China in the 1950s and tried to keep lines of communication and a small trading relationship alive. Then in 1970 Japan
was shocked to learn of President Nixon's sudden and secret reversal of U.S. policy toward China. But Japan adjusted quickly to the
new reality and moved to normalize its own relations with China
while at the same time working closely with the U.S. to develop a
strategic triangle with China to counter Soviet expansion.

As Oksenberg points out, however, this long period of cooperation took place in the context of great asymmetry in U.S. and
Japanese power. Now that there is no longer an imminent Russian
threat and Japan no longer sees itself in as unambiguously a subordinate role to the U.S. as it did in earlier years, the challenges to
cooperation are much more difficult.

Oksenberg stresses in his chapter the importance of close but
quiet and nonprovocative consultations between the U.S. and
Japan about China policy. He also cautions both countries to
avoid the temptation to use China policy as a kind of card in
dealing with each other. Such an approach would give Beijing the

opportunity to play Washington and Tokyo against each other and well might raise the general level of tensions in the region. The lesson of history that Oksenberg stresses is that the United States and Japan share an interest in seeing China unified and effectively governed and integrated into the emerging Pacific community. Of course the question of what the U.S. and Japan should do in the way of developing new approaches to deal with China depends on what China does in its foreign policy. Oksenberg points to several enduring features of China's goals and attitudes in dealing with Japan and with the United States. He notes, among other things, Chinese determination to avoid dependence upon either the United States or Japan and the considerable degree of suspicion with which it views the motives of both the U.S. and Japan.

Oksenberg also discusses the domestic uncertainties that confront China. There is the question of what kind of leadership structure and what leaders will emerge after Deng Xiaoping is gone. There is also the question of what will happen to the Communist party itself given the fact that it is riddled with corruption and resented by the populace. How the central government will manage its relations with local regions and whether and, if so, how civilian leaders will exercise control over the military are also key questions facing China in the coming years. And there of course are enormously difficult questions of economic management that the regime has to confront. Oksenberg cites the need to reform the industrial sector, minimize the urban-rural income gap, and absorb vast numbers of new entrants into the job market.

The conclusions Oksenberg draws from this assessment of China's likely developmental course are not entirely reassuring. He sees the United States and Japan having to deal with a China that is culturally confident but socially undisciplined, economically vibrant and politically messy, huge in size but territorially amorphous, in short, a difficult neighbor whose cooperation is essential for regional and global stability and prosperity.

Nonetheless, Oksenberg concludes his analysis on a cautiously optimistic note. Washington and Tokyo currently are embracing approaches toward Beijing that differ in degree but not in kind. They are both aware that China is going to be a difficult partner to deal with in world affairs, and they are both conscious of the need to avoid conflict over China. There is a strong basis for the U.S. and Japan to cooperate in their approaches to China as long as they continue to recognize the need for consultation, extensive and high-level dialogue with China, and a mixture of realism and patience and firmness in dealing with the complex issues that China is certain to pose in the coming years.

Bruce Stokes and C. Michael Aho analyze the dynamic interactions among the Asian economies and their implications for the United States. Their message is straightforward: the United States government has to do more to engage the U.S. business community in the region, or the opportunity to be a key part of the fastest growing economic area in the world will be lost. Stokes and Aho stress the competitive dimensions of United States and Japanese involvement in the economic life of the Asian region, and the advantages the Japanese have in industries such as automobiles. They warn that the United States must reverse what they see as a trend of declining U.S. economic fortunes in the region, or Americans will not long support a major U.S. security role there.

Stokes and Aho stress the importance of building institutions in the Asian-Pacific that can encourage greater economic openness and cooperation among countries there. They argue the need for better coordination of macroeconomic policies, for more energetic government programs to encourage exports to the Asian-Pacific region, and for regional agreements on investment rules and codes of conduct for multinational corporations. They also emphasize the positive role that the Asia-Pacific Economic Cooperation organization (APEC) can play in defusing some of the tensions in the bilateral U.S.-Japan relationship and providing additional leverage on Japan to open its markets to more imports. They conclude by stressing that the most fundamental challenge faces the American public and American business, which must recognize that being able to compete with the dynamic economies of the Asian-Pacific region will require sacrifice and a recognition that the United States is no longer in a league of its own.

Charles Morrison looks at Southeast Asian views of Japan and at the implications of Japanese-Southeast Asian relations for the United States. He points out that traditional links between Southeast Asia and Japan were very weak, and that the four-year period of Japanese control during the Second World War created a legacy of hostility without producing any kind of positive Japanese cultural orientation among Southeast Asian elites. It was on such a base that Japan had to build its postwar relationships with Southeast Asian countries.

The turning point in Japan–Southeast Asian relations came with the riots against Prime Minister Tanaka in Bangkok and Jakarta in 1974. These events led both Japanese and Southeast Asians to put a great deal of effort into getting their relations onto a new and more constructive track. Those efforts have paid large dividends in strengthened ties between Japan and Southeast Asia. Morrison makes the especially important point that the Association of Southeast Asian Nations (ASEAN) sees Japan as an important counterweight to China and as the critical strategic link to the United States. Without Japan as a strategic partner, the United States' presence in the region would lose its credibility, Morrison emphasizes. Morrison gives many examples of the mutually beneficial economic relationship that is developing between Southeast Asia and Japan and their expanding cultural ties. While pointing to sources of conflict and controversy, he offers a generally upbeat assessment of Japan's relations in this part of Asia.

In looking at the implications for the United States of Japan's relations with Southeast Asia, Morrison points out that the United States supported expanded ties with Japan and Southeast Asia when Japan was relatively weak and the United States was the dominant power in the region, but that it now looks with concern at Japan's increasing influence in the region. Morrison finds American concerns to be exaggerated and more reflective of American ambivalence about its own position in the world than Japan's position in Southeast Asia. In conclusion, Morrison notes that Japanese still give priority to their relationship with the United States, that Southeast Asian leaders are sometimes frustrated by what appears to them to be an unnecessary degree of Japanese deference to the United States, and that the issue for the United States is not to attempt somehow to limit Japan's role in the region, but to ensure an appropriate and consistent level of U.S. engagement in the region.

Ezra Vogel traces the evolution of Japanese policy in China and

Southeast Asia from the reparations agreements of the 1950s and the early development of Japanese export markets in Asia to the investments in Asia of the 1980s for exports to the rest of the world. Vogel underscores the economic thrust of Japanese policy in the region and the reluctance to exercise political leadership there. One question is how much the end of the cold war and Japan's search for a larger role in international affairs will change this pattern of relations between Japan and Asia. Vogel concludes by noting that although Japan is likely to emphasize strengthening relations with the rest of Asia in its foreign policy, its governmental and business leadership are well aware that Japan's major economic and security interests lie with the United States. For some time to come, Japan is likely to be number one in Asia, and to rank relations with the United States as the number one priority of its foreign policy.

Thomas McNaugher focuses his attention on U.S. strategic interests in Asia. He notes the uncertainties that characterize the region and that surround the missions of U.S. military forces there. McNaugher's view is that in addition to its role in defending Korea and Japan, U.S. forces have a role to play in encouraging China's cooperative engagement with its neighbors.

McNaugher discusses the sharply opposed globalist and realist perspectives on international relations, the former optimistically envisaging a world pacified by economic integration, the latter seeing disintegration proceeding from the end of cold war bipolarity and the erosion of U.S. economic hegemony. Even realists, McNaugher notes, recognize that with the existence of nuclear weapons and the global spread of technology, new approaches to thinking about security are needed. Nowhere is this truer than in Asia where, as McNaugher stresses, the United States is better positioned to deal with the region's key security problems than are the regional powers themselves.

In the case of Japan, McNaugher stresses the buffer role the United States plays between Japan and its neighbors. A break in the U.S.-Japan security relationship would not only create instability in the region, but might produce instability in Japan itself, since it would force Japan to confront security issues that it has been able to avoid due to the presence of the U.S. nuclear umbrella. McNaugher argues that the United States and Japan have two choices. They can try to sustain the security relationship in the absence of an identifiable threat, or they can allow Japan to become more like other countries at the risk of destabilizing the region. This issue has not been faced squarely. With the U.S.–Japan security relationship seemingly being sustained more by its own momentum than by rigorous strategic analysis, the problem of Japan, McNaugher argues, remains to be faced.

McNaugher's major focus, however, is on China, which, with its central location, vast population, and rapidly growing economy, is East Asia's strategic center of mass, the region's "natural hegemon," in McNaugher's view. Tensions between China and its neighbors are likely to grow, McNaugher maintains, as China grows stronger and richer, making relative gains that will be seen as threatening by Japan and Russia in particular. McNaugher emphasizes that concern over China arises not necessarily from assumptions of Chinese malevolence, but from uncertainties about the future course and policies of a state of enormous size and power potential. The dilemma is that smaller neighbors cannot hope to match China's power, and larger neighbors, Russia and Japan, may try to match it by relying on nuclear weapons. None of this is likely to serve U.S. or regional interests in stability.

McNaugher points out that the challenges posed by China and Japan are exacerbated by East Asia's notable lack of overarching multilateral security institutions, and this in turn reflects the traditionally weak sense of regional identity and of regional economic integration in East Asia. Even where regional coordination has occurred, it has taken the shape of what McNaugher refers to as "multiple bilateral" interactions rather than multilateral discussions, with the United States often playing the role of mediator between local states.

McNaugher stresses the important role U.S. military and economic engagement can play in balancing Chinese power, and thereby countering the forces now driving East Asia's "fledgling arms race," gaining some leverage over Sino-Russian tensions, and potentially having great leverage over Japan's response to China's growing power. In McNaugher's view, U.S. engagement thus substantially improves the prospects for regional stability.

The U.S. goal should be to help "to bring China into the world in a productive way, as part of the global economy and, ideally, as a cooperative partner in security discussions at both the global and regional levels." The question is what kinds of leverage can the United States bring to bear to coax China toward such goals. Economic leverage is limited. Conditioning most favored nation (MFN) treatment or in other ways "punishing" China for behavior the United States finds abhorrent can stimulate the kind of regionalism the United States should be seeking to avoid, and hurt U.S. business interests more than anything else.

As far as military and strategic leverage is concerned, McNaugher stresses the importance of involving China in nuclear arms control dialogues, of finding ways to build constraints on the expansion of China's conventional forces, and of engaging China in discussions with Japan and others aimed at maximizing cooperation in dealing with the issue of eventual Korean unification. McNaugher also reiterates the importance of the U.S.–Japan security relationship in dealing with China, and he stresses the importance of ameliorating economic tensions in order to obtain U.S. public support for continued military alliance with Japan.

McNaugher's conclusion is that "the central strategic challenge in East Asia is that of accommodating China" and coaxing it into a constructive, cooperative regional and global role. In order to do that, there must be continued U.S. military involvement in East Asia. It is not possible to say now what the specific shape of the U.S. force structure in the region should be several years from now. But it is certain that without the United States being engaged militarily and economically, Asia will become a more unstable and dangerous region.

In the concluding chapter, I examine the importance of Asia to the United States and Japan, analyze alternative visions being proposed for U.S. policy in Asia in a post–cold war era, and make a number of suggestions for how the United States should develop its relationships with Japan in the context of a broader Asian policy. The end of the cold war and the end of an era of U.S. economic dominance raise important questions both about what is actually happening in Asia, and what policies the United States should adopt to deal with the dynamic and changing Asian scene.

Asia's economic achievements have been dramatic, and they have made this region the fastest growing economic area in the world. Part of the challenge in analyzing Asia's regional economy is to maintain a balanced view of what is going on. Extreme views are popular because they are sensational and dramatic. Thus there is much talk about a "power shift" across the Pacific to Asia comparable to the shift in economic power from Europe across the Atlantic to the United States earlier in this century. There is also much talk about Japan's economic "hegemony" in Asia, and the U.S. "failure" to be economically competitive there.

Yet the reality is much more complex. Economic power is becoming more diffuse, with the share of world gross national product produced by countries in the Asian region now approaching that of North America and Western Europe. This is an important development, but not a power shift from one side of the Pacific to the other. Moreover, trends in Asia do not suggest growing Japanese hegemony. Japan is the most important country in the region economically, and is certain to remain in that position for some time to come. But China's rapid growth and the explosive expansion of trade and investment among Asian countries are evidence of the region's dynamism. The United States is also important for Asia economically and Asia has grown in importance for the U.S. economy. The United States continues to be the largest export market for most Asian countries. It also is a significant investor in Asia. Japan is the largest overseas market for U.S. exports, and over 40 percent of total U.S. exports goes to countries that lie on the other side of the Pacific Ocean. The challenge to the United States is to improve its competitive position in this, the fastest growing region of the world.

There are several fundamentally different perspectives on U.S. policy in Asia vying for support in the United States. I review the key ones: the view of those who optimistically maintain that economic integration will create such strong vested interests in maintaining stable relationships that tensions and conflicts are bound to be contained; those who argue quite the opposite, that the United States should retreat from its intimate relationship with Japan and assume the position of a balancer of a regional balance of power; and those who believe that the policies pursued by the United

States during the cold war remain basically sound even in the new international environment that now exists.

I suggest that a framework for U.S. policy toward Japan in Asia should consist of several major components: strengthening U.S. economic competitiveness; continuing the alliance with Japan; encouraging the development of APEC and other multilateral mechanisms and approaches to deal with economic issues; developing more extensive consultative mechanisms with Japan on key regional issues; and promoting new arms control arrangements in the region. I stress the importance of responding positively to the growing interest in Asia in the development of new multilateral mechanisms to deal with regional economic and security issues, and I also emphasize the need to work closely with Japan in pursuing our interests in the region. The basic challenge to U.S. policy in Asia is to find realistic ways to play a leadership role in the region that promotes regional stability and economic growth and serves U.S. national interests. Its goal should be to weave a complex web of entangling relationships with Japan and China and with other countries that encompass commercial, financial, political, and security affairs. The United States can accomplish this goal only if it is an active player—in all these dimensions—in Asia.

1

The United States
and Japan in Asia:
A Historical Perspective

AKIRA IRIYE

The Emergence of a Tridimensional World

One useful way of looking at the history of U.S.–Japanese relations is to put it in the framework of two large themes in modern international relations: the emergence of the two nations as great powers, and the growing assertiveness of what is called the Third World. What is remarkable about these themes is that they made their appearance at about the same time, i.e., the end of the nineteenth century and the beginning of the twentieth. Thus from the moment that the United States and Japan emerged as major powers in the world arena, they were faced with the question of how best to meet the challenge of the Third World. The often troubled pattern of U.S.–Japanese relations in Asia can best be understood in such a context.

AKIRA IRIYE is Charles Warren Professor of American History and director of the Edwin O. Reischauer Institute of Japanese Studies at Harvard University. He has held Woodrow Wilson, Guggenheim, and ACLS Fellowships, and was president of the American Historical Association in 1988. Dr. Iriye is the author of several books in both Japanese and English, most recently *China and Japan in the Global Setting*.

Until toward the end of the nineteenth century, world affairs had been dominated by the European powers. They were called "great powers" because of their unrivaled military power, their involvement in all parts of the globe through their colonies and other forms of control, their worldwide economic activities (trade, shipping, investment), and their cultural influence (in such areas as technology, ideology, religion, scholarship, and arts and letters). They entered into various alliances and agreements among, and frequently against, each other, but even such division did little to lessen the overall superiority of the European powers, for no outsider was able or willing to take advantage of it. Moreover, the powers were often united on colonial issues, entering into several ententes to protect their respective colonies and spheres of influence. Neither the United States nor Japan could be considered a great power in such terms, not to mention other countries and regions. Africa, the Middle East, Asia, the Pacific, and the Western Hemisphere (even including the United States) were receptacles of European power and influence. None of them involved itself in global affairs.

In one of the most remarkable coincidences in modern history, the United States and Japan challenged this pattern of European supremacy at about the same time, from the 1890s through the first years of the new century. The former annexed Hawaii and the Philippines, established a protectorate over Cuba and other Caribbean countries, and quickly developed a modern navy, while the latter fought wars against China and Russia, acquired Taiwan and South Sakhalin, obtained exclusive rights in southern Manchuria, and annexed Korea. Japan's navy established itself as the most powerful in the western Pacific, replacing the hitherto dominant positions held by the British and Russian navies, just as the U.S. Navy challenged British and German naval power in the Western Hemisphere.

The great powers of Europe might have responded to the challenge of the newcomers in unison, by cooperating to keep the United States and Japan, or at least one of them, in check. Instead, the European nations solicited their cooperation both in colonial matters and in their antagonistic alliance systems. Britain's alliance with Japan and solicitousness of the United States in Asian and Caribbean affairs are good examples. In other words, the United States and Japan were welcomed and coopted into the existing system of international relations. Neither Washington nor Tokyo resisted such overtures; after all, the two nations had decided to become great powers, and that status by definition entailed playing the game of big-power politics. Both the United States and Japan would undertake further naval armament, seek to extend their influence over nearby areas, play a role in affairs farther away, and expand trade and investment activities abroad. International politics that had been dominated by Europe would now become trilateralized, an arena for a tridimensional exercise of power and influence. One characteristic of twentieth-century world affairs, tridimensionality, had clearly emerged.

The Awakening of the Third World

Even so, it could be argued that at least until 1914, European affairs were dealt with by the Europeans without much direct interference by Americans or Japanese. That the United States and Japan had emerged as world powers neither prevented nor brought about the eruption of the European war, and to that extent the impact of the two new powers was still limited. (One could argue, of course, that even before 1914 the two new powers had assured Britain of their neutrality in the event of a European war and enabled the British navy to be concentrated closer to home, thereby making the position of Britain and its allies, France and Russia, more belligerent toward Germany and its allies than it might have been otherwise. But neither the United States nor Japan was involved in three of the immediate causes of the war: the Balkan crisis, the French-German dispute over Alsace-Lorraine, and the colonial question involving the disposition of Morocco and other parts of North Africa.)

It was, rather, in the Third World, especially in Asia and the Pacific, that the new power of the United States and Japan made itself felt. No sooner had they decided to acquire overseas colonies than they found themselves fighting colonial wars, the former in the Philippines and the latter in Taiwan. The anticolonialist sentiments in these countries combined with an antiforeignism of the more traditional sort in China (the Boxer uprising), and gave rise to an incipient Third World nationalism confronting the United States and Japan, as well as the European powers, with a serious challenge. Because the great-power status of Europe, the United States, and Japan had taken the form of colonial acquisitions, the maintenance of this status would hinge, to a great extent, on their handling of Third World nationalism. They could cooperate in meeting the challenge, whether forcefully suppressing nationalistic movements or somehow responding to them in a more accommodating fashion, or they could act separately, each devising its own policy toward this phenomenon. For the United States and Japan, in particular, the test would come in Asia and the Pacific, where their newly acquired colonies and spheres of influence lay, and where their emergence as great powers had the effect of awakening nationalistic sentiments. In the end, the two nations' failure to work together in dealing with this phenomenon was to prove of fateful consequence.

One can see this already during the first years of the twentieth century. To be sure, the United States and Japan did cooperate in a number of areas. They joined the European powers in sending an international expedition to China in 1900 to suppress the Boxers. The resulting Boxer protocol provided for the payment of indemnities to the powers and gave them the right to station troops in the Peking-Tientsin area to safeguard the capital's access to the sea. Washington did not encourage Korean nationalists when they turned to them for help against Japanese ambitions, any more than Tokyo aided Aguinaldo in his struggle against American rule in the Philippines. The Taft-Katsura memorandum of 1905 specified that the United States would not interfere with Japan's protectorate over Korea, and that Japan in its turn would not meddle in Philippine affairs. In 1908 another note (the Root-Takahira agreement) reaffirmed the two powers' commitment to upholding the status quo in the Pacific. In 1910, when Japan formally annexed Korea, the United States made no response.

Already at this time, however, divergent approaches to China, and to Third World nationalism in general, were becoming apparent. Japan was determined to "manage" Taiwan, Korea, southern Manchuria, and South Sakhalin so as to assist the home country economically and militarily. Japanese leaders viewed their home-land as overcrowded and poor in resources, including food. The new colonies and spheres of influence would provide the nation with a steady supply of food and raw materials that it needed to undertake industrialization, as well as markets to sell manufac-tured items. Furthermore, the empire was strategically situated to cope with an imaginary threat, which initially was assumed to lie in Russia but increasingly came to imply the United States.

The idea that Third World areas were to serve the economic and strategic interests of "metropolitan" nations was nothing ex-ceptional and was accepted by all the great powers, including the United States. They shared a hierarchical view of the world, with the West defined as the most powerful and the most "civilized," the definitions of power and civilization being interchangeable at that time. Other countries were accorded lower ranks in propor-tion to the degrees of their "civilizedness." Japan was among the top group because it was "civilized"; it was "civilized" because it was powerful. (There was, to be sure, much debate then, as now, as to whether Western civilization and Japanese civilization were essentially similar or qualitatively different. In the context of our discussion, however, their differences were less critical than the fact that Japan had joined the ranks of the great, "civilized" pow-ers.)

Europe, the United States, and Japan thus collectively estab-lished their superiority over the rest of the world. Their self-identi-fication as the most powerful, the richest, and the most advanced would not change for a long time. Americans and Japanese did not differ on this point. Where they did begin to diverge was on the question of whether the two nations should jointly try to respond to the awakened nationalism of Third World countries, especially China. Once the Boxers had been suppressed, the Ch'ing court made some belated attempts at political and economic reform, including the setting up of a constitutional regime. Late Ch'ing reformers were ardent nationalists and sought to "recover national rights," as they said, rights that had been lost to the imperialist powers. Other groups and individuals in China despaired of sig-nificant reforms under the dynasty and began advocating its over-throw and replacement by a republican government. Regardless of specific agendas and ideologies, these Chinese were engaging themselves in "nation-building" efforts, to turn their traditional society into a modern nation. China was not the only country thus engaged in modernizing efforts; Turkey and Persia in the Middle East, Siam in Asia, and, although not quite in the same category, American states like Mexico and Brazil were similarly active. But China was the most conspicuous example because of its size, its history, and its potential power and resources. If modernization worked there, others would follow, and the whole Third World would be transformed.

Should the great powers welcome and encourage such transformation? Or should they fear the consequences of the rise of the Third World? Did they have any choice in the matter in any event?

One interesting thing about the United States' policy toward the Third World was that, more than any other power, it had assumed it did have a choice, that it could make a difference in the destiny of Third World countries, and, therefore, that it was possible to steer them toward a less violent and more constructive direction of change.

This was already becoming apparent in U.S. approaches to China in the early years of the century. While the sense of great-power superiority did not change, and while the United States continued to enjoy special privileges in China like other powers, there also developed an approach that sought to extend American economic and cultural influence in such a way as to help promote that country's nation-building efforts. One can see this in the steady stream of American educators, doctors, and philanthropists who crossed the Pacific and joined missionaries already there in various attempts to reform the educational and medical practices in China. There was also the movement of students and scholars in the opposite direction. One should recall that the United States was the first power to remit the unpaid balance of the Boxer indemnity to China so that the latter would use the funds to send students to American colleges and universities. In the meantime, the American business community as well as the government in Washington welcomed China's economic modernization efforts. As Secretary of War William Howard Taft declared in a speech in Shanghai in 1908:

I am not one of those who view with alarm the effect of the growth of China with her teeming millions into a great industrial empire. . . . [It] is a pleasure to know and to say that in every improvement which [China] aims at, she has the deep sympathy of America, and that there never can be any jealousy or fear on the part of the United States due to China's industrial or political development, provided always that it is directed along the lines of peaceful prosperity and the maintenance of law and order and the rights of the individual, native or foreign.[1]

Here, in a nutshell, was a statement of the United States' basic policy toward China, and by extension toward other Third World countries. It is not surprising that under Taft, various activities were undertaken by American bankers and businesspeople to help China's economic transformation.

Nor is it surprising that it was around this time that tensions grew between the United States and Japan in China. Not that the Japanese were in strong opposition to the kind of ideas Taft expressed. After all, they were themselves busily engaged in various educational and economic projects in their colonies, just as Americans were trying to modernize the Philippines. But the Japanese felt they, too, had a special stake in China's transformation, and thought the United States was interfering with their work. Part of the sentiment was historical, derived from the shared literary tradition of the two Asian countries. There was a sentiment that the Japanese "knew" more about China than others because they used the same characters. Moreover, as the only Asian country that had successfully modernized itself, Japan, it was thought, had much to teach others in the region. Western words and concepts like "society," "sovereignty," "citizenship," even "nation" had first been translated into Japanese (in Chinese characters) and then exported to China. After Japan's victory over China in 1895, thousands of young Chinese had come to study at Japanese schools, universities, and military academies.

This sense of special relations based on cultural affinity was, however, seriously challenged not only by the Americans but also by many in China who resented Japan's growing power and influence and who turned to the United States to balance it. From around 1910, more Chinese students went to the United States than to Japan to study. Chinese nationalists eyed America's superior economic power and sought to make use of it to undermine

Japan's special position in southern Manchuria. In contrast to the Japanese, the Americans were confident of their economic affluence and their ultimate success in the China market so long as the principle of the "open door" prevailed, and the Chinese encouraged the infusion of American capital and technology. The Japanese were clearly on the defensive, knowing full well that they could never compete with the Americans in this regard. While both participated in an international banking consortium to lend money to China, Japan was heavily in debt and could spare little outside its colonies and spheres of influence, whereas the United States, though still a net capital importer, had a much stronger private sector intent on investing in Chinese railway development, among other projects.

When the revolution of 1911 overthrew the Ch'ing dynasty—ironically, it was triggered by the local gentry's opposition to the dynasty's railway construction scheme with funds borrowed from the powers—it was the United States, not Japan, that inspired the revolutionaries and gave them a model after which to pattern their new government. The Japanese had, of course, not been unaware of internal developments in China and even secretly subsidized some revolutionaries. But Japan's policy after 1911 was imperialistic, involving an attempt at detaching the Manchurian provinces from China proper and otherwise taking advantage of the Chinese turmoil to extend its control. The United States under President Woodrow Wilson was the first major power to extend recognition to the new Republic of China, America's "sister republic," as many referred to it. Here was, from the American perspective, clearly a Third World country trying to turn itself into a modern nation, and it seemed axiomatic that the United States should take the initiative to help the effort.

Competition for Asia's Future

This historical background has been offered at some length as it helps explain much that followed in U.S.–Japanese relations. By the time World War I broke out—an event that confirmed Europe's relative decline in international politics and the rise to greater influence of the United States and Japan—these two powers had already begun to pursue different policies with regard to China, and by implication toward other Third World countries. Whereas Japan continued to view China narrowly, in terms of its military strategy and economic interests, the United States had taken steps to incorporate an agenda for Chinese modernization into its Asian policy. The Great War if anything accentuated the differences. Japan declared war on Germany, drove German forces out of Shantung province as well as from Pacific islands such as the Marianas, the Carolinas, and the Marshalls, and imposed on China a series of demands (the "twenty-one demands") that, if accepted *in toto*, would have turned that country into Japan's protectorate. The United States, in contrast, was eager to promote China's railway and industrial development and to aid its nation building by sending advisers and establishing schools. Many Chinese reformers—Young China as they were called—considered the United States their spiritual home; some had studied there, and others had been students in American funded institutions at home. Japan, in contrast, represented aggressive imperialism that had no interest in seeing China develop as a modern nation. No wonder that U.S.–Japanese relations deteriorated during the war—despite the fact that the two nations became nominal allies in 1917 as the United States entered the war against Germany.

China, too, joined the allies in the war. This fact was of momentous significance, as it enabled the country to emerge from the hostilities as one of the victors over the mighty German empire. In this regard, the Paris peace conference was a real landmark. For the first time, as a Chinese historian noted recently, China participated in "the process of shaping a new international order." The Chinese believed that "China was coming out of subordination and capitulations to be accepted by the West as a member . . . of the emerging international society."[2] The United States obviously welcomed such a development, President Wilson's wartime and postwar proclamations clearly indicating support for the "national aspirations" of China and other countries whose destinies had hitherto been controlled by outside powers. Although the Wilsonian principle of "national self-determination" was not meant to be applied literally to all colonial and dependent peoples, the message was unambiguous. The United States would espouse

the rights and interests of Third World countries as a key aspect of
the new international order. It was not that the distinction between the great powers and the Third World would be obliterated.
The United States itself would retain its status as a great power,
perhaps the greatest power in the aftermath of the European war.
The American proposed League of Nations contained a council
whose permanent members were to consist of the United States,
Japan, and three European nations. But the League would be
open to all other independent states, and besides, it would turn the
former colonies of Germany and the Ottoman empire into mandated territories, rather than distributing them among the victors.
The idea was that eventually, the mandates would be able to gain
full sovereignty. (One of them, Iraq, attained independence as
early as 1932.)

Given such a policy on America's part, Japan's insistence at the
peace conference on maintaining its forces in Shantung and inher-
iting German rights there could not have done more to illustrate
the contrast between the two nations' approaches to China. Japan
was still behaving within the framework of big-power control over
the Third World, whereas the United States was intent upon rede-
fining that relationship, to bring both groups of nations into a
larger international community. That community might still be
led by the powers, but they would now cooperate to assist other
countries to develop politically and economically. Japan's policy in
Shantung showed that it was not interested in such a project. It is
to be recalled that this was the time when the United States Congress passed a law to prepare the Philippines for eventual independence—and when Japanese authorities brutally suppressed an
uprising in Korea seeking an end to Japan's rule.

An Internationalist Solution

If the divergent approaches of the United States and Japan to
the Third World had remained, the two nations might have found
themselves in serious conflict within a short span of time. A potential U.S.—Japanese clash over China at this time was avoided,
however, as all three countries accepted, partially if not totally, the
postwar international order. Japan, which initially had not ac-

cepted it, came around by the time of the Washington conference of 1921–22, which was convened to discuss both big-power and Third World (Asia and the Pacific) questions. A major achievement in the former category was the naval treaty limiting the sizes of the navies of the United States, Japan, Britain, France, and Italy. In the latter category, numerous agreements were worked out to promote China's development in the framework of international cooperation. By then Japan's leaders had come to accept the inevitable; they could not afford to antagonize the United States. Although Japan had emerged from the European war as a net creditor nation, and its export trade had expanded phenomenally, it was still far behind the United States and most European countries in per capita income and other indicators of wealth. Japan's need for China's resources and markets was as great as ever, but, given the latter's awakened nationalism and America's support for it, it would be unrealistic to continue unilateral, imperialistic practices. Rather, it would make more sense to emulate, belatedly, the American example and court Chinese goodwill.

Whether this meant a fundamental shift in Japanese policy toward the Third World can be debated. Much depends on how one views the Washington conference. If it can be said to have laid the groundwork for a new regional order in Asia and the Pacific as a subsystem of the postwar international order, then it seems clear that Japan was very much part of it and, hence, its approach to China was also different from the earlier, more blatant imperialism. If, on the other hand, one argues, as a Chinese historian did recently, that "the break with the pre-war past was by no means complete, and a new order worthy of the name was yet to emerge,"[3] then it follows that Japanese policy remained essentially the same. After all, Japan's colonial empire was kept intact throughout the 1920s, and its special interests in Manchuria were asserted time and again.

Nevertheless, there are grounds for arguing that U.S.–Japanese–Chinese relations were never the same after World War I because the overall international community was now much more ready to accommodate Third World countries. To be sure, this postwar internationalism was rather loosely defined. For one thing, the League of Nations, the symbol of postwar international-

ism, had to do without U.S. participation. Neither did Britain or
Japan always defer to the League for solving contentious issues.
Nevertheless, there were mechanisms, such as the Washington
conference treaties, that supplemented the League and established
a basis for international cooperation. As if to anticipate the Kel-
logg-Briand pact of 1928, which was a typical internationalist document of the time in that the signatories pledged not to use force as
a means for settling disputes, Japan withdrew its forces from Shantung, and the United States its marines from Central American
countries. Moreover, American individuals and groups were very
active in promoting economic and cultural internationalism.
Bankers were busy internationalizing U.S. economic affairs, while
scholars, artists, tourists, and students built extensive networks for
cultural exchange. They met and worked closely with their counterparts elsewhere, including Japanese bankers and intellectuals.
American, Japanese, and Chinese men and women met at the
League and at other institutions such as the Institute of Pacific
Relations to discuss political and cultural matters of mutual concern. (This was the time when American women, having acquired
the right to vote, spearheaded the movements for peace, internationalism, and social issues like birth control. They found willing
converts among Japan's and China's increasingly urbanized and
educated women.) It was also at this time that Japan, Britain, and
others emulated the United States and remitted Boxer indemnity
funds to China, further enabling them to promote educational and
cultural exchanges with the latter. While such instances of internationalism did not in themselves guarantee a long period of stable
U.S.–Asian relations, they at least pointed to an alternative approach to the kind of animosity that had characterized prewar and
wartime Japanese relations with China and with the United States.

China's Nation Building Frustrated

China, as the most conspicuous of the Third World countries,
was in many ways a test case of the new internationalism. If it
worked there, it would be feasible elsewhere. As of 1929 it did
seem as if the United States, Japan, and other powers were intent
on coordinating their policies toward China, now under the Kuo-

mintang regime. They all recognized the latter and signed commercial treaties explicitly restoring tariff autonomy to that nation. Negotiations for the termination of foreigners' extraterritorial privileges also began. In the meantime, the powers, in particular the United States, sent experts in finance, taxation, bridge construction, and other fields as advisers to Nanking. The Nanking government still faced enormous obstacles in building China as a modern nation. Some historians have argued that while China now had a state, it had not yet become a nation, not to mention a power. Nevertheless, all signs pointed to its eventual emergence as a unified, modernized nation state—if favorable international circumstances prevailed.

Unfortunately, this prerequisite was not fulfilled in the 1930s. Internationalism, the essential condition for China's successful nation building, collapsed, and it found itself a victim of renewed foreign aggression as well as a global economic crisis, forcing it to remain weak and underdeveloped—in other words, in Third World conditions—much longer than would otherwise have been the case.

The United States and Japan were directly, if differently, responsible for China's plight. The Wall Street crash and the consequent Depression made it virtually impossible for the United States to continue to aid China financially; the government in Washington was so preoccupied with the domestic economic crisis that it even countenanced action, such as the Silver Purchase Act of 1934, that caused serious damage to the Chinese economy. The Chinese effort at economic modernization was stalled, and the central government lacked sufficient revenue to unify the country administratively. In a way, the United States was abandoning its policy of promoting nation building in Asia and elsewhere, at least for the time being; with the earlier optimism and self-confidence gone, it was no time for maintaining a sustained strategy toward the Third World.

If the United States found it difficult to aid China's nation building, Japan reverted to the practice of frustrating the project outright. The fear of China becoming a unified, modernized nation was a theme that ran through all phases of renewed Japanese imperialism on the continent. Whereas the civilian authorities during the 1920s had accepted the idea of China developing as a modern nation, the military and their supporters were determined to block the development, reasoning that a politically and economically modernized China would be incompatible with Japan's own requirements, especially as the Depression was spreading worldwide. To deal with China's apparently inevitable modernization in an internationalist framework was not going to work, the military argued, for the very reason that internationalism and China's nation building had become interchangeable. Rather, Japan must once again act unilaterally to protect its own position in Asia, an objective that necessitated control over the continent's resources and markets. This was the same type of anti-Third World logic that had characterized earlier Japanese imperialism, but now it seemed to gain even greater urgency as Chinese public opinion was much more nationalistic, and as the globe was fast becoming divided into economic blocs.

All groups in China bitterly denounced the new Japanese aggression that threatened to nullify the recent efforts at nation building. As they could no longer count on the friendly support of the United States, they turned in other directions and sought to obtain aid where they could: from Germany, the Soviet Union, and Britain. Ultimately, however, the Chinese would have to save their nation by themselves, and, as recent studies show, the desperate struggle to develop technology, industry, and commerce against all odds gave rise to a large number of experts in and out of government who would play important roles in China's economic rehabilitation and development under the Communists.

While Japan brutally suppressed Chinese nationalism, it also tried to turn Asia against the West. The pan-Asianist rhetoric of the 1930s was, in a way, Japan's answer to the Third World question. If China, Southeast Asian countries, and other parts of Asia were suffering from years of misgovernment and underdevelopment, Japanese propagandists asserted, it was because they had for too long been subjugated by the West. The time had come for all Asians to unite and rise together to put an end to Western domination. Japan, of course, would take the lead because it had already successfully accomplished the task. It would show the way to other Asian countries so that they would all cooperate to create "a new East Asian culture," as the Showa Research Association declared.[4] Takada Yasuma, a well-known sociologist, wrote that a reunified Asian world would aim at eliminating poverty, eradicating oppression, and putting an end to racial inequality. Royama Masamichi, a political science professor at Tokyo Imperial University, argued that a new Asia must aim at industrial development, popular welfare, and the advancement of science and technology. Such ideas suggest that Japan's ideologues were aware of the need to put the aggression in China in the context of a policy toward the Third World. In other words, the Chinese war was justified as an attempt to end the West's long suppression of Asian aspirations. It was as if one of the great powers had broken rank and decided to identify itself with Third World causes.

That view would be echoed even after Japan lost the war. Many Japanese, particularly of the wartime generation, still harbor the idea that the Great East Asian War, as the nation called the Asian-Pacific theater of the Second World War, helped liberate Asians from Western colonialism. The reality, of course, was far otherwise. Japan's pan-Asianism, even as an ideal, did not envision an Asia consisting of independent nations. Rather, Japanese spokespersons emphasized the problematic nature of modern nationalism and insisted that new Asia under Japanese leadership would do away with sovereign states. Instead, the whole region would become an integrated whole, with each contributing its part to the general well-being. This sort of regionalism, it was argued, would help avoid inevitable clashes of national interests and promote the welfare of all. The vision was clearly at odds with the nation-making aspirations of Chinese and other Asians and, therefore, inherently anti–Third World. The Asians knew it; except for a few "collaborators," they were under no illusion that Japan's replacement of Western colonialism would hasten their independence. On the contrary, nationalistic leaders in China, Korea, Southeast Asia, India, and elsewhere believed the defeat of Japanese imperialism was an essential condition for attaining their goals, and cooperated with the United States, Britain, and their allies in the war.

Decolonization

Contrary to such expectations, however, the Western powers did not fight against Japan and its Axis partners (Germany and Italy) in order to bring freedom to the Third World. To be sure, the United States reaffirmed the Wilsonian principle of self-determination, and the Atlantic Charter declared that the victorious allies would pledge to make sure that "sovereign rights and self-government [would be] restored to those who had been forcibly deprived of them." This fell short of an unequivocal declaration in support of colonial liberation. The United States had, in 1934, passed a law promising independence to the Philippines in twelve years, but it did not oppose the European powers' reclaiming their colonies in Asia once Japanese forces were driven out. The colonial leaders in India, Indochina, and Indonesia, having assisted in frustrating Japanese ambitions, were forced to turn against the victorious European powers to struggle for independence. Even China, to whose survival the United States had once again committed itself, reversing the posture of indifference adopted during the 1930s, was no exception. Although American officials and public opinion favored the idea of having China as a major power and partner in Asia after the war, little was actually done to bring this about. Of course, the United States did what it could to provide China with military force, equipment, and advice to win the war against Japan, but it also compromised Chinese sovereignty by trying to impose an American general (Joseph W. Stilwell) on all Chinese armed forces and by agreeing to the Soviet Union's regaining certain rights and privileges in Manchuria that it had lost to Japan in 1905. The United States did little to help promote political reform or control rampant inflation in wartime China.

The United States might nevertheless have taken up the cause of the Third World after the Second World War but for certain circumstances that brought about the cold war. After all, the nation was now more committed to the new international organization, the United Nations, than it had ever been to the League of Nations, and the U.N. included many more Third World countries. China, despite its political division and economic underdevelopment, was duly seated on the U.N. Security Council as a permanent member. American public opinion, inspired by wartime internationalism such as that envisioned in Wendell Willkie's *One World* (1942), would have welcomed a strong policy of support for national independence movements in the Middle East, Africa, and Asia. But the emergence of the new Soviet threat pushed Third World issues to the background. Washington determined that the economic recovery, political stability, and pro-American orientation of the European nations and Japan were much more important. In other words, the restoration of some of the traditional great powers to their preeminent status was deemed more critical than new initiatives toward the Third World. In terms of U.S. relations with Japan and China, this could only mean giving priority to the reconstruction and security of Japan over promoting China's development as a modern nation. It is not surprising that the postwar Japanese leadership welcomed such a trend, or that the Chinese, both Nationalist and Communist, were bitterly disappointed. While a more or less smooth transition took place for Japan, from a defeated and occupied nation to an ally of the United States, American commitments in China were progressively reduced. The United States did not extend substantive help either to the Nationalists or to the Communists in the civil war. Some officials in Washington even contemplated the use of force to overthrow the Kuomintang regime in Taiwan, to which the Nationalists had fled, and to detach the island from mainland China. Such a strategy amounted to viewing China as a backward Third World nation, a far cry from the lofty wartime enunciations.

The United States did not totally lose interest in Third World matters. It expressed support for Indonesian and Indochinese efforts at obtaining greater autonomy, and it warmly welcomed India's independence in 1947. In fact, for a while the U.S. government looked to India rather than China as a model Third World country that could develop along liberal, pro-Western lines. By the same token, however, Communist China was not Washington's idea of Third World development.

Ironically, the Korean War and the resulting division of China had the effect of making Taiwan (the Republic of China) into a model Third World country deserving of U.S. support. If it could transform itself politically and economically without becoming

Communist, it would present a nonradical alternative of modernization. There was, then, a stake in the successful transformation of Taiwan, an objective that may be said to have been largely achieved. Likewise, the United States extended military and economic assistance to non-Communist regimes in South Korea, the Philippines, South Vietnam, and elsewhere to promote their nation-building enterprises.

What is interesting about postwar U.S. policy in Asia is that there was a great deal of cooperation, direct or tacit, between Washington and Tokyo. Reversing the historical pattern of U.S.–Japanese antagonism in the Third World, the two nations often coordinated their policies. For instance, the United States insisted that Japan maintain diplomatic relations with Taiwan, not with the People's Republic on the mainland; encouraged Japanese-Korean rapprochement through the signing of a normalization treaty; and promoted close economic ties between Japan and Southeast Asia. (The two seemed to be in a symbiotic relationship; Japan would need Southeast Asia's resources and markets for its economic recovery and expansion, while the latter could make use of Japanese goods, capital, and technology for their own development.) Even when Japanese businesspeople resumed contact with mainland China on an unofficial basis, Washington did not object, accepting Tokyo's argument that the Chinese market, although less significant than before the war, was still of vital importance to the Japanese economy.

Japan may even be said to have defined a clearer approach to the Third World—at least insofar as Asia was concerned—than the United States during the 1950s and the 1960s, in the sense that the latter's overall preoccupation remained the cold war. Japan, secure under the American "nuclear umbrella" and eschewing military involvement overseas under the postwar pacifist constitution, was able to concentrate its energies on economic development and expansion. The Third World for Japan meant resources, markets, and investment opportunities. Of course, the same was true for the United States, where "developmental economics" became quite influential. But developmental assistance always had to be balanced by the requirements of cold war strategy, as was demonstrated most graphically by the Vietnam War. The U.S.

government justified the war as necessary for containing Communist (in particular, Chinese) expansionism, but few Third World countries saw the conflict that way. Combined with American interventions in Lebanon, Cuba, and the Dominican Republic, the Vietnam War seemed to suggest a shift away from the traditional policy of support for Third World nationalism. Many Third World countries were alienated from the United States and even embraced the Chinese (Maoist) doctrine of national liberation warfare, with the globe pictured as having become divided into "the cities" and "the countryside," in which the majority of humanity living in the latter areas would unite and rise against the oppression by the former.

Japan was a passive player in all this drama. It neither supported the U.S. war in Vietnam nor departed from the policy of not recognizing the People's Republic of China, no matter how supportive Tokyo was of private trade agreements between the two countries. Still, it may be said that by "separating politics from economics" in dealing with China and other countries, and by focusing on industrialization, trade, and investment, the nation managed to show that it was possible to define an alternative approach to the Third World. The problem was that there was no ideological or intellectual basis for this economic approach. Japan gave the impression that all it cared about was its own economic interests. Somehow it was thought that Japanese trade and investment would benefit Third World countries, but what this would mean in terms of overall international relations was not clear. Still, in the history of U.S.–Japanese relations in Asia, the postwar decades were in sharp contrast to the prewar pattern, with the United States now much more active politically and militarily, and Japan content to pursue economic objectives. In a way the two nations reversed their prewar priorities, but this time the situation did not give rise to serious conflict in U.S.–Japanese relations.

Economic and Cultural Transformations

The contrasting policies of Washington and Tokyo, however, were sowing the seeds of potential trouble across the Pacific. International relations after the late 1960s, from tentative steps toward a U.S.–Soviet detente and the Washington-Beijing rapprochement to the ending of the Vietnam War and the collapse of the Soviet Union, came to be characterized more and more by economic factors, and Japan had been assiduously preparing itself for such a time. By the time the United States reconciled itself to the People's Republic of China (PRC) and ended the war in Vietnam, economic indicators—productivity, competitiveness, rates of exchange—emerged as critical determinants of international affairs. Here not just Japan but many other Asian countries proved to be enormously successful, whereas it took much time and effort to convert the U.S. economy from a cold war orientation to a post–cold war strategy.

During 1965–80, the U.S. economy grew by an average annual rate of 2.7 percent. The rates for Japan, South Korea, Taiwan, Hong Kong, and Singapore were 6.5, 9.6, 9.7, 8.6, and 10.1 percent, respectively. Clearly, the Asian countries were making impressive gains, despite the fact that during the 1970s, the "oil shocks" initiated by the Organization of Petroleum Exporting Countries (OPEC) hit them directly, for none of them had substantial domestic petroleum resources and had to pay for imported oil at unprecedentedly high prices. It would be too simplistic to attribute Asia's impressive economic performance to a single cause, but at least these countries shared an export oriented industrial policy, high rates of domestic saving, a close government-industry-labor relationship, and a disciplined work force with a nearly 100 percent literacy rate. First Japan, then the NIEs (the newly industrialized economies, or South Korea, Taiwan, Hong Kong, and Singapore), and then the countries belonging to the Association of Southeast Asian Nations (ASEAN) successfully transformed themselves economically. Although this cannot be attributed to any conscious design on Japan's part, the fact remains that Japan's example was closely watched and then followed in large outline by other Asian countries. In time even China joined the movement away from a rigid Socialist system of production to one in which private initiatives were to combine with state direction to energize the economy. The Chinese economy grew by an annual average of 6.4 percent prior to 1980, and then by 10.3 percent thereafter. While U.S. trade grew at an annual rate of 1.2

percent during the 1980s, China's grew at 11.9 percent, Japan's at 5.3 percent, South Korea's at 14.7 percent, and Taiwan's at 15.0 percent.[5]

U.S.–Japanese relations after the late 1960s cannot be discussed apart from this phenomenon. Clearly, some Asian members of the Third World were in the process of transforming themselves from underdeveloped to developed economies. They had left the Third World and, while not yet reaching the ranks of the most advanced nations of Europe, North America, and Japan, were steadily narrowing the distance separating the two groups. Such an outcome was by no means a product of Japan's, or America's, conscious design, but at least it could be said that Japan had played a role in the transformation, for Japanese trade with the NIEs and the ASEAN countries grew more rapidly than with the United States.

That situation presented a formidable challenge to the United States. Concealed underneath the more melodramatic trade friction across the Pacific was the genuine concern in the nation that Japan was fast turning Asia into a collective economic superpower, somewhat like the abortive Great East Asian Coprosperity Sphere, from which American and other outside influences would be shut out. Although such an analogy was patently wrong—if for no other reason than that no Asian country now would tolerate any resurgence of Japanese militarism—there was something to the image, for it could be argued that Japan in the recent decades, just as in the 1930s and the 1940s, was trying to convert Asian countries from their Third World status into something different. It remained to be seen whether such an Asia would be one the United States would be able to fit into its own global strategy. Would the United States and Japan, as two advanced economic powers, be able to cooperate together in steering Asian transformation in a desirable direction, or would they once again pursue divergent strategies and end up colliding in the region?

The question was ultimately a cultural one, for to answer it required a philosophy, an idea of how the future of the Asian-Pacific region was to be viewed. Japan's wartime pan-Asianism was a dismal failure, while the postwar developmentalism espoused by the United States had often been compromised by cold war calculations. Would there emerge an alternative vision, one that included opportunities for cooperation between the United States and Japan? Could the two nations really undertake cooperation when their ideological orientations and cultural traditions appeared to be so different? Could Asia, itself a land of diverse religions, languages, and ethnic groups, expect to develop a sense of identity comparable to the European Community or the North American free trade area?

Such questions were much more than exercises in abstract theorizing, for they related to a central phenomenon of recent history: the growth of cultural issues in national and global affairs. In addition to the critical importance of economic questions, international relations after the 1960s had been increasingly characterized by religious, ethnic, and racial conflicts. Put another way, the "Westphalian system" of interstate relations in which, for more than 300 years after the Thirty Years' War (1618–48), sovereign states pursued their respective "national interests" and together constituted an international system, began to be undermined by the new cultural forces. The authority of the modern nation state as the basic institutional unit for human activities is increasingly challenged by "civil societies" within each nation as well as by transnational groupings. The international community made up of independent entities with inviolable sovereign rights has had to accommodate itself to the rising importance of global issues like the protection of human rights and the preservation of endangered species, issues whose solution sometimes necessitates intruding upon sovereign states, forcing them to alter their ways. Asian affairs would evolve in such an environment in which not just economic but cultural questions would determine the shape of the region.

Here is an opportunity for the United States and Japan to make a fresh start in their relationship. They are being faced with the need to refine their cultural perspectives and to determine whether or not they would be able to work together in the cultural, as well as in security and economic spheres. Pessimists might argue, as Samuel Huntington has, that "the clash of civilizations" is an inevitable trend of world affairs at the end of the twentieth century and, therefore, that "the West" would have to "maintain the economic and military power necessary to protect its interests" from the non-Western civilizations "whose power approaches that of the West but whose values and interests differ significantly from those of the West."[6] He is evidently including Japan and other Asian countries among "the non-Western civilizations." But such a dichotomy, as old as history, would seem to be less useful than the modern division between the advanced powers and the Third World, for this latter dichotomy allows for change, whereas the former dichotomy only gives rise to fatalistic determinism.

The real challenge today is not whether the United States and Japan, representing "the West" and "the non-West," can manage their bilateral relations without too much friction in trade and other economic matters, but rather whether they, both as members of the advanced powers, can cooperate in steadily transforming the Third World. In a sense they have accomplished much in Asia, albeit through their individual, rather than collective, initiatives. There may be hope in this. If they clearly recognize the history of the bilateral relationship in the context of modern Asian transformation, then they may gain some satisfaction from the achievement.

By the year 2010, it has been estimated, the whole of East Asia and the Western Pacific would come to account for about 27 percent of the world's total gross domestic product. That would be about the same share as the combined GDP of the United States and Canada, the remaining 46 percent being accounted for by Europe, Africa, the Middle East, and Central and South America.[7] If the resources of the whole Asian-Pacific region were put together, it would create an enormous opportunity for development, welfare, and, one would hope, peace. The region, by obliterating the odious distinction between West and non-West, North and South, or the great powers and the Third World, might contribute to the making of a new world community. The United States and Japan could share a mission in promoting such an enterprise. On the other hand, a serious rupture in U.S.–Japanese relations would adversely affect Asian economic performance and create cultural tensions that would make it impossible for an Asian-Pacific community to emerge. It seems obvious which of the two alternative futures Asians would prefer. Only shortsightedness would prevent Americans and Japanese from listening to their voices.

Notes

1 Iriye (1972), pp. 198–99.
2 Zhang (1991), p. 97.
3 Fung (1991), p. 19.
4 These quotes are taken from Iriye (1993).
5 Sakamoto (1993), p. 215.
6 Huntington (1993), p. 49.
7 Sakamoto (1993), p. 218.

2

Trading with an Ally: Progress and Discontent in U.S.–Japan Trade Relations

MERIT E. JANOW

Introduction

Together, the United States and Japan now represent approximately 40 percent of the world's gross domestic product. Japan's economic achievements since the end of World War II and the global prowess of Japanese firms have raised fundamental questions about the relative competitiveness of the U.S. economy and the appropriate role of governments in fostering or hindering competitiveness.

MERIT E. JANOW is a senior research associate at Columbia University's East Asian Institute, with research and instructional responsibilities at the School of International and Public Affairs and the School of Law. From February 1990 through July 1993, Ms. Janow was deputy assistant U.S. trade representative for Japan and China. Before joining USTR, she was an associate with the law firm of Skadden, Arps, Slate, Meagher & Flom, specializing in mergers and acquisitions and international corporate transactions. From 1980–85, Ms. Janow was a member of the professional staff of Hudson Institute, based initially in Tokyo and then in New York. She is the author of a number of articles and books on U.S.–Japanese and U.S.–Asia business and economic relations. The viewpoints expressed in this chapter are Ms. Janow's, and should not be interpreted to represent official government policy, past or present.

Although few can agree on the reasons for Japan's economic success and its impact on the United States, many Americans believe that, first, the condition of the U.S. economy is primarily the result of actions taken in the United States and will be in the future, and second, despite the substantial opening of the Japanese economy that has occurred in recent years, the Japanese market remains by many important measurements closed to foreign goods and services compared with the U.S. economy, and this should be corrected.

There is a vigorous debate in the United States on what corrective measures are necessary in Japan, and what tools should be employed by U.S. policy makers to encourage the further opening of the Japanese economy.

The U.S.–Japan economic relationship is important not only for bilateral relations but also for growth and economic relations in the Asian-Pacific region as a whole. For a number of East Asian countries, Japan's economic experience has served as a partial model for their own development strategies. Increasingly, countries in the Asian-Pacific region are being called upon by the United States, in part because of its experience with Japan, to dismantle formal and informal barriers to trade. In this sense, the U.S. economic experience with Japan has had important implications for U.S. trade policy toward other parts of Asia.

Development strategies aside, greater access to the Japanese market is not only a U.S. concern, but it is shared by many nations, including those in other parts of Asia that depend heavily on exports as a source of domestic growth. Thus far, sales to the U.S. market have been a major engine of growth for these late-developing economies, but sales to the Japanese market far less so. Future growth prospects for other economies in Asia will depend in no small measure on future access opportunities in the Japanese market. For U.S. firms, as the second largest economy in the world, their ability to compete in the Japanese market is essential, since Japan is the home market of their major global competitors in the United States, Europe, and increasingly in other Asian markets. The ability of U.S. and other Asian firms to compete in Japan has important consequences for U.S. global competitiveness and for economic growth in the Asian-Pacific region.

This chapter focuses on the specific trade policy initiatives that have been undertaken by the Bush and Clinton administrations to improve access to the Japanese market. It seeks to answer the questions: (1) What were the Japan trade objectives and priorities of the Bush administration, and how have these changed with the Clinton administration?; (2) What has been accomplished since 1988 and how?; and (3) What does the recent record suggest will be the likely policy challenges facing U.S. government officials and business executives in the years ahead as they seek expanded access to the Japanese market? This chapter concludes with observations on options available to U.S. policy makers.

The Bush Administration's Trade Policy toward Japan

When the Bush administration came into office, trade tensions with Japan were near an all-time high. In 1988 the U.S. was faced with a $55 billion bilateral trade deficit with Japan, down from a historic peak of $59 billion in 1987. Although there was (and is) little disagreement among economists that the causes of large U.S. aggregate and bilateral deficits are largely attributable to macroeconomic factors such as exchange rates, interest rates, differences in business cycles, and savings and investment levels, the trade deficit with Japan had remained stubbornly high despite shifts in macroeconomic policies. High deficits coupled with continuing allegations from U.S. business interests about the closed nature of the Japanese market were resulting in serious domestic political pressures for improved access to the Japanese market.

Suggested remedies for dealing with the "Japan problem" ran the gamut of the policy spectrum. Several policy proposals were aimed at seeking dramatic reductions in the bilateral trade deficit with Japan. Representative Richard Gephardt advocated amending the 1974 Trade Act to seek annual and specific reductions in the bilateral surpluses of Japan and other "excess surplus" countries. In a similar vein, former Secretaries of State Henry Kissinger and Cyrus Vance argued in an article in *Foreign Affairs* in 1988 that the United States and Japan should seek to "establish an overall trade balance the United States would find tolerable; within that balance, Japan would have the choice of either reducing its exports or increasing its imports, thus removing the need for sector-by-sector industrial negotiations."[1] These proposals and others assumed that the United States should decide (or threaten to decide unilaterally) what level of trade was acceptable, and then leave it up to the Japanese government to correct the situation, or the U.S. government would impose mandatory trade reductions. This perspective was buttressed by the emergence of "revisionist" theories about the Japanese economy, which argued that the Japanese market was essentially "different," open only to those Japanese that are part of the Japanese system and requiring different approaches in U.S. trade policy than those pursued with other nations.[2]

Already enacted were the so-called super 301 provisions of the 1988 Trade Act, which required the U.S. trade representative, by specific dates, to initiate investigations against unfair foreign trade practices, the elimination of which would likely result in significantly increased U.S. exports. This law was aimed in no small measure at Japan, and reflected congressional dissatisfaction with the executive branch's management of trade issues.

An important expression of preferred policy approaches toward Japan came in the form of a February 1989 report of the Advisory Committee on Trade Policy and Negotiations (ACTPN), the U.S. trade representative's most senior private sector advisory committee. The ACTPN report called for a multifaceted trade agenda with Japan that included macroeconomic and microeconomic elements. In its macroeconomic recommendations, the ACTPN report called for gradual and steady reductions in the U.S. budget deficit, greater stimulation of the Japanese economy through domestic demand-led growth, and the implementation of structural reforms, among other measures. On the sectoral agenda, the ACTPN report argued that it was essential for the Bush administration to adopt a "results oriented trade strategy." The U.S. government should identify those sectors where the United States is competitive globally, but unable to penetrate the Japanese market. The "sectors should then be prioritized based on the extent to which an increase in U.S. exports could be expected if Japan were to act like other industrial countries with similar economic attributes," and it should define what constitutes "successful outcomes" in a given sector prior to entering into negotiations. Then, it should "insist on appropriate sectoral import levels that properly reflect the international competitiveness of U.S." and other foreign suppliers. Failure by Japan to implement fully an agreement or understanding should result in either unilateral action by the United States under section 301, or a General Agreement on Tariffs and Trade (GATT) complaint. This approach was needed, it was argued, because imports play a less significant role in Japan than would be expected of an industrial economy of Japan's size and importance, and because traditional trade barriers were not the factor driving Japan's trade behavior, except perhaps in the case of agriculture.[3]

In this highly charged domestic trade policy environment, the Bush administration's overall trade policy objective toward Japan was, simply put, to seek expanded market access for U.S. goods and services. Consistent with that objective, the United States would seek a dismantling of Japanese barriers to trade and investment wherever discernible, without regard to whether the United States was experiencing deficits or surpluses bilaterally. As then U.S. Trade Representative Ambassador Carla A. Hills said time and time again in congressional testimony, the Japan trade agenda was "to create open, competitive market environments in which the decision to buy or sell is based on price and quality, not collusion or protective industrial policies."[4]

This objective was pursued through a three-pronged approach of multilateral, sectoral, and structural initiatives. The pursuit of increased access to the Japanese market through the simultaneous use of this policy triad was seen as complementary and mutually reinforcing. What followed during the four years of the Bush administration was a period of unprecedented negotiating activity with the government of Japan. The rest of this section briefly reviews the Bush administration's trade approach toward Japan and comments on its results.

Multilateral Trade Negotiations:
The Uruguay Round

Arguing that approximately one-third of world trade was not adequately covered by international rules, the successful conclusion of the Uruguay Round was identified by the Bush administration as its highest trade priority. Negotiations covered four broad categories: agriculture; market access (e.g., traditional tariffs, nontariff measures, textiles, and tropical products); the new issues of intellectual property rights, services, and investment; and the reform of GATT rules (e.g., those covering safeguards, balance of payments, subsidies, antidumping, and dispute settlement).

Japan's participation in the Uruguay Round was vigorously pursued by the Bush administration and was essential, given the importance of the Japanese market. Meaningful commitments by the Japanese government in areas under discussion in the Uruguay Round offered the promise of significant market-opening consequences for the United States and other trading nations—for example, through the so-called market access reductions in tariff peaks and the elimination of tariffs in certain sectors; through the negotiation of a framework of binding commitments in agriculture; through expanded coverage of government entities and procurements subject to rules on government procurement; through agreement on rules of fair play for services in areas such as telecommunications, transportation, professional services, architectural services, engineering and construction services, and financial services; and through agreement on strong standards of protection of intellectual property.

At the political level, the government of Japan was an active participant in and supporter of the numerous Group of Seven (G-7) economic summit statements announced in 1990, 1991, and 1992 that underscored the shared commitment of the G-7 leaders to the successful conclusion of the Uruguay Round. This collective effort was important in the attempts by the G-7 countries to move the process of multilateral negotiations forward. Yet it seemed that the U.S. government was constantly encouraging the Japanese government to be more ambitious in its offers in the Uruguay

Round, and to take more of a leadership role in bringing the Uruguay Round to a successful conclusion.

For example, the linchpin of the negotiations during this period centered on agricultural reform, an issue that had the United States and the European Community (EC) at nearly constant loggerheads. The government of Japan, both in the context of the agricultural discussions and elsewhere, often tended to hang back and wait to see if the United States and the European Commission were able to reach a breakthrough. Even aside from the particularly difficult issue of agricultural reform, it often seemed that where the government of Japan chose to be vocal on specific issues, it took positions that were either opposed to outcomes sought by the United States or less ambitious than those hoped for by the United States—for example, on antidumping and countervailing duty rules, on intellectual property, and on government procurement code coverage, among other issues. In this sense, Japan's contribution to the Uruguay Round was often, in my view, disappointing.

This is not to say that the responsibility for the lack of completion of the Uruguay Round falls primarily on the shoulders of the government of Japan. The inability of the GATT member countries to conclude successfully the Uruguay Round by December 1990 as initially expected stemmed from many causes, with ample credit and blame to share among the world's trading partners. The gains to Japan, however, of a successful Uruguay Round (and the risks of failure) were so overwhelmingly apparent that one suspected that at the end of the day, once it became clear that there was momentum on the core issues (e.g., on agriculture, especially between the United States and the EC), the government of Japan would ultimately come forward with offers that would enable the Round to successfully conclude. Yet despite intensive stop/start periods of negotiations that continued well into January 1993, that endgame scenario did not crystalize during the tenure of the Bush administration.

Sectoral Negotiations

Sectoral trade negotiations are what trade officials usually do for a living, and the history of U.S.–Japan trade relations has witnessed a seemingly constant stream of sectoral negotiations. The 1988–92 period brought the negotiation and conclusion of thirteen new bilateral agreements with the government of Japan and numerous other undertakings by the Japanese government through bilateral consultations. These included four agreements covering Japanese government procurement practices and procedures (supercomputers, satellites, construction services, and computer hardware and software); five agreements covering Japanese government telecommunications standards, regulations, and licensing procedures (third-party radio and cellular telephone, telecommunications equipment, and three agreements on international value-added telecommunication services); one agreement covering technical standards (wood products); and three agreements covering market access problems involving both government policies and private practices (amorphous metals, semiconductors, and paper products).

All of the agreements were negotiated on a most favored nation (MFN) basis so that the agreements would potentially benefit all countries trading with Japan. MFN treatment was also required in order for the agreements to be consistent with the GATT system. Yet many of the agreements went beyond matters covered by multilateral rules. For example, invisible barriers to market access identified in semiconductors, amorphous metals, and paper products, among others, were not covered by multilateral rules, and many of the government procurement agreements went beyond existing GATT obligations. The bilateral trade agenda with Japan was essentially a GATT-plus approach to the special problems of access to the Japanese market.

In keeping with its basically free trade approach, Bush administration officials were decidedly cool to the microeconomic recommendations contained in the ACTPN report that called for bilateral agreements with Japan that identified appropriate levels of import penetration. Nor did the Bush administration seek to rank those sectors of the U.S. economy that it believed were important for its future competitiveness, and negotiate bilateral agreements on the basis of that assessment. For the most part, although the specific tactical approaches varied, negotiations occurred in those areas where barriers to market access had been identified by U.S. firms or by the U.S. government or mandated by U.S. trade laws, and covered a diverse array of manufacturing and service sectors.

In negotiating these agreements, the leverage provided by U.S. trade laws was seen by Bush administration officials as making an important contribution to progress bilaterally with the government of Japan.[5] The use or threatened use of U.S. trade laws was an important component of the tactics employed by the Bush administration in many instances of sectoral dispute with Japan.[6] At the same time, a number of these bilateral agreements were concluded without the use or threatened use of U.S. trade laws.[7] Despite its support for existing trade laws, the Bush administration was vigorous in opposing new trade legislation (such as HR 5100 and various new super 301 bills, among others) that it believed would limit necessary flexibility required to negotiate market opening agreements, trigger cycles of retaliation by foreign countries, and close markets.

The agreements negotiated with the Japanese government varied substantially in their approach, even with respect to the same type of problem, such as government procurement practices. For example, in the supercomputer, satellite, construction services, and computer accords, the U.S. government sought and obtained modifications in what it believed to be exclusionary Japanese government procurement procedures. The resulting agreements were aimed at ensuring that future procurements would occur in a transparent, nondiscriminatory, open, and GATT-consistent fashion. In specifics, the agreements differed greatly, as they were aimed at correcting the particular problems that had arisen in each of these sectors. The agreements also differed in scope. In the satellite, supercomputer, and computer agreements, the Japanese government agreed to new procedures that would be used by almost all government entities and relevant quasi-governmental entities. The construction agreement of 1991, however, which modified and expanded an earlier agreement, only applied to a limited universe of forty government projects. The computer agreement of 1991, which was the last procurement agreement reached with the Japanese government under the Bush administration, was similar to other procurement agreements in that it contained highly detailed changes to Japanese procurement procedures; yet it broke new ground by covering both hardware and services—the latter not yet subject to GATT disciplines. Equally important, unlike other procurement agreements, the computer accord stated explicitly that its objective was to expand Japan's procurements of competitive foreign computer products and services, and it included various quantitative criteria to be used to assess implementation of the agreement.[8]

Only one agreement, semiconductors, contained an explicit reference to a specific foreign market share figure. However, this reference in the 1991 accord stemmed from an earlier reference in the 1986 agreement and the particular history of U.S.–Japanese semiconductor trade friction. In order to understand the 1991 agreement, it is worthwhile to review briefly the 1986 semiconductor accord, which was probably the most scrutinized and controversial of the many bilateral trade agreements between the United States and Japan.

The overall purpose of the 1986 accord was twofold: first, to facilitate increased market access for foreign semiconductor firms in Japan through government efforts to promote long-term relationships between Japanese and foreign semiconductor manufacturers, and second, to prevent dumping of semiconductors in the United States and in third-country markets. Although not part of the text of the public agreement, a confidential side letter (that did not remain confidential for long) contained a reference to the expectation of *foreign* (not just U.S.) semiconductor market penetration of the Japanese market in excess of 20 percent by the end of 1991. The dumping provisions of the agreement were implemented through Japanese government monitoring of costs and prices of Japanese semiconductor exports from Japan to the United States and third-country markets.

In 1987 the U.S. government determined that the third-country dumping had not ceased, and that access to the Japanese market continued to be restricted. This resulted in the imposition of retaliatory tariffs on certain Japanese imports into the United States, only the second such case where the United States imposed economic sanctions against Japan. The dumping portion of the sanctions, amounting to $135 million, was lifted in two stages in 1987, but the market access portion of the sanctions, amounting to $165 million, was only suspended when the 1991 arrangement came into effect in August 1991.

Views on the 1986 agreement are extremely varied. It is credited by some Americans with saving the U.S. semiconductor industry from near-total elimination, and criticized by others for driving up prices of some semiconductors to the detriment of semiconductor users.

The negotiation of a new semiconductor agreement that commenced in 1991 was perhaps the most delicate bilateral negotiation with the Japanese government during the Bush administration. Negotiations occurred without recourse to the use of U.S. trade laws such as section 301, although the failure of foreign semiconductor manufacturers to reach the 20 percent market share expectation by the end of 1991 as referenced in the 1986 accord raised the possibility that the U.S. government would interpret this lack of foreign penetration as a breach of the 1986 agreement.

The objectives of the resulting 1991 accord were first, to expand access to the Japanese market for foreign semiconductor suppliers and second, to deter dumping of Japanese semiconductors in the U.S. market. It eliminated Japanese government monitoring of third-country dumping, and introduced certain other modifications to the dumping provisions aimed at reducing the role of the government while continuing to deter injurious dumping. The modifications to the dumping provisions were designed to correct complaints by semiconductor users that the previous system had increased the costs of semiconductors.

The market access provisions of the 1991 accord emphasized the importance of design-ins (the development of new semiconductors for use in future products), and other types of long-term business relationships between foreign semiconductor suppliers and Japanese user companies. The Japanese government explicitly recognized the U.S. industry "expectation" that foreign semiconductor market share was to exceed 20 percent by the end of 1992, and stated in the 1991 accord that it "considers that this can be realized." However, the 1991 agreement states that this 20 percent figure is neither a floor, nor a ceiling, nor a guaranteed market share. The accord further states that when assessing progress under the agreement, both sides will pay "particular attention" to market share, but a variety of other "quantitative and qualitative factors" such as design-ins of foreign semiconductors and long-term business relationships, among other factors, will be taken into account to evaluate progress under the agreement.

Both the 1986 and the 1991 agreements tend to be praised as accords that have contributed to increased foreign penetration of the Japanese semiconductor market and demonstrated the ability and commitment of both governments and private sectors to work together to address an area of serious bilateral friction. Some Americans have attributed the success of the semiconductor agreements to the inclusion of a specific market share number. Others have argued that it is not so much the inclusion of that 20 percent reference, but the fact that the agreements properly emphasized the importance of long-term relationships and created an effective context in which government and private sector collaboration could occur. Some have argued that this combination of elements would not have been sufficient if the U.S. government had not imposed economic sanctions in 1987, thereby demonstrating to the Japanese government and Japanese industry that the agreement had to be taken seriously.

Whatever one's views of the 1986 and 1991 semiconductor accords, the specific foreign market share reference in the 1986 semiconductor accord was a sore point for senior members of the Bush administration. The targeting of specific foreign market share outcomes was seen by many as arbitrary and ultimately self-limiting. As Ambassador Hills said later in an editorial in the *Wall Street Journal:*

A negotiated target is by its very nature a compromise, it is always lower than what U.S. exporters could achieve were the market open. And even though the 20% "expectation" in the 1991 agreement is explicitly termed "not a floor, nor a ceiling, nor a guaranteed market share," few Japanese companies are buying more than the "expected" 20%.[9]

Indeed, no other bilateral agreement negotiated during the Bush administration, whether covering government procedures or aimed at a combination of government and industry practices, contains a reference to a particular foreign market share target. For example, the 1992 paper accord, which was negotiated after the second semiconductor agreement and which covered Japanese market access and business practices somewhat akin to those identified in semiconductors, contains no reference to a specific foreign market share expectation.

In that accord, the government of Japan committed to a set of measures to "substantially increase market access for foreign firms exporting paper products to Japan." Most of the specific measures were acts of "encouragement" by the Japanese government to increase the utilization of foreign paper products by Japanese companies. The 1992 paper agreement identifies a number of quantitative and qualitative factors that will be used to evaluate progress toward meeting the agreement's stated objectives.[10] Change in the level of import penetration is one such factor that will be examined, but six other very broad factors are also identified.

Other Sectoral Commitments
by the Government of Japan

Apart from the aforementioned sectoral agreements, the Bush administration also worked with the Japanese government to bring about improvements in market access in a variety of other sectors without a formal agreement. The following are a few major examples. In 1990 the U.S. government obtained a commitment from the Japanese government to amend its copyright laws to extend the term of protection for sound recordings, to provide protection for foreign sound recordings before 1978, and to protect against unauthorized rental of foreign sound recordings.

Another important initiative was aimed at increasing access to Japan's auto and automotive parts market. Under the so-called Ministry of International Trade and Industry (MITI)/Department of Commerce market-opening sector-specific (MOSS) consultations, the two governments developed a framework of industry-to-industry and government-to-government consultations aimed at facilitating relationships between U.S. parts suppliers and Japanese auto manufacturers in the early "design" stages of vehicle production, the stage at which parts procurement decisions are largely determined. In addition, efforts were made to expand Japanese procurements of U.S. produced auto parts, to remove technical barriers to parts and vehicle sales in the Japanese market, and to improve access to the Japanese distribution system for U.S. vehicles.

Under the pressure of the January 1992 trip to Japan by President Bush, the Japanese government encouraged the Japanese automotive industry to pledge to increase its procurements of U.S. made automotive parts, which the Japanese industry pledged to more than double from $9 billion in JFY 1990 to $19 billion by JFY 1994, and, perhaps even more important, to increase the U.S. content of the vehicles they build in the United States to 70 percent. Japanese automobile dealers also reconfirmed their willingness to sell U.S. automobiles in their dealerships, and Japanese auto manufacturers reaffirmed that they had eliminated the prior consultation requirement clauses in contracts with the dealerships. Although these pledges were made by Japan's automotive industry, not the Japanese government, they occurred in the important political context of a presidential visit, and the pledges were announced at the same time as the official communique. A number of countries complained that these automotive undertakings were discriminatory in that they were specifically aimed at increasing sales and access by U.S. firms.

A variety of other sectoral commitments was contained in the 1992 Action Plan announced by President Bush and Prime Minister Miyazawa. For example, the Japanese government committed to substantially increase access to Japan's glass market, and to resolve issues surrounding the treatment of foreign lawyers in Japan. These undertakings and others reflected areas of ongoing sectoral negotiation.

Structural Impediments Initiative

The Structural Impediments Initiative (SII) was the broadest bilateral initiative with the Japanese government during the Bush administration. It was launched by President Bush and former Prime Minister Uno in July 1989 to "identify and solve structural problems in both countries that stand as impediments to trade and to balance of payments adjustment with the goal of contributing to the reduction of payments imbalances." As this broad phrasing suggests, the SII covered an enormous range of issues. Instead of focusing on the usual grist of trade negotiations such as tariffs, quotas, or sectoral barriers to market access, SII focused on underlying structural impediments to trade and balance of payments adjustments. Although it was never deemed an agreement for purposes of section 301 of U.S. trade laws, it too, like the sectoral agreements, was negotiated on an MFN basis. However, it was unusual both in the way in which negotiations occurred and in the subjects that were addressed.

For example, the degree of constant high-level interagency participation on both sides of the Pacific was unique to the SII process. The SII was chaired at the subcabinet level on the U.S. side, and at the vice ministerial (or equivalent) level on the Japanese side. It had the participation of senior members of the Departments of State, Commerce, and Justice; the USTR; and the Council of Economic Advisers. On the Japanese side, the ministries of Foreign Affairs, Finance, International Trade and Industry, and Justice; the Economic Planning Agency; and the Japan Fair Trade Commission participated on an active and ongoing basis. Further, the SII from its inception was a two-way street. That is to say, both governments were free to raise issues of concern to it regarding structural issues in the other country.

SII covered areas that had, until then, been considered domestic matters where foreign views have seldom been taken into account or welcomed. The substantive issues raised by the U.S. government were encompassed in six broad areas and resulted in specific undertakings by the Japanese government in each of these areas. Specifically, the United States raised concerns in savings/investments, keiretsu,[11] exclusionary business practices, pricing, distribution, and land policies. In identifying specific issues under these respective headings, the U.S. government drew heavily from the writings of Japanese academics, government advisory committees, journalists, opinion leaders, consumer groups, and business groups, as well as numerous U.S. business and academic sources.

The issues raised by the Japanese government focused on matters that it believed to be impediments to U.S. competitiveness. The Japanese government raised, for example, its concerns about perceived low levels of private savings; damaging U.S. budget deficits; the short planning horizons of U.S. corporations; insufficient attention to research and development by U.S. companies; insufficient attention to export promotion by the U.S. government; and a flawed U.S. educational and work force training system.

Results of These Initiatives

Uruguay Round. Including more than 100 countries, the Uruguay Round was unquestionably the most ambitious overall trade initiative pursued by the Bush administration. Although the Round can make important contributions to the world trading system and to certain trade issues with Japan, it is not well geared to the particular types of market access problems in Japan, since the constraints faced in Japan tend so often to go beyond matters that are fully addressed by current or even proposed modifications to the GATT system. Thus, although the Uruguay Round may address a number of formal barriers to trade in Japan that need to be addressed, it is unlikely to result in broad based commitments that will remedy structural Japanese market access issues.

Sectoral Negotiations. The sectoral negotiations have been, in my view, the most obviously successful part of the Bush administration's Japan trade agenda, although even the sectoral agreements have not been uniformly successful, and specific improvements are often difficult to measure. In the aggregate, by some reports across the thirteen sectors covered by agreements, U.S. exports increased by 57 percent, about twice as fast as exports to Japan overall.[12] In addition, aggregate U.S. exports of goods and services to Japan grew from approximately $59 billion in 1988 to approximately $72 billion in 1992—with the fastest growth occurring in services exports. How much of this growth can be attributed to bilateral agreements versus some combination of market trends and changes in government policies is difficult to ascertain. This is a topic that warrants serious additional analysis by economists.

More detailed data are somewhat more illuminating, as illustrated by the following examples. In the case of telecommunications equipment, exports to Japan rose from $528 million in 1989 to $699 million in 1991. Sales by Motorola of third-party radio systems in Japan have increased very substantially since the 1989 agreement. Motorola had sixteen third-party systems licenses in place in mid-1989, and 125 systems licenses in place by mid-1993. On the other hand, in the area of cellular telephones, Motorola has seen some improvements, but believes that greater sales and profits should have occurred and will not be apparent for some years.[13]

In construction services, since the first Major Projects Agreement was concluded in 1988, U.S. firms have won approximately $505 million in contracts, compared to virtually no presence in the market beforehand. Since the June 1990 satellite agreement was signed, there have been two satellite procurements awarded, both to U.S. firms. The first is valued at approximately $600 million, the second at approximately $70 million.

U.S. firms have won three of fifteen Japanese supercomputer public sector procurements since the June 1990 supercomputer agreement was signed. Prior to the agreement, U.S. supercomputers were chosen in only two of forty-three awards. Results in computer procurement are still anecdotal. Although it may be too early to see results of the computer accord, the U.S. computer industry stated when the accord was announced that it expected that the computer procurement agreement would result in increased sales of $3.5–5.5 billion annually by 1995. In the case of semiconductors, foreign market share has increased from approximately 8.6 percent in 1986 to over 20 percent in the fourth quarter of 1992. In value terms, this has amounted to increased U.S. sales from $920 million in 1986 to $2.6 billion in 1992.

In the case of sound recordings, the Recording Industry Association of America believes the ability to prohibit unauthorized rental of foreign sound recordings could, over the medium term, result in increased sales of $1 billion a year. There are, however, no precise current measurements, and it is very difficult to measure sales largely attributable to the changes in the enforceability of Japanese laws, given certain other changes that have occurred in the record retailing business in Japan—e.g., the growth of megastores such as Tower Records, Virgin, and others.

In the case of paper products, since the agreement was only concluded in April 1992, it may be too early to assess future prospects for improvements in sales in Japan. However, to date neither other foreign nor U.S. firms have seen an appreciable increase in market penetration.

Although noticeable improvements in market access appear to have occurred in a number of sectoral areas, and perhaps particularly in those sectors where agreements had been reached, in many of these areas U.S. firms have achieved far greater market penetration in the U.S. and third-country markets. Many U.S. industries continue to allege serious market access difficulties in Japan, including in many of the areas subject to bilateral agreements.

By the end of the Bush administration, serious questions were being raised about the Japanese government's implementation of the supercomputer and construction agreements, and continuing concerns remained regarding autos and auto parts, glass, legal services, paper products, and semiconductors, among others.

SII. As noted before, the SII represented the broadest attempt ever undertaken to address underlying differences in structure between the U.S. and Japanese economies. As a consequence of its breadth, the results of SII for U.S. commercial interests are perhaps the most difficult to evaluate. One can identify numerous specific changes in Japanese laws, regulations, government practices, and even the nature of public discourse in Japan that would not have occurred but for SII. For example, Japanese antitrust enforcement activities have increased to a degree perhaps unimaginable before SII with heightened prestige for the agency responsible for enforcement, the Japan Fair Trade Commission (JFTC). Prior to SII, Japan's Anti-Monopoly Act was intended to discourage collusive practices, but its effectiveness was constrained by inadequate penalties, less than vigorous enforcement, and numerous exemptions. As a result of the SII process, there have been increases in formal actions, both administrative and criminal, and increases in administrative and criminal fines—albeit from a low base. There have also been some improvements on technical legal barriers to litigation (e.g., lowering of court filing fees, which can be very large, especially in antitrust cases, since they represent a percentage of anticipated damages).

In the area of distribution practices, certain bottlenecks in the Japanese distribution system have been substantially reduced. For example, revisions to the Large Scale Retail Store Law have occurred, substantially reducing the time it takes to obtain a permit to open a large store. There have been certain improvements in import clearance procedures. In the area of government/business relations, the government of Japan introduced a comprehensive administrative procedures law that has the potential, if passed, to be an important step toward greater transparency and accountability in the administrative actions of the Japanese government. The Japanese government also introduced new financial disclosure rules, requiring 5 percent holders of shares to disclose their holdings, and affiliated parties to disclose their transactions. These are but a few examples of specific changes engendered by SII.

More generally, and more important, the SII process brought to light the challenges facing the U.S. and Japanese economies in reconciling structural differences in the two systems and necessary for the future integration of the two economies. SII also stimulated a broad public debate in Japan about issues such as government transparency and accountability, deregulation, antitrust enforcement, and minority shareholder rights, among others. Through this debate, a linkage was established between the interests of Japanese consumers and foreign companies. This stemmed in part from the fact that the U.S. government actively took its case to the Japanese public, seeking to mobilize constituencies in Japan supportive of U.S. proposals for domestic reasons.

For a time, SII witnessed strong support in Japan from the Japanese media, from the political leadership, and from a variety of diverse interest groups in Japan and in the United States. There was a time when U.S. officials commonly received letters from Japanese citizens encouraging the U.S. government to keep up its efforts to stimulate further changes in Japan. Japanese newspaper editorials on SII subjects supported (and still continue to support) some SII subjects—not because they were U.S. issues, but because many of the structural problems were similarly seen by many Japanese as inhibiting consumer choice, raising prices, and resulting in intrusive and nontransparent government practices. The resulting public support in Japan of SII was a welcome departure from the usual bilateral trade negotiation dynamic of U.S. pressure, Japanese government resistance and ultimately some accommodation, accompanied by the feeling or perception in Japan that it had been forced to capitulate to U.S. demands.

These positive aspects notwithstanding, after a few years of high visibility, the effectiveness of SII as a vehicle for addressing structural issues diminished. Some diminution in energy may be inevitable in any trade initiative, since with the passage of time it loses its "newness." But another factor that contributed to its declining effectiveness was the growing opposition within the Japanese government to the SII. Japanese government officials became increasingly critical of what they perceived to be the failure of the U.S. government to implement its SII undertakings, and used this as grounds for resisting a revitalization of the SII process. Some U.S. officials (myself included) came to feel that this stance by the Japanese government was unfortunate and in neither country's interest. While failure to implement U.S. undertakings was a serious problem for the United States, it had limited direct impact on Japanese consumers or Japanese firms. Japan's failure to implement structural reforms, on the other hand, not only harmed the Japanese consumer but also had serious consequences for U.S. firms doing business in the Japanese market. Further, the nature of the changes sought by the U.S. were in many instances more fully within the hands of the Japanese government to remedy than those sought by Japan.

By the end of 1991, with personnel changes in senior officials occurring on both sides of the Pacific, some of the chemistry of SII diminished. As an initiative that was already several years old and subject to increasing criticism from Japanese government officials about U.S. undertakings, it became increasingly difficult to revitalize the SII process. The U.S. side tried to do so (as is reflected in the communique issued by President Bush and Prime Minister Miyazawa in January 1992),[14] but the second annual report of SII, released in the summer of 1992, was a far less ambitious document than the Joint Report of 1990, and the process of achieving even those commitments contained in the 1992 report was extremely difficult to arrive at for both governments.

I believe that on balance the benefits of the SII were substantial and more comprehensive than can be given adequate coverage here, and that despite the diminution of bilateral momentum on some SII subjects, it started a process of change in Japan that continues to this day (e.g., the emphasis on deregulation, corporate governance reforms, antitrust enforcement, reduction of antitrust exemptions, improved transparency, alternative dispute settlement mechanisms, and infrastructure investment, among other areas). One wonders what the results of SII could have been if the level of political commitment to SII in both the United States and Japan had been maintained.

Clinton Administration Trade Policy toward Japan

Although certain issues were raised by then Governor Clinton in the course of the 1992 presidential campaign, domestic economic issues—the budget deficit, health care reform, and educational policy, among others—dominated the presidential campaign. Trade policy did not receive much attention. There was some discussion of the North American Free Trade Agreement, the Uruguay Round, most favored nation treatment for China, super 301, and tariff classification for minivans, and only glancing discussion of U.S. trade policy toward Japan in particular. Once in office, this emphasis on the domestic agenda soon translated into a linkage of the domestic economic agenda (particularly U.S. competitiveness and the creation of jobs) to U.S. trade policy objectives.

In President Clinton's first major address on international economic and trade issues at American University in February 1993, he stated that the United States must rise to the challenge of the global economy and engage internationally. He said, "In the face of all the pressures to do the reverse, we must compete, not retreat." The United States, he stressed, "remains the world's strongest engine of growth" and must "be the engine of global growth and be the leader." This requires, first and foremost, that the

United States "get our own economic house in order." It also requires that the United States make "trade a priority element of American security." Trade policy was defined as part "of an integrated economic program, not just something we use to compensate for the lack of a domestic agenda. We must enforce our trade laws and our agreements with all the tools and energy at our disposal. But there is much about our competitive posture that simply cannot be straightened out by trade retaliation." He put aside what he called "the distracting debates over whether efforts should be multilateral, regional, bilateral, or unilateral" saying that "each of these efforts has its place."

While making the U.S. economy the number one priority, the president committed his administration to a trade policy agenda that sought simultaneous pursuit of multilateral, regional, and bilateral measures. As was the case during the Bush administration, these prongs of U.S. trade policy were seen as complementary and mutually reinforcing. The presumption that the Japanese market is not effectively open to competitive imports has also continued. This section briefly reviews Japan trade initiatives under the Clinton administration.

Tone and Philosophy

An important general point made by President Clinton in the American University speech described above was that just as the United States must assume responsibility for its own economic ills, it is incumbent upon its trading partners to do their part to contribute to global growth, and see to it that their markets are comparably open to foreign goods and services. Although Japan was not specifically mentioned in that context, that vision of the enhanced responsibilities of America's trading partners clearly applies to Japan.

President Clinton himself has made some of the most pointed public remarks about the closed nature of the Japanese market of any U.S. president in recent memory. For example, in remarks to the press following his first meeting with Japan's then Prime Minister Kiichi Miyazawa in April 1993, President Clinton called for a "rebalancing" of the relationship requiring "an elevated attention to economic relations." He stressed that he was "particularly concerned about Japan's growing global current account and trade surpluses and . . . deeply concerned about the inadequate market access for American firms, products, and investors in Japan." While acknowledging that these are complex issues, he said quite plainly, that "the simple fact is that it is harder to sell in Japan's market than in ours. America is accepting the challenge of change, and so, too, must Japan." The implication of this statement was that as the United States was holding itself up to a different and higher standard of economic achievement, it was incumbent upon Japan to do the same with respect to growth and improved market access opportunities for foreign suppliers.

The president has also stressed that macroeconomic measures alone are not enough. In the same press conference he stated that he was concerned "not only about how much we sell, but about what we sell." This point is important as a number of senior Clinton administration officials have suggested that some sectors of the economy are particularly "strategic," or more important for the future competitiveness of the nation than other sectors, and should receive priority attention in trade policy.[15] To my knowledge, there has been no public identification of priority sectors.

Another difference between the Clinton administration and the Bush administration is reflected in the Clinton administration's support of new super 301 legislation. Like the Bush administration, the Clinton administration has shown no enthusiasm for a trade policy toward Japan or other countries centered on specific mandatory reductions in trade deficits. However, President Clinton and U.S. Trade Representative Mickey Kantor have publicly supported renewed super 301 legislation. It remains to be seen what form of super 301 will get this administration's endorsement, and whether such legislation, if passed, will be used vis-à-vis practices occurring in Japan.

Another important shift in trade policy emphasis with Japan is the Clinton administration's focus on the need for improved results and new and concrete ways of measuring the results flowing from existing and future bilateral agreements. In the April 16, 1993 press briefing with Prime Minister Miyazawa, the president cited favorably the existing semiconductor agreement as a results oriented agreement that "gave some hope that this approach could work."

The recommendations of the ACTPN group in its January 1993 report to the new administration provide an important context. The latest ACTPN report, like its 1989 report, contained both macro and microeconomic recommendations. Once again, its sectoral recommendations appeared to have received the greatest attention in the media and in U.S. and foreign government circles. Unlike its 1989 report, however, the 1993 report was very favorably received by the new administration.

The 1993 ACTPN report recommended that where invisible barriers to trade exist, both countries should develop and use "temporary quantitative indicators" (TQIs) to measure progress toward achieving an open market. The report argued that such indicators would be used as tools for both countries to simulate market conditions, and should be mutually arrived at and eliminated once imports reached identified levels. Failure to reach such benchmarks would result in internal U.S. government review and/ or bilateral discussions to determine necessary actions. Retaliation is identified as one possible action.[16]

The Japanese media and government appear to have welcomed the president's renewed attention to domestic U.S. economic matters (since many of the problems identified by the president were matters of concern raised by the Japanese government in SII). However, the Japanese government's early reactions to the ACTPN report as well as to the Clinton administration's emphasis on obtaining concrete improvements in market access were extremely negative. It apparently interpreted references to "results" as a call for numerical market access targets—akin to those contained in the domestically unpopular semiconductor agreement. In response, the Japanese government launched a major media campaign in Japan and abroad, which sought to paint the United States as drifting away from multilateralism and free trade toward unilateralism and managed trade outcomes.

Prime Minister Miyazawa himself pointedly stressed in his public remarks at the press briefing in April 1993 that the U.S.–Japan relationship needed to be nurtured with a "cooperative spirit based upon the principles of free trade. This cannot be realized with managed trade nor under the threat of unilateralism."

The public manner in which the Japanese government reacted to the Clinton administration's emphasis on achieving improved results was unusual in its vehemence and in its very public nature. In fact, the early aggressive media efforts by the Japanese government occurred before senior officials of the two governments had had an opportunity to discuss in detail the specific bilateral agenda proposed by the U.S. government. Since then, the Japanese government has continued to paint a picture to its public of a United States that is departing from a long-held commitment to the multilateral system.

The Japanese government may have succeeded in putting U.S. policy makers on the defensive—at least to the extent of initially obliging U.S. officials to comment publicly in international fora such as the Organization for Economic Cooperation and Development (OECD) that they were not seeking managed trade outcomes. Some observers, myself included, felt that there was no shortage of irony about the Japanese government waving the free trade banner and alleging that the United States was becoming a managed trader—this coming as it did from a country that has had perhaps the most pronounced and successful record of a heavily regulated market economy in modern economic history. In this sense, although Japan as the global champion of free trade tended to be discounted by many Americans, the Clinton administration's early pronouncements on Japan trade policy had the effect of raising serious concerns in Japan that the United States was embarking on a trade strategy toward Japan that included the negotiation of specific market outcomes, irrespective of market forces. This concern continues in Japan and in some circles in the United States.[17]

Specific Initiatives with Japan

Beyond a sharper tone on economic issues, expressions of a higher standard of performance expected of Japan, and shifts in nuance on trade philosophy, what specific trade policy priorities with Japan have been identified by the Clinton administration?

First, from its earliest days in office, the Clinton administration (primarily through Ambassador Kantor) has pressed the Japanese government on the importance of full implementation of existing bilateral agreements and pledges such as the semiconductor, supercomputer, and construction agreements, the 1992 Bush-Miyazawa Action Plan undertakings, and the automotive issues, among others. In April 1993 continuing difficulties in construction services led Ambassador Kantor to cite Japan under Title VII of the 1974 Trade Act for alleged discrimination in its procurement of construction, architectural, and engineering services. He called for a sixty-day period of consultations during which the U.S. government would seek to rectify the situation. At the end of June, retaliation was postponed until November 1, 1993, because the Japanese government indicated a willingness to negotiate further on the issues identified by the U.S. government, which retaliation was further posponed in October 1993 because of indications of further reforms in Japan's public sector construction market announced by the government of Japan in October.

Also in April 1993, continuing concerns about the Japanese government's implementation of the supercomputer agreement led Ambassador Kantor to announce a review of upcoming Japanese government supercomputer procurements pursuant to section 306 of the Trade Act of 1974. After the completion of the review, the U.S. trade representative (USTR) will determine whether or not Japan is in compliance with the terms of the 1990 supercomputer agreement. If Japan is determined not to have complied with the agreement, the U.S. trade representative has stated that he will initiate trade action against Japan under section 301.

Most important, President Clinton and Prime Minister Miyazawa called, in April 1993, for the negotiation of a broad based new framework for U.S.–Japan economic relations. The resulting Joint Statement on U.S.–Japan Framework for a New Economic Partnership (Framework), which was concluded in July 1993, outlines U.S. trade and economic policy priorities with the Japanese for the next several years.

The Framework Agreement

The Framework identifies necessary improvements in macroeconomic outcomes and areas of sectoral or structural problems. It contains commitments on macroeconomic policies, outlines an agenda on bilateral sectoral and structural negotiations, and outlines a timetable and structure for further meetings, which include meetings twice a year between the heads of government. On macroeconomic measures, the Japanese government agreed to pursue

the medium-term objectives of promoting strong and sustainable domestic demand-led growth and increasing the market access of competitive foreign goods and services, intended to achieve *over the medium term a highly significant decrease in its current account surplus* [emphasis added], and at promoting a *significant increase in global imports of goods and services* [emphasis added].

The United States agreed to pursue the medium-term objectives of substantially reducing its fiscal deficit, promoting domestic savings, and strengthening its international competitiveness. The Framework states that it will be used by the two governments as a "principal means for addressing the sectoral and structural issues covered within it." It itemizes five broad substantive areas for negotiations on sectoral and structural areas, including (1) government procurement, including computers, supercomputers, satellites, medical technology, and telecommunications; (2) regulatory reform and competitiveness, including reform of government laws that impede foreign market access, financial services, insurance, competition policy, government transparency, and distribution; (3) other major sectors such as the automotive sector; (4) a variety of issues under the heading of economic harmonization and including foreign direct investment, intellectual property rights, access to technology, and long-term buyer-supplier relationships; and (5) the implementation of existing bilateral arrangements and measures, including SII. It also identifies a number of areas for joint cooperation on global problems.

Assessing the implementation of measures and policies taken in the above areas is to be "based on sets of objective criteria, either qualitative or quantitative or both as appropriate, which will be established using relevant information and/or data that both Governments will evaluate."

Ambassador Kantor, in describing the Framework in his July 13, 1993 testimony to the Subcommittee on Trade of the House Ways and Means Committee, stated that the Framework agreement addresses the four basic concerns of the president. First, it is "a results oriented policy," evidenced by the Japanese government's commitment to highly significant decrease in its current account surplus and significant increases in global imports of goods and services. Second, it contains reference to "quantitative and qualitative measures," thereby establishing the principle of obtaining and measuring results through objective criteria. Third, through its five baskets, the Framework allows for the "intersection of sectoral and structural approaches within each basket," and fourth, it provides tight "time frames to complete negotiations." He went on to say:

> By itself, it constitutes no market opening, guarantees no future success, and represents no panacea for the bilateral differences that have characterized our relationship with Japan. Hard bargaining on important issues remains, including the enforcement of agreements already in effect.

It was no secret that these were difficult negotiations—although not necessarily more so than has been the case historically in bilateral negotiations. Areas of particular difficulty that received considerable publicity are worth brief mention because they are likely to point to future problems.

The Japanese government resisted references to specific levels of current account surplus reductions and import increases. Japanese government officials remarked publicly that they believed they could not commit to specific current account surplus reductions because this went beyond matters in the hands of the government to address on its own. The resulting language described above states the direction of future policies, which U.S. government officials say is the critical point, but it does not contain specific macroeconomic or import targets. U.S. administration officials have indicated that they believe that "highly significant" decreases in current account surpluses would mean a reduction to historic levels of 1.5–2.0 percent of GDP.

The U.S. government's emphasis on identifying objective criteria or benchmarks was also a chronically difficult element in the negotiations. The Japanese government perhaps did not want to prejudice its position in future sectoral negotiations or deviate from its general reluctance to set specific targets. It may have felt that agreeing to "results" in the context of the Framework could later translate into U.S. government arguments that Japan had already agreed to include specific numerical targets in future agreements. But this entire debate seems somewhat muddled in light of the remarks on July 10, 1993 of Deputy U.S. Trade Representative Charlene Barshefsky to the press upon the announcement of the Framework:

We have never in this negotiation said or asked for numerical targets. That is to say, for market-sharing arrangements or for a specific result-oriented outcome. What we asked for and what we got in this agreement is agreement on mutually agreed upon series to be negotiated of objective criteria, qualitative and quantitative, which would be used to measure progress towards market access.

A third area of difficulty had to do with the legal status of the Framework and future agreements negotiated under it. As usual, the government of Japan wanted an explicit exemption from U.S. trade laws. This was rejected by the U.S. government, although some accommodation to Japanese concerns appears to be reflected in language of the Framework that states that both sides intend to use the Framework as the principal means for addressing the various bilateral issues between the United States and Japan. In this way, it suggests that the two governments will seek to resolve their differences through intensive consultations. Trade actions are not precluded, however. In public side letters, Ambassador Kantor stated that the U.S. government reserved its right to use U.S. trade laws as it saw appropriate, and Ambassador Kuriyama, the Japanese ambassador to the United States, stated that the Japanese government reserved its right to withdraw from any negotiation or nullify any measures it had previously agreed to if the United States invoked its trade laws. Thus the Framework does not foreclose any number of approaches that might be available to policy makers in either country.

Future Challenges

This section offers a few perspectives on what the recent record of U.S.–Japan trade relations suggests are the challenges facing U.S. policy makers (and by implication business executives) as they seek to implement the current Japan trade agenda.

Uruguay Round

Concluding the Uruguay Round will be a major challenge. Although it is not part of the bilateral Framework process, it will affect the overall bilateral trade environment as well as a number of sectors that are being addressed both bilaterally and multilaterally (e.g., financial services and government procurement). The Clinton administration, like the Bush administration before it, has identified the Round's successful conclusion as a top priority. However, it has identified some issues in the Uruguay Round that it intends to handle differently. It obtained from the U.S. Congress an extension of fast-track negotiating authority until December 15, 1993. It also achieved what the U.S. government and other G-7 countries have called a breakthrough in one of the four principal areas of the Uruguay Round, market access—e.g., tariffs. However, a great deal remains to be negotiated.

If the Uruguay Round is successfully concluded, it can result in important gains for the world trading system and certain improvements in access to the Japanese market. If negotiations are not successfully concluded, the president will have to decide whether or not to seek additional fast-track negotiating authority from the U.S. Congress. Given the seven-year negotiating history of the Round and the controversy surrounding it and other trade agreements requiring congressional approval (e.g., NAFTA), obtaining an additional period of negotiating authority is likely to be extremely difficult. If the Round is not successfully concluded, and particularly if Japan is seen as having contributed to its failure, U.S.–Japan economic relations are likely to be under still greater strain. Bilateral political tensions are likely to rise, and new trade cases may be brought by those U.S. interest groups that have long waited for multilateral remedies to specific problems of access to the Japanese market—e.g., access to Japan's rice market. However, for reasons outlined earlier, the fate of the Round is likely to be an important but not decisive factor in bilateral trade relations.

Sectoral

A second challenge ahead is achieving progress in the sectoral areas identified in the Framework. The Framework provides both governments with an opportunity to try to resolve a number of difficult trade issues through intensive negotiations. Through regular heads-of-government meetings, it also gives additional primacy to bilateral economic issues.

Although much hard bargaining lies ahead, the likelihood of successful resolution of a number of the issues identified in the Framework is enhanced by the fact that the government of Japan itself can remedy many of the specific problems identified by the United States. For example, further deregulation of financial services and insurance services, as well as modifications to the Japanese government's own procurement practices in areas such as computers, construction services, and telecommunications, among others, are matters purely in the hands of the government of Japan to correct.

In general, the likelihood of successful resolution is enhanced by the fact that important groups within the Japanese business community, such as the Federation of Economic Organizations (Keidanren) and other consumer interests, along with the Hosokawa government, have for their own reasons stressed some of the themes being pressed by the U.S. government—for example, the need for greater deregulation and improved transparency. These domestic based pressures reflect ongoing changes in the Japanese economy and a desire to see a diminution of Japanese government interference in the economy. U.S. encouragement of further deregulation and increased transparency is likely, therefore, to find domestic supporters in Japan—even as other Japanese interest groups are almost certainly likely to resist deregulation if it implies increased competition in previously protected markets.

A third challenge to policy makers and business executives stems from practices in Japan's private sector. These pose particularly complex and knotty problems. The forthcoming bilateral consultations on competition policy could break new ground with respect to business practices that are or should be covered by antitrust laws. Thanks in part to the SII process and to the regular consultations between the Department of Justice and the Japan Fair Trade Commission, enforcement actions by the JFTC have increased significantly. Furthermore, many of the instruments for an effective antitrust enforcement regime in Japan are now in place—e.g., increases in fines and in numbers of enforcement personnel. Japan still has a long way to go, however, before it establishes an enforcement record comparable to that of the United States or other OECD countries. If the Japanese government fails to effectively pursue antitrust problems affecting U.S. companies, U.S. policy makers will be faced with the question of whether or not to pursue remedies under U.S. trade or antitrust laws. Although no such case has been brought under Section 301 of the 1988 Trade Act, that section contains a cause of action for foreign government toleration or encouragement of anticompetitive conduct. With respect to antitrust remedies, in April 1992 the Department of Justice restored its pre-1988 position of enforcing U.S. antitrust laws with respect to anticompetitive conduct abroad that injures U.S. export commerce. It is now Justice Department policy to challenge conduct abroad that restricts U.S. exports of goods or services where certain criteria are met. The Japanese government's reaction to this change in U.S. antitrust policy was that such "extraterritorial" application of U.S. antitrust laws was unacceptable to the government of Japan. Achieving meaningful cooperation between U.S. and Japanese antitrust and related agencies will be a significant challenge.

Even aside from practices that might be covered by Japan's antimonopoly act, the U.S. and Japanese governments have engaged in numerous efforts—some contained in bilateral agreements, others pursued under more informal consultative mechanisms—to influence Japanese private business practices and improve market opportunities for foreign firms—e.g., in semiconductors, paper products, glass, autos, and auto parts. All of these measures seek proactive steps by the Japanese government to encourage new business relationships between Japanese and foreign firms and an increased use of imported items. The receptivity of Japanese firms to these initiatives has varied. Often, they have been perceived by Japanese business as triggering unwelcome increases in the role of the Japanese government in the microeconomic decisions of private firms. Unless and until these problems are self-correcting, however, the U.S. government has little choice but to continue to press for still greater efforts by the Japanese government and the Japanese private sector to increase foreign access to the Japanese market. This is likely to be resisted by the Japanese government, which will doubtless continue to assert that it lacks the power to force Japanese private sector compliance (an issue that it defines as one of "government reach"), and resented by the Japanese private sector groups that tend to argue that U.S. pressures for government action are contradictory to calls for deregulation and in any event result in unwelcome increases in Japanese government interference in the economy.

These goals are not inherently contradictory, but they require U.S. policy makers (and perhaps U.S. business groups) to engage in active public diplomacy in Japan. Further, efforts are needed to mobilize domestic groups in Japan that are in favor of the reforms sought by the U.S. government. For example, deregulation of heavily regulated industries such as financial services and insurance does not require more government intrusion but less. Greater openness should benefit some Japanese business groups, consumers, and foreign firms. Japanese government encouragement of greater openness does not imply increased regulation of the Japanese economy. It might require the exercise of existing governmental authority for purposes other than industrial development or the management of competition between purely domestic companies—that is, the exercise of existing authority to promote increased penetration of competitive imports. Such encouragement need not occur in "secret," known only to the affected parties— that has simply been the customary pattern of Japanese government exercise of administrative guidance.

A fourth policy challenge relates to the specific benchmarks or indicators that will be contained in future agreements. The U.S. government has made plain the importance that it attaches to "results" and agreements that contain quantitative and qualitative criteria by which to measure such results over time. It will have to decide what benchmarks it believes represent the appropriate barometers of progress—presumably with much U.S. industry input. Japanese government officials have agreed in general terms to the inclusion of both quantitative and qualitative criteria in future agreements. However, one can safely assume that there will be substantial differences between those criteria deemed appropriate by the government of Japan and those identified as necessary by the U.S. government.

The Japanese government is concerned that the United States is treating Japan as an outlier nation in trade terms, representative of a "different" type of economic system than other OECD nations, in other words, seeing Japan as a "special case" requiring more specific commitments as to future outcomes than is required of its other trading partners. Japanese officials may also be concerned that other countries will follow the U.S. example. The United States is not alone, for example, in seeking greater quantification of results and improvements in Japanese market access. The EC, for example, is itself in the midst of active negotiations with the Japanese government on various sectors that it believes are experiencing inadequate access in the Japanese market, and is developing a new and complex statistical system of measuring results in Japan and in third-country markets as a means of identifying what it believes to be Japanese market anomalies.

If it turns out that the U.S. government seeks greater quantification in agreements, but not fixed market share targets, this would build upon earlier approaches such as those taken in the computer and paper products accords. If, on the other hand, the U.S. government tries to garner Japanese government agreement to specific market share targets, it will likely encounter stiff resistance from the Japanese government, which will likely claim that such specificity is inconsistent with free trade, and otherwise beyond the reach of governments. At this juncture, the specific benchmarks and results that will be sought by U.S. policy makers have not been fully disclosed, and the successful negotiation of meaningful sectoral agreements is far from certain. There is likely to be considerable divergence of views between the U.S. and Japanese governments regarding the specific benchmarks selected, as well as the types of commitments that each side will view as being within the reach of the Japanese government.

The heightened publicity (and scrutiny) on the issue of benchmarks runs the risk of constraining the negotiating flexibility on the Japanese side, making negotiations more difficult to conclude. As noted, some previous bilateral agreements have included benchmarks. Negotiation of those specific benchmarks has always been controversial and difficult since they serve as important bases for possible U.S. trade retaliation, if progress in market access is not achieved. Now, however, public attention is riveted on the benchmarks that will be selected by the U.S. government and agreed to by the Japanese government, which may have the effect of focusing attention from the outset of negotiations on the most controversial aspects of the negotiations.

Attitudes

A fifth challenge facing U.S. government officials arises from the discernible stiffening in Japanese official attitudes about the need for meaningful commitments by the United States on matters of concern to the Japanese government. As noted in the SII discussion above, Japanese government officials have been critical of the United States for what they believe to be a failure to implement measures that will improve the state of the U.S. economy. This complaint will have less credibility as the Clinton administration takes steps toward deficit reduction and improving U.S. competitiveness. However, even aside from complaints about U.S. competitiveness, since SII the Japanese government has become increasingly resistant to making unilateral concessions, and assertive in seeking undertakings from the U.S. government on matters that the Japanese government believes are problems in U.S. government practices. Examples often cited by Japan in this category include the Exon-Florio regulations and the Buy American Act, which the Japanese government claims are counter to GATT principles. How much of this stiffening is negotiating strategy rather than points of principle essential to the Japanese government is unclear, but certainly both are involved. U.S. policy makers will need to decide whether or not they are willing to put any or certain U.S. practices on the negotiating table as inducements to gain Japanese government engagement on issues of importance to the United States. The lessons from SII suggest that such an approach has both benefits and hazards.

A sixth challenge facing U.S. policy makers and the U.S. business community is when and how to use foreign pressure, or *gaiatsu*. Although *gaiatsu* has been an indispensable element in securing progress on the bilateral U.S.–Japan trade agenda, and, as many Japanese complain, has been necessary to achieve some changes that even Japanese believe to be necessary, it is also a source of considerable resentment in Japan. Over the long term, progress in achieving expanded market access can only be assured if the market-opening measures have some domestic support in Japan.

Arguably, U.S. trade policy initiatives are most effective when they reinforce long-term market trends, and when policy makers in their efforts to improve access to the Japanese market seek results that create incentives for Japanese government officials and business executives to see those initiatives as a net gain to the Japanese economy. Thus a fundamental challenge facing policy makers in both countries, but particularly in the United States, is to ensure that their negotiating priorities are supportive of market based trends, and are understood as such by the Japanese public.

Macroeconomic

A seventh challenge ahead is managing public expectations in the United States (as well as in Japan) in the short term, as macroeconomic conditions may push the United States to wider trade deficits in the near term. A number of forecasters are predicting further deterioration in U.S. merchandise trade deficits over the next several years.[18] The U.S. economy is ahead of most other industrial countries, including Japan, in recovering from the recession, and foreign demand for U.S. exports relative to U.S. demand for imports is likely to result in a further deterioration of the U.S.

trade balance. If there is an increase in investment in the United States but little improvement in savings, one can reasonably expect to see increasing net capital inflows to the United States and larger trade deficits.

If Japan's economy recovers and the Japanese government implements policy measures to reduce its current account surplus and increase imports, this could prove of great importance over the medium term. (Hence, perhaps, the emphasis in the Framework on medium-term results.) Early signs coming from the government in Japan suggest a recognition of the importance of policy measures along these lines. However, success is far from certain, and policy failures on both sides of the Pacific could imperil macroeconomic adjustments and global growth prospects.

In the short term, therefore, U.S. global trade deficits may increase substantially, and it is questionable whether U.S. domestic budget deficit reduction and Japanese demand stimulation will result in a reduction of the U.S. nominal trade deficit with Japan. Macroeconomic adjustments will only occur over the medium term. If the U.S. public or Congress were to expect short-term improvements in bilateral trade balances from either macroeconomic measures or trade policy initiatives, this is likely to produce disappointment and frustration.

Conclusion

Bilateral trade friction has become a constant feature of U.S.-Japan economic relations. To some extent this is both natural and unavoidable, given the interdependence of the two economies and the differences in the two economic systems. Trade friction is not just an issue between the United States and Japan. The United States has serious trade frictions with most of its other major trading partners, especially Europe but also including other countries in the Asian-Pacific region.

In Japan's case, recent years have brought some notable improvements in access to the Japanese market, attained through the hard work of entrepreneurs and governments in both the United States and Japan. For the U.S. government, the Bush administration defined its trade goals in terms of a reduction of barriers,

improved market access, and increased sales for U.S. firms. It
pursued this goal through multilateral, sectoral, and structural
initiatives. It rejected the use of specific market share targets as the
single criterion for judging whether or not the Japanese market
was sufficiently open to imports. A number of agreements have,
however, included a variety of quantitative and qualitative indicators by which progress will be evaluated over time. The Bush
administration used a variety of tools, including multilateral and
bilateral negotiations under and outside of U.S. trade laws, to
achieve improved access to the Japanese market for U.S. goods
and services. It did not believe that the executive branch needed
additional or new tools to negotiate effectively on trade matters,
such as renewed super 301 legislation or any of a number of tools
proposed by members of the U.S. Congress.

There has been no single formula for success in trade negotiations with Japan. Sectoral trade negotiations that have been the
most successful have tended to have one or more of the following
features: first, a globally competitive U.S. industry committed to
penetrating the Japanese market, prepared to provide the U.S.
government with solid analysis and detailed information about
their market access difficulties in Japan (often at perceived risk to
their ongoing business activities), prepared to stay the course in
negotiations that could become highly contentious, and prepared
to take advantage of increased market opening; second, a willingness on the part of the U.S. government to apply bilateral and
multilateral economic and political pressure on the Japanese government for corrective measures; third, the ability of the Japanese
government to deliver on those requests; fourth, the existence of
constituencies in Japan that see U.S. demands as in their economic
interests or at least legitimate on their own terms; fifth, the negotiation of measures that provide an effective context for ongoing
monitoring efforts by U.S. and Japanese government officials; and
sixth, an identification of sectoral market access priorities that
reinforce rather than buck market trends.

Yet despite the economic improvements that have come to pass
in recent years, many Americans believe that access to the Japanese market remains inadequate. Japan's current account surpluses, its levels of imports compared to other industrial countries,

and its sectoral and structural policies and practices remain sources of serious and continuing political and economic friction.

The Clinton administration has suggested that it intends to be more results oriented than the last administration, and to hold itself and Japan up to higher standards of performance. The Framework agreement embodies the bilateral agenda for the next several years. In the short term, tensions may escalate as both countries engage on the specific issues. Given the policy priorities identified to date, the following factors might reasonably be the implied standards by which the Clinton administration believes that its policies and Japan's responsiveness to U.S. concerns should be judged: (1) increases in exports of U.S. goods and services to Japan; (2) increases in exports in negotiated sectors; (3) improved performance measured by the identified benchmarks of progress contained in existing and new agreements; (4) reductions in Japan's current account surplus and U.S. budget deficits over the medium term; and (5) increases in Japan's global imports over the medium term.

What mix of policy tools will be used by Clinton policy makers to achieve these objectives? Bilateral and multilateral approaches will obviously be pursued. The Framework Agreement suggests that the U.S. government will try to resolve problems through intensive negotiations without recourse to trade action, unless such efforts fail to achieve results.

What is U.S. leverage going forward? Threatening to close the U.S. market (and meaning it) is a significant form of available U.S. leverage in any trade negotiation. Trade negotiations then become subject to game theory, with the U.S. consumer being among the potential hostages. The assumption is that the willingness or perceived willingness to impose economic costs not only on Japanese (or other foreign) exporters, but also on U.S. consumers if the problem is not satisfactorily resolved will increase the likelihood of successful resolution. If economic retaliation occurs, however, it means that negotiations have failed and either the other side backs down or everyone loses. Economic sanctions also raise other hazards, including the risk of counter retaliation. Furthermore, depending on the nature of the sanctions imposed and the circumstances of their imposition (e.g., whether they are or are not

applied to matters covered by GATT rules, and are unilateral or
after resort to multilateral remedies), sanctions can also result in
strains on the multilateral trading regime.

If a particular dispute centers on a subject covered by GATT
rules, U.S. trade laws, especially Section 301, require the simultaneous pursuit of multilateral remedies. Historically, the United
States has never determined unilaterally that another country has
violated its GATT obligations. It has always based such determination on a GATT panel finding of a violation. Multilateral dispute settlement is therefore another option required in certain
circumstances where GATT rights are involved, and available in
other instances to U.S. policy makers in their efforts to increase
their negotiating leverage vis-à-vis their trading partners. The use
of multilateral mechanisms is an important option to consider, as it
will demonstrate the United States' continued commitment to the
multilateral trading regime. However, GATT remedies are perceived by many Americans as currently inadequate, and in any
event many areas of trade friction with Japan stem from practices
that are not covered by GATT rules. This allows U.S. policy makers to take certain forms of unilateral action without violating
GATT rules. What is more debatable is whether or not such actions are effective and whether or not they reinforce or undermine
the GATT system—a judgment call that depends in part on the
practices under dispute.

Political pressure can also be applied without threat of economic sanctions. The record suggests that in many instances of
negotiation with Japan, bilateral pressure can be very influential.
Not all countries care whether or not they are seen by the United
States as bad actors in international trade terms. Japanese government officials have historically cared a great deal about Japan's
standing in the international community, and in particular its
standing with the United States. This concern on Japan's part has
perhaps been more important than the economic consequences of
potential trade sanctions in specific sectoral cases. The reasons for
this are perhaps obvious.

The United States has been the principal champion of the
strengthening of the multilateral trading system and of the global
reduction of barriers to trade. It has taken this position for its own

reasons, but by virtue of its open market and its commitment to global trade expansion, the United States has been perhaps Japan's best ally in international trade. U.S. policy has always assumed that the continued vitality of the Japanese economy was important not only for Japan, but for U.S. global foreign and economic policy objectives. The United States has welcomed Japanese imports and investment, and has not, for the most part, conditioned access to the U.S. market on strictly comparable access to the Japanese market. Other countries have been far more willing to erect or maintain barriers to trade in general, and with respect to imports from Japan in particular. Although such actions have limited the choices available to their consumers, and constrained growth prospects for affected U.S., Japanese, and other exporters, that choice has reflected domestic trade-offs that many countries have been prepared to assume. If the United States, on the other hand, were to adopt a similar stance, other nations might follow, leading to a weakening of the international trading system. For Japan, such actions by the United States, especially if aimed primarily at Japanese imports, would foreclose a major market for Japanese firms, and potentially imperil future growth prospects.

With the end of the cold war, the greater emphasis on economic well-being could mean far less American tolerance for the domestic costs associated with perceived inequities in trade. Arguments in favor of selective reciprocity are now being seriously debated in the United States. The United States may be less willing to provide its trading partners with unlimited access to the U.S. market without obtaining comparable access to foreign markets. Such is the political tone of much of the debate in the United States about the problems of trade with Japan. This puts U.S.-Japan trade friction in a different context than in earlier periods. The importance of the U.S.-Japan trade relationship for both countries, and the global economy notwithstanding, a continuation of the status quo ante in U.S.-Japan economic relations cannot be assumed.

Notes

[1] Kissinger and Vance (1988), p. 913.
[2] In a different approach, former U.S. Ambassador to Japan Michael Mans-

field promoted the negotiation of a free trade agreement with Japan, similar to that that had been recently negotiated with Canada. A number of economists argued, meanwhile, that the Japanese economy was becoming increasingly open, and the best course of action was simply to manage the political aspects of the relationship and let the market take its course. These perspectives, however valid, carried little weight in policy debates in the late 1980s.

[3] Advisory Committee for Trade Policy and Negotiations, *Analysis of the U.S.– Japan Trade Problem*, February 1989. With the exception of a labor dissent, the ACTPN explicitly rejected the Kissinger/Vance recommendations of managed reductions in the bilateral imbalances. The ACTPN members stated that such an approach was too extreme in that it dealt with symptoms rather than underlying problems, and would force the two countries into a managed economic relationship that, in turn, could trigger the unraveling of the international trading system.

[4] Testimony of Ambassador Carla A. Hills, U.S. trade representative, before the Committee on Finance, U.S. Senate, April 25, 1990.

[5] Testimony of Ambassador Carla A. Hills, U.S. trade representative, before the Committee on Energy and Commerce, Subcommittee on Commerce and Competitiveness, House of Representatives, May 10, 1990.

[6] For example, the satellite, supercomputer, and wood products agreements were the result of self-initiated super-301 investigations by the Bush administration in 1989. The 1991 Major Projects Arrangement, which covered construction services, was the result of a legislatively mandated Section 301 investigation. The 1989 agreement on cellular telephone and third-party radios resulted from a U.S. industry petition to identify Japan under the so-called telecommunications 301 embodied in Section 1377 of the 1988 Trade Act. The four other telecommunications agreements developed from concerns expressed by U.S. firms in the course of the annual telecommunications agreements review process, and thus can be seen as cases that might have triggered the initiation of trade action, but were concluded through negotiations without explicitly invoking U.S. trade laws. The amorphous metals agreement arose from a 301 petition by a U.S. firm that was withdrawn when the U.S. government announced in April 1990 that the U.S. and Japanese governments would begin immediate talks to seek solutions to the identified problems within 150 days. In September 1990 the two governments announced an agreement. In only two cases involving Japan during the Bush administration—construction services and cellular telephones and third-party radios—did the U.S. government actually publish a list of products that would be subject to increased tariffs, should negotiations fail to conclude successfully.

[7] For example, the computer and paper accords were negotiated and concluded without the explicit threat of U.S. trade law remedies.

[8] For example, it states that information relevant to the assessment of implementation includes: "annual purchasing data for all Japanese public sector procurements . . . broken down by two categories (i.e., foreign computer manufacturers and domestic computer manufacturers) of computer products and services; similar such data publicly available for private sector procurements; the efforts by foreign computer manufacturers to increase their Japanese public sector participation in terms of availability, specifications, performance, users' evaluation of the products and services; the growth in the Japanese public and private sector markets; and levels of foreign computer manufacturers' participation in the public and private sectors in Japan." See: Measures Related to Japanese Public Procurement of Computer Products and Services, January 22, 1992.

[9] Carla A. Hills, "Targets Won't Open Japanese Markets," *Wall Street Journal,* June 11, 1993.

[10] For example, some of these factors include: disaggregated trade data for paper products; change in the level of imports of foreign paper products in the Japanese paper product market; change in the level of import penetration of foreign paper products in the Japanese paper products market; efforts made by foreign producers of paper products; efforts made by Japanese distributors, converters, printers, and corporate users; efforts made by both governments to implement the measures; market conditions of the Japanese paper market; and other relevant external factors.

[11] In the context of SII, discussions on *keiretsu* included concerns about certain exclusionary effects of Japanese corporate groupings, constraints on minority shareholder rights, and constraints on investment, among other issues.

[12] Carla A. Hills, "Targets Won't Open Japanese Markets," *Wall Street Journal,* June 11, 1993.

[13] Tyson (1992), p. 71.

[14] Specifically, in the January 1992 Global Partnership Plan of Action, it was stated that "both governments intend to reinvigorate the SII through strengthening policy initiatives including new commitments to address the aspects of the business environment of both countries that might impede structural reform including market access, foreign investments and competitiveness, while fulfilling the commitments in the Joint Report of June 1990."

[15] For example, the chairperson of the Council of Economic Advisers published a book shortly before entering the government that argues that technology intensive industries make special contributions to the U.S. economy and should deserve priority trade and domestic policy attention. Tyson (1992).

[16] See *Major Findings and Policy Recommendations on U.S.–Japan Trade Policy.* Report of the Advisory Committee for Trade Policy and Negotiations. January 1993.

[17] For example, in an open letter to Prime Minister Hosokawa and President Clinton in September 1993, a group of prominent economists led by Professor Bhagwati of Columbia University urged both leaders to reject quantitative trade and surplus reduction targets.

[18] DRI's recent forecast expects that the U.S. current account deficit will increase from $66.4 billion in 1992, to $85.6 billion in 1993, $116.2 billion in 1994 and $158 billion in 1995. Data Resources Inc. *Review of the U.S. Economy,* August 1993.

3

China and the
Japanese-American Alliance

MICHEL OKSENBERG

The governments of the United States and Japan face a complex challenge. Can Washington and Tokyo manage their relations toward China in ways that reinforce or at least do not jeopardize the Japanese-American alliance? Or will the China issue be an additional, acerbic factor in Japanese-American relations, perhaps even serving to drive the two apart? The answers to these questions require an examination of Washington and Tokyo's approaches toward China, a sensitivity to East Asian diplomatic history of this century, and an understanding of China's uncertainties and current condition. This chapter addresses each of these topics in successive sections.

The questions posed above are neither idle nor irrelevant. A

MICHEL OKSENBERG is president of the East-West Center. Previously, he was director of the Center for Chinese Studies at the University of Michigan, where he remains an adjunct professor of political science. He also has taught at Columbia University and Stanford University. Dr. Oksenberg was a senior staff member of the National Security Council from 1977–80. His research specialties include Chinese domestic affairs, China's foreign policy, and Sino-American relations.

cursory review of modern East Asian history provides a powerful reminder that the policies Tokyo and Washington adopt toward China can either deeply divide the two capitals or help bring them together. Further, the historical record reveals that frequently in this century, Tokyo and Washington made decisions about China without taking into adequate account how the other capital would react, and the unanticipated responses often proved costly. The historical record also suggests that the long-term or enduring interests and objectives of the United States and Japan toward China do not entirely coincide. If pursued without coordination, American and Japanese policies toward China could easily diverge. It is important for Washington and Tokyo to identify their areas of overlapping interests toward China and to understand the differences in their perspectives and interests.

Although lessons from history are important, their utility is also limited. In several respects, the strategic situation in Asia is unprecedented. For much of this century, Moscow sought to influence China's internal developments and secure positions of influence both within China and on its periphery. Both Tokyo and Washington developed their China policies in part to thwart Moscow's designs toward China and Asia more generally. In the early and mid-1990s, at least, Tokyo and Washington fortuitously can fashion China policies while Moscow is in temporary eclipse.

Another major strategic change involves the economic rise of South Korea and the isolation of the North. Korea has been a major factor in the Japanese-American-Chinese triangle. Throughout the past hundred years, the leaders of China and Japan have perceived that their national security was at stake in Korea, and the two nations—as well as the United States in the post–1945 era—have struggled over Korea. Throughout this period, Korea itself was a victim of great power rivalry: focal point of Sino-Japanese competition in the 1880s and early 1890s, then a Japanese colony from 1895 to 1945, and until the early 1990s, divided between the American protected South and Russian and Chinese backed North. Throughout this period, Korea had little say in its own fate. In the years ahead, however, Korea's destiny is more in the hands of the Korean people. The South has become an economic power with global economic reach and considerable political autonomy. It has constructive relations simultaneously with Washington, Beijing, and Tokyo. Meanwhile, North Korea is neither a client of China nor Russia and exists outside the international system. Exactly how the changed and evolving situation in the Korean Peninsula will affect the Sino-Japanese-American triangle is unclear, but clearly the consequences will be profound.

Further, the China toward which Japan and the United States must design its policies presents unparalleled challenges and opportunities. From the 1880s to 1927, China was in decay and chaos. From 1927 to 1945, it was in a process of national unification, which Japan sought to halt through force of arms. After the intense civil war between Communist and Nationalist parties (1945–49), the victorious Communists allied with the Soviet Union and emulated the Soviet pattern of economic and political development. Then, from 1960 to 1970, the regime pursued a self-reliant development strategy that defied both Moscow and Washington. From 1970 to the late 1980s, China was in the initial stages of economic reform and integration into the international economy and aligned itself strategically with the United States and Japan. Thus far in the 1990s, the processes of economic reform and opening to the external world have accelerated. And China has sought good relations with all of its neighbors. The emerging China bears some resemblance to each of its past phases, but in many respects, the emerging China is a new phenomenon. To be sure, much about the Chinese future is uncertain, but its contours are taking shape. Both the uncertainties and the unprecedented challenges that this China will pose for Japan and the United States should be made explicit.

The Seeds of Divergence and Convergence

From June 4, 1989 until late 1993, Japanese and American government policies toward China have diverged somewhat. The government of the United States tended to be confrontational in its approach toward China, issuing demands and imposing conditions. It sought to alter Chinese external and internal behavior in the areas of weapons proliferation, human rights, and trade. Following the military suppression of popular demonstrations in Beijing in 1989, the United States ceased having extensive, regular high-level dialogue with Chinese leaders. Despite the strains in government-to-government ties, however, Chinese exports to the United States continued to skyrocket, and American interest in investing in China reached new heights. The overall public and private American approach lacked coherence and consistency. Rather, the diverse agencies in the executive branch, the Congress, and the private sector pursued contradictory and uncoordinated policies that, in their sum, somewhat baffled the Chinese.

The Japanese government too was somewhat divided on China policy, with some agencies focusing more on the threats that China's growth poses while others saw China as offering extraordinary opportunity. But on balance, the Japanese approach was nonconfrontational and muted, typical of Japan's preferred low posture in the conduct of its diplomacy. Regular high-level contact was resumed after a decent interval following the June 4th tragedy. And the Japanese government was at the forefront in restoring development assistance in the months following the violent crackdown.

While Washington tended to denigrate China's strategic importance in post–cold war affairs, Tokyo tended to focus on the growing importance of China in regional and world affairs. Many in the United States endorsed the pleas for Tibetan autonomy and Taiwan's effort to attain greater international status, while these causes were approached very cautiously in Japan.

While Tokyo treated China with dignity and respect, Washington ceased doing so. With the noticeable exception of President George Bush, high American officials tended to look upon China with disdain and scorn. For all his many accomplishments, Secretary of State James Baker spent more nights in Ulan Bator, flying over China to go hunting in Mongolia, than he spent either in Beijing or Tokyo. And, at this writing, after ten months of the Clinton administration, not a single top member of the foreign policy team—Warren Christopher, Les Aspin, Lloyd Bentsen, Mickey Kantor, or Anthony Lake—had met his Chinese equivalent in Beijing or Washington. The only contact has been two brief meetings between Secretary of State Warren Christopher and Foreign Minister Qian Qichen, first at the July 1993 Singapore

Post-Ministerial Conference of the Association of Southeast Asian Nations (ASEAN) and then in New York at the October 1993 U.N. General Assembly meeting. Meanwhile all the active leaders of China have visited Japan since 1989, and Japanese visitors to Beijing included the emperor himself.

In his widely heralded speech of September 21, 1993, the President's National Security Advisor Anthony Lake divided the world into three types of countries: the market democracies; those becoming market democracies such as in Eastern Europe; and "backlash states" that resist the inevitable trend toward market democracy. Lake singled out five countries as belonging in the latter category: Burma, Iran, Iraq, North Korea, and China. Two days later, without mentioning specific states, United Nations Ambassador Madeleine Albright echoed the same analytical scheme, but clarified the rhetoric, referring to "rogue states" rather than "backlash states." One can hardly imagine similar officials in Tokyo referring to the Chinese government in such provocative and derogatory terms.

The United States spoke loudly about issues of human rights and democratization in China, but Japan took a more quiet stance that in contrast approached benign neglect. To be sure, the Japanese government had many concerns about the Chinese scene, extending to military expenditures and weapons acquisition, environmental degradation and erosion of the state's capacity to control population migration. Tokyo launched major efforts to assist China in the environmental sphere, while in contrast, due to China's human rights record, the United States government has excluded China from its assistance to developing countries in the environmental and population realms.

The differences between Tokyo and Washington on China policy were kept within manageable proportions. Tokyo and Washington consulted frequently on China policy, and the Japanese government had on occasion—such as with respect to World Bank lending—deferred to American preferences. But many Japanese officials questioned the wisdom of the American approach. If that approach veered further in the direction of imposing sanctions, Tokyo would have given serious consideration to adopting a more independent stance toward China.

In early fall 1993, however, the United States government initiated a significant effort to reverse the downward spiral in Washington-Beijing relations. Five days after categorizing the People's Republic as a backlash state, Anthony Lake met with Liu Dayu, the Chinese ambassador to the United States, to outline an ambitious effort to address the diverse issues confronting the two countries. Without altering the American stance on the substantive issues at stake—security issues, trade, and human rights—the Clinton administration signaled a willingness to engage in a renewed, broad based dialogue with Beijing, including a resumption of military contacts that had been suspended in 1989. The Chinese response was swift, and within weeks different delegations in the trade, defense, and human rights spheres were in Beijing.

Even more significantly, Chinese President Jiang Zemin met President Clinton both privately and at the Asian leaders' summit in Seattle in November 1993. Those occasions marked the first time since February 1989 that the leaders of the United States and China spoke directly to each other. In short, in late 1993 American policy toward China no longer diverged sharply from that of Japan. And one reason for the change was the increasing concern in both Tokyo and Washington—as well as Seoul— of the dangers posed by North Korea's apparent efforts to develop nuclear weapons. No solution to the dangers posed by North Korea could succeed without at least tacit cooperation from China. And that required the leaders in both Washington and Tokyo to engage in extensive dialogue with the Chinese.

Thus the seeds exist for significant divergence or major convergence in the China policies of Japan and the United States. China can serve as either a divisive or unifying issue for the Japanese-American alliance.

The Lessons of History

China as a Divisive or Unifying Issue

From the mid-1880s to 1945, with a few brief exceptions, the United States and Japan pursued sharply divergent China policies.

In fact, Japan's brutal aggression against China and the eventual American response were crucial factors leading to the Japanese attack on Pearl Harbor. To oversimplify, beginning in the 1880s, Japan joined the Western powers in the race for territory and treaty privileges in China. As its presence expanded, Japan gained Taiwan as a colony and carved positions of privilege in Shandong and southern Manchuria. Although deep divisions existed within Japan over China policy and the domestic balance continually altered, for much of the time (except in the 1920s), the Japanese government believed that a weak and divided China offered opportunity for Japan to secure markets and access to supplies of raw materials. As a corollary, it believed that a unified and nationalistic China—or one under British, Russian, or American domination—would be threatening to Japan.

As a near and huge neighbor, moreover, and one with deep historical and cultural links, China loomed large in Japanese minds and in the Japanese strategic calculus. For many Japanese, the national involvement in China had an altruistic and even noble dimension. The Japanese mission was to save China from its own inadequacies and excesses. Gradually the differing and contradictory strands in Japanese thinking about China became interwoven in an elaborate rationale for the Japanese occupation of China itself—an effort to unify China under Japanese aegis, driving out Western imperialists in the process and bringing about an East Asian Coprosperity Sphere.

The American approach to China from the 1880s to 1945 also had its elements of massive self-delusion. But it contrasted sharply with that of Japan. First of all, China was of secondary, even tertiary importance to the United States. Trade was small, and the military presence minimal. A few American companies and family firms did make money, and missionaries flocked to China in significant numbers. But China was a peripheral concern to the United States in the pre–World War II era. And to the extent there was a concern, the United States saw itself as a protector of China's political unity. To be sure, it participated in the rush for foreign privilege, but it did not seek its own treaty ports. In contrast to Japan, once it was assured in 1927 that the Kuomintang (KMT) was not under Communist influence, Washington welcomed China's reunification under nationalistic rule.

In the 1930s Japan became ever more deeply involved in the Chinese quagmire as it sought to prevent the emergence of a unified, nationalistic China. We need not recite that tragic history here. It is worth recalling however that for a decade, Washington dithered, reluctant to back up its sentiment for China with muscle against Japan. Rather late in the sequence, only after Japan had irreversibly committed itself to its military penetration of China and was extending its appetite to Southeast Asia, did the United States decide to deter the Japanese advance through economic sanctions and trade embargoes. The miscalculations on both sides were enormous. When Japanese officials embarked on their project to rule China, they did not calculate—nor could they have calculated—that the United States would eventually galvanize itself and threaten to deny Japan with the flow of resources necessary for Tokyo to achieve its imperial ambitions. And certainly the decision makers in Washington did not fully understand that their belated actions would trigger Japanese aggression against the United States.

The era of Japanese and American conflict over China, part of the underlying struggle for dominance of the Asian-Pacific region, ended with Japan's defeat in 1945, the Chinese Communist victory in 1949, and the Sino-Soviet alliance of 1950. During the subsequent three decades, Japan essentially subordinated its foreign policy—especially its policy toward China—to American policy, in exchange for the American nuclear umbrella against the Soviet threat and for access to the American market. Many Japanese officials enthusiastically and voluntarily supported the American policy toward Taiwan and Communist China of the late Truman, Eisenhower, and Kennedy years. They harbored a sense of guilt over the fate of the KMT, which had retreated to Taiwan after its loss to the Communists. They perhaps also desired to keep Taiwan out of mainland Chinese hands. Moreover, opposition to the Soviet bloc made strategic sense. But as Russia and China drifted apart, many Japanese leaders became increasingly eager to cast aside the straightjacket that Washington had imposed on their China policy.

Then came President Nixon's 1970 reversal of American China

policy. The suddenness and secretiveness of his move shocked the Japanese government, but it accommodated itself to the change rapidly, establishing full diplomatic relations in 1972, seven years before the United States undertook the same move. With explicit encouragement from the United States in 1978, Japan signed a peace and friendship treaty with the People's Republic. One powerful motivation for these moves of the 1970s was the shared desire of Washington and Tokyo to nurture a strategic triangle of economic and military cooperation among the United States, Japan, and China to counter Soviet expansionism. This bold and creative diplomacy enhanced the security of both Japan and the United States. These allies entered the 1970s with the senior partner bogged down in Vietnam and the junior partner criticized at home for its support of America's Indochina policy. By the end of the decade, Soviet expansionism and altered China policies reinvigorated the Japanese-American alliance.

In short, China policy has been a source of tension and a source of cooperation between Tokyo and Washington. But the cooperation was achieved when Tokyo subordinated its foreign policy to Washington's interests and when both capitals felt imperiled by Russia. Neither condition exists today. Russia no longer is an imminent threat, and Japan is decreasingly willing to serve as Washington's loyal agent in Asia.

Japan and American Interests

Under the new circumstances, it becomes particularly important for Washington and Tokyo to understand the enduring interests of each with respect to China. Recognizing that interests are not "objective" but grow out of perceptions and beliefs, nonetheless it is instructive to examine the past century to identify certain underlying objectives and concerns that repeatedly have motivated Tokyo and Washington in their behavior toward China. We have already touched upon this subject, noting that their interests and particularly their priorities have tended to differ.

For Japan, the foremost interest has been a China that is amenable to Japan's economic influence. It has desired access to the natural resources and markets of China. Japan has felt its security endangered when it has perceived that China was becoming dominated by or allied with an adversary of Japan. It has demonstrated relatively little concern for whether China is authoritarian or democratic. Rather, it has sought leaders capable of fulfilling their commitments. But, it has feared a nationalistic, expansionist, or militaristic China. It has sought a Korea that is not under Chinese domination. And in the post–World War II era, it has reluctantly exhibited an ill-defined sense of obligation or responsibility for the war it waged against China. And in the most recent period, it has been concerned that were China to become unstable, the chaos would affect the entire region.

The abiding American interests only partially overlap with those of Japan. The United States certainly has sought a China that was not allied with or dominated by an adversary. It has usually sought a China that did not threaten its neighbors, although it has welcomed a China that troubled an American adversary. Until recently, its economic interests were minimal. The most striking feature of American interests has been its highly ideological component. Except for the period from 1970 to 1989, the United States has sought to remold China in accord with the American ideal. A major purpose of the private sector involvement in China from the mid-1800s to the early 1900s was to make China a Christian country. Americans found comfort in the knowledge that Chiang Kai-shek was a convert to Christianity and that his wife Sung Mei-ling came from a Christian family. While the religious missionary zeal has subsided somewhat, even in the 1990s numerous Americans have gone to China to spread the gospel. In the 1920s and 1930s, American intellectuals in China took on another cause: to make China liberal and pragmatic. This impulse remains quite strong among academics involved with China today. And since the 1940s, important strands of the American cause have been to make China democratic and capitalist (or to use Anthony Lake's phrase, a market democracy) and to rid China of communism's oppressive yoke. It is a fascinating question as to why the United States has hoped and upon occasion demanded that the world's oldest civilization reject its past and embrace the values of the world's youngest civilization. One wonders too why the United States has repeatedly exhibited such intense anger and animosity toward the Chinese government on those occasions such as in 1949–50 or in 1989 when the leaders of China have rejected American values. To be sure, American foreign policy in general has exhibited a greater degree of moralism than the policies of most other countries, but American policy toward China—in comparison to its posture toward Europe or Latin America—has seemed particularly prone to episodes of moral fervor.

This is not the place to explore the wellsprings of America's often emotional, sentimental, and ideological posture toward China. For our purposes, the important consideration is the contrast with Japan. Both Japan and the United States have long exhibited security interests toward China. Beyond their somewhat different security considerations, Japan's interests have tended to be economic, while America's have been ideological and sentimental.

Intelligence Failures about China

History teaches another lesson. Both the United States and Japan have committed major policy blunders due to failures of intelligence. Both Tokyo and Washington have repeatedly underestimated the strength of Chinese nationalism: the determination of China's leaders to attain political unity, to resist foreign domination, and to obtain a voice in the councils of nations commensurate with China's size and history. Nationalistic Chinese leaders have frequently demonstrated a willingness to accept and endure great damage in order to avenge foreign insults.

Relatedly, on several occasions Tokyo and Washington have overestimated regionalism and localism. Some Japanese strategic thinkers and China specialists in the 1920s and 1930s encouraged an ardent wooing of individual warlords in belief that Japan's interests could be secured within a fragmented China. Clearly, Japanese leaders did not foresee the galvanizing effect its invasion would have. Some American strategists and China specialists during the 1945–50 civil war and more recently toyed with the ideas of helping divide China into northern and southern political identities. Advocates of such policies focus upon strong underlying regionalist forces at work in China; ethnic and linguistic differences; natural macroeconomic areas focusing on distinctive metropolitan centers (Guangzhou and the Pearl River delta; Shanghai and the lower Yangtze, Wuhan on the middle Yangtze, and so on); and on disparities in income levels and levels of economic development between the coast and the interior and between cities and remote rural areas.

Chinese politics indeed occur on a terrain that encourages regionalism and fragmentation. But deeply etched in the minds of most Chinese leaders, policy advisers, and intellectuals is the strong belief that the nation's eras of greatness coincide with periods of political unity. Weakness, chaos, and foreign aggression coincide with moments of disunity. Chinese history honors those who unified the far-flung empire, while those who prompted its disintegration are scorned and reviled.

Decentralization of authority within the context of a unified China and even federalism and provincial autonomy within a single political system are compatible with nationalistic aspirations, but the break-up of China into separate political entities would produce a civil war among those seeking to reunify the realm. Tokyo and Washington are well advised to resist fascile thoughts about encouraging the political disintegration of China.

Both Tokyo and Washington have repeatedly overestimated their capacities to influence China's path of political development. Each has overestimated its leverage over China's leaders and fastened too readily upon evidence that China was receptive to its influence. Leaders who were thought to be "pro-American" or "pro-Japanese," or even "pro-Soviet" proved to be primarily "pro-Chinese." These leaders used their foreign connections to advance their often well veiled domestic purposes. The error has been for either Washington or Tokyo to believe that it was more central to the concerns of China's leaders or the populace than in fact was the case. Chinese domestic politics have always been very opaque, and foreigners tend not to understand the powerful internal forces that overwhelmingly structure and narrow the choices available to China's leaders.

Americans and Japanese, especially in commercial realms, have tended to overestimate the attractiveness of the China market.

Europeans have exhibited the same propensity. The images of a near limitless number of consumers, a vast, untapped market, and rich undeveloped resources have lured investors for over a century. Some have found wealth, but most have proven overly optimistic about the size of the market and about the ease of exploiting it.

Both Japan and the United States also have misjudged Chinese military intentions and capabilities. Tokyo and Washington have underestimated Chinese willingness to use force and to absorb huge losses on the battlefield in order to damage an adversary. China's strategic culture—the Chinese predispositions to use force, their traditional and contemporary military doctrines, and their theories of deterrence—remains ill understood in either Japan or the United States. But this much is clear. In this century, whether the nation is divided or united, whether the Chinese commander enjoys a position of advantage or suffers from a position of lesser strength, Chinese have not been adverse to the use of force. The use of force typically has been disciplined, limited, and resolute. Use of force also has been part of a larger protracted strategy against an adversary. Further, while much has been written about the priority Chinese attach to human will, the record suggests they keenly appreciate modern arms. An underlying theme of modern Chinese history has been the quest for advanced weaponry.

Both Japan and the United States have come in conflict with China because of miscalculations over Chinese interests and intentions in regions that Beijing considers core to China's security (Vietnam and Korea) or that it believes to be a part of Chinese territory (Taiwan, Manchuria, and Tibet). Some Japanese and American strategists have focused on the notion of "core China"—the Han populated regions of mainland China south of the Great Wall. They erroneously concluded that Han interests in the areas beyond this core are in some sense negotiable and subject to modification. To differing degrees, the leaders of core China have believed that their national identity and security interests are inescapably at stake in their border regions and adjacent states. Both Japan and the United States have stumbled badly when they ignored these Chinese perceptions.

Summary

The lessons from history are sobering. China can be a deeply divisive issue in Japanese-American relations, but it can also serve to bring the two together. Moreover, enduring American and Japanese interests do not entirely coincide. Both have security interests at stake. The United States has brought an emotionalism and ideological dimension to the relationship that Japan has escaped, while Japan has attached a primacy to its economic involvement in China that the United States has not exhibited until recently. Both Tokyo and Washington also have suffered intelligence failures in their assessments of Chinese intentions, capabilities, and strategies in regional affairs.

These lessons have two important policy implications. First, the United States and Japan must consult closely and at high levels on China policy. But given the dangers of an aroused Chinese nationalism and Chinese fears of both Japan and the United States, the consultation must be quiet and nonprovocative. That is, Tokyo and Washington must not inadvertently stimulate Chinese fears that the two are establishing a condominium against China. Rather, Tokyo and Washington should portray themselves as coordinating policies that are intended to enhance their respective abilities to be constructively engaged in and with China.

Second and relatedly, neither Tokyo nor Washington should look upon China as a counterweight to the other. Such strands of thought exist in both capitals. Thus some Americans advocate cultivating ties with China as a way of checking Japan. On occasion, for example, Richard Nixon, Henry Kissinger, and Alexander Haig have all given voice to this view. Some Japanese see in China an alternative to the United States, should the Japanese-American alliance sour. More specifically, China offers an attractive market and place of investment. Our reading of history cautions against such views. Efforts to use China for tactical advantage give Beijing excessive influence. The strategy yields Beijing the opportunity to play Washington and Tokyo against each other. Such a strategy also assumes a greater capacity to manage tensions within a triangle than the three capitals possess.

The effort to foster and manipulate tensions may work too well, producing instability in the region. Rather, the goal ought to be— as it was from 1970 to 1989—to create constructive relations among all three powers, thereby depriving any of the three of incentives to create rivalry and tension in the region. The overwhelming lesson of history is therefore rather simple: the United States and Japan share a major interest in cooperating to facilitate the development of a unified and effectively governed mainland China and to integrate it into the emerging community of Pacific nations.

The Emerging China

China is not passive in the triangular relationship, however. Its leaders have their own strategies, intentions, and capabilities. And its nature, as we have earlier noted, is constantly changing. History therefore cannot serve as a total guide to the present. One must ask: what kind of a challenge will China present to Tokyo and Washington in the years ahead? Where is that nation headed? Will its future leaders be willing to cooperate with the nascent Pacific community? How can they be encouraged to play such a role? We now turn to these questions.

Chinese National Interests

Despite the enormous vicissitudes in its domestic evolution during the past century and despite the wide range of views with China as well as among its successive generations of leaders, a few common elements have characterized Chinese conduct toward the United States and Japan. These might be called China's enduring interests, and Beijing can be expected to act upon these in the years ahead.

First, China has sought to avoid dependence upon or entangling alliances with the United States or Japan. It has been and will remain committed to forging an independent posture in world affairs rooted in its own economic and military strength. Second, given China's century-long humiliation at the hands of the West, it has approached both Japan and the United States with suspicion.

Its leaders are inclined not to trust the intentions of either country. Third, with misgivings, its leaders have tended to prefer the United States over Japan or Russia as a strategic power providing a balance of power simply because it is the distant power. Distant military powers are easier to keep at arms length, though the era of missiles and nuclear weapons has changed that traditional calculation somewhat. Fourth, both Japan and the United States are seen as sources of technology, equipment (including arms), and capital. These are their most attractive features, but the challenge has been to extract them without humiliation, surrender of independence, or erosion of China's cultural distinctiveness. Fifth, China is sensitive to Tokyo and Washington's persistent and largely successful efforts to win positions of influence in domains it considers within its sphere: Korea, Taiwan, and the Indochina peninsula. And sixth, in response to domestic political pressures, the central government has facilitated the flow of immigrants and students to the United States and Japan, despite the fact that many of these Chinese then stimulate dissident movements in their native lands. All of these considerations guarantee that both the United States and Japan will continue to loom large in Chinese national security policy.

Uncertain Dimensions

Uncertainty is a permanent condition of modern China. Its size, the complexities of its governance, the episodic disorderliness of its people, and the intractability of its problems give a tenuousness to any set of institutions and policies that might exist in the Chinese landscape. But it seems that China is entering a particularly uncertain period in the mid-1990s.

A major political succession looms ahead. The Deng Xiaoping era is drawing to a close. Who and what will come after him is unclear. No orderly succession arrangement is in place. Jiang Zemin has been designated as the heir apparent and holds the positions of head of the state, general secretary of the party, and chairman of the Military Affairs Commission. But Hua Guofeng held similar positions upon Mao Zedong's death in 1976, and they did not yield him the authority to ward off the challenge from

Deng Xiaoping and his supporters—even though Deng held no formal position until mid-1977 and for three years thereafter was nominally Hua's subordinate. Power at the apex in China resided then and still resides in individuals, not institutions.

Others appear ready to contest Jiang for preeminence, such as Premier Li Peng, Vice Premier Zhu Rongji, and Politburo member Qiao Shi. But it is not clear who among the possible successors possesses the four requisites to be the preeminent leader of China: a lust for power, ruthlessness, a vision relevant to the Chinese condition, and personal connections to the key bureaucracies (army, party, and government) in Beijing and the provinces. For inexplicable reasons, Deng Xiaoping ousted three heirs apparent whom he had anointed and who had begun to exhibit the requisites to be a plausible successor. He removed Hu Yaobang in 1986–87, turned upon Zhao Ziyang in 1988–89, and demoted Yang Shangkun in 1991–92. Anyone who aspires to be China's preeminent leader would be foolish to exhibit his full range of talents at this time. Thus we do not know who, if anyone, has the ability to become the dominant leader of China. Will the struggle that typically yields such a leader be confined to the corridors of power, or will elite strife spill onto the streets? Will the struggle be protracted and debilitating? If no towering figure emerges, what will be the result? And does it even matter? Has the center of political gravity in China shifted in the past decade to the provinces and the mammoth bureaucracies, so that what happens in the Zhongnanhai—the Kremlin of China—is not all that significant?

Even more profound political uncertainties exist. The Communist party is not in healthy shape. It is riddled with corruption; the populace resents the nepotism practiced by its leaders. Reform of the party clearly is necessary if it is to regain popular support and remain an effective instrument of rule. But how and in what direction is this reform to be undertaken?

Central-provincial relations also require attention. So much authority has gravitated to the provincial level and below that the central government now lacks easily employable mechanisms for guiding the economy. Further, several of the techniques employed in the Mao era to discipline the provinces—especially the propaganda apparatus and the personnel management system—have eroded. Are the grants of authority to the provinces irretrievable? Can Beijing create a central banking system and national revenue system so it can effectively regulate the economy? These are open questions. Civil-military relations in the post-Deng era are also problematic. The Ministry of National Defense exists on paper only. The real chain of command goes from the chief of staff to the Communist party's Military Affairs Commission and thence to the Politburo. No effective civilian control of the military exists below the pinnacle of power, and many civilian officials owe some allegiance to military commanders. (Hundreds of thousands of People's Liberation Army officers have transferred to government and party positions in the past decade.) In this sense, the Chinese chain of command resembles that of Prussia or pre–World War II Japan. The Chinese military enjoys direct and unmediated access to the country's supreme leader. Mao and Deng were able to make this system work because of the enormous prestige they enjoyed within the military and their deep knowledge about how the military worked. Not only will support from at least a portion of the military be essential for any successor to Deng, but the military is extensively involved in China's economy. Extensive efforts have been undertaken to convert plants from military to civilian production, but the military establishment retains control over the converted factories and derives profits from their sales. The military also retains the foreign currency earned from arms sales abroad. The relationship between the civilian and military sectors in the post-Deng era must be included as a significant uncertain element of the Chinese future.

Economically, too, much is uncertain. All of Deng's likely successors seem committed to expanding the marketplace and to introducing labor, capital, real estate, and technology markets. But they differ over the desirable pace and extent of the reforms. The end point of the economic reforms remains quite unclear to the Chinese. The result will be some eclectic mixture of Stalinist, East Asian, capitalist, and traditional systems, but it is premature to conclude that its capitalist portions will be dominant. After all, most economic systems in East Asia even now entail considerable government intervention.

Further, economic growth of the early Deng era was based on

agricultural reform, the development of rural, small-scale industries, and rapid expansion of exports. In the mid- and late 1980s, attention shifted to the urban sector, with the stimulation of the service sector pioneered by private entrepreneurs. Each of these largely successful policies has generated nettlesome new problems that demand solution.

Efforts have also been made to reform the large, state owned enterprises. While sophisticated economic studies reveal that the urban industrial reforms have yielded better results than conventional wisdom suggests, nonetheless a major task looms ahead to transform the state enterprises into profitable undertakings rather than being a drain on the state treasury. A substantial portion of the government budget is devoted to subsidizing these enterprises. How to reform the industrial sector, how to increase peasant income in order to minimize the currently widening urban-rural income gap, and how to absorb the vast numbers of new entrants into the job market are major challenges that will consume the talent of Deng's successors. And the danger of social unrest lurks behind each of these challenges. In short, the policies that produced spectacular growth in the 1980s and early 1990s are inadequate in themselves for the mid- and late 1990s.

In the ideological sphere, too, uncertainty prevails. Since ancient times, the Chinese government has disseminated a set of values—a moral code—that helped unify the nation and welded the bureaucrats, intellectuals, and local elites into a cohesive whole. In imperial times, the state ideology was Confucianism. From 1949 to the 1980s, it was communism. Today, Marxism-Leninism-Maoism has lost its appeal. Even its articulators no longer believe in the doctrine. Can China endure without the state propagating a unifying ideology? Will Deng's successors be able to articulate a set of inspiring beliefs beyond crass materialism? And if so, what will the content of the new ideology be? Deng's successors may seek to use some form of nationalism—an assertion of Chinese greatness—in an attempt to elicit a popular response and enhance their legitimacy. This nationalism could be relatively harmless and patriotic, or it could take a more menacing, muscular, and xenophobic turn. If guided by such an ideology, China's leaders could become quite assertive, seeking a large voice in the affairs of all the countries on its periphery.

Predictable Qualities

While the precise shape of China's evolving political and economic system is uncertain, not all is problematic. In my view, several aspects of the Chinese future are predictable. First, China is unlikely to abandon its opening to the outside world. Its economic expansion depends upon the import of commodities, technology, and capital. To sustain its growth, China will need to import petroleum, food, and steel (or iron ore and cooking coal), as well as such manufactured products as airplanes and petroleum equipment to remedy bottleneck sectors of the economy. Too many regional and bureaucratic interests now have a stake in foreign trade for China's leaders to turn away from the international economy. And even if the regime sought to impose isolation, the worldwide telecommunications and transportation transformations preclude such an effort from being successful.

Second, it would be very difficult to reverse the domestic economic reforms. The state lacks the organizational capacity and trust to reimpose a highly regimented collectivist form of agriculture, and restriction of the free markets in the rural areas and urban service sector would deprive tens of millions of their livelihood. The leaders could not control the resulting unrest.

Third, the leaders of the central party and government apparatus are unlikely to have the same power concentrated in their hands as in the Mao and early Deng era. Beijing's old fashioned propaganda machine, its command over allocation of key economic commodities, and its extensive control over personnel assignments are probably irretrievably lost. The coercive instruments of the state will probably remain in place. Effective central banking and financial systems await creation, and their construction is not beyond hope. Other reforms could eventually restore central authority, such as strengthening the national representative assembly or wisely using the new mass media (especially television). The system is not at an equilibrium. Either the center will become even weaker, or its authority will be restored through major institutional reforms. In either case, Beijing will not assert totalitarian control over the country. Rather than the center controlling the nation's destiny, the agenda of a porous China will be set in large measure by forces emanating from its periphery.

Fourth, for the foreseeable future China will lack a well-developed legal system and independent judiciary, effective civilian control over the coercive apparatus, and a vibrant parliament. As a result China's human rights record will probably fall abysmally short of international standards. I am not suggesting that Chinese culture somehow encourages such abuses of human rights as torture, detainment without notification of kin, and widespread use of the death penalty. Rather, I am simply stating the obvious: basic human rights can not be guaranteed and are likely to be violated when a country lacks an independent judiciary, the rule of law, and a disciplined police force. And the creation of these institutions takes time. Thus the outside world should and indeed must prod China to improve its human rights record and to establish the requisite institutional infrastructure to do so. Progress is a realistic expectation, but actual performance is likely to fall short of the ideal.

Fifth, despite the political and economic uncertainties and the likely continued harsh nature of the system, the economy is likely to continue to grow rather rapidly. China will rank with the United States and Japan as one of the world's three leading economies. Several aspects of the current economic scene are worrisome, and the growth is likely to be cyclical rather than steady. But the underlying fundamentals for rapid growth are sound: an entrepreneurial population, a high savings rate, a vast internal market, the magnetic pull of the region, and the financial and managerial contributions of the overseas Chinese. China's dramatic rise and its phenomenal growth must be seen, after all, as part of the dynamism of the entire region stretching from India to Japan.

Sixth, the growth will generate severe environmental degradation. Already air quality in Chinese cities is low, and most inland waters are polluted. Toxic wastes are poorly handled. China's heavy reliance on coal means it will be a major new contributor of greenhouse gases. Its sulfuric dioxide emissions already produce acid rain in Korea and Japan. The pressures that the Chinese people will place on their ecological systems can only grow.

Seventh, social unrest can be expected. The surprising aspect of China is how little unrest occurred during the Deng era, when one considers all the change that has occurred. This is unlikely to continue. After all, urban strikes, ethnic strife, peasant protests and uprisings, and rampant crime and corruption are daily fare in most developing countries. As government controls over the populace erode and geographic mobility increases, social disorder and its suppression will become more common place. This is the natural consequence of economic and political liberalization.

Eighth, the connections among ethnic Chinese residing in mainland China, Hong Kong, Taiwan, and Southeast Asia will continue to grow. Investments by overseas Chinese throughout mainland China, especially along the coast from Guangdong to Shanghai, are likely to increase, and this involvement can be expected to spread further north, to Shandong, and to such interior locales as Wuhan municipality, Sichuan, and Yunnan. This process is already beginning. The Chinese versions of the Japanese *keiretsu* and the Korean *chaebol*—the Chinese answer to Mitsubishi or Hyundai—are beginning to arise. Originating in diverse locales—Beijing, Taipei, Hong Kong, or Bangkok—huge Chinese firms have been founded in the last two decades by such entrepreneurs as Li K'ai-hsing, Gordon Wu, and Rong Yiren. Chinese firms typically are organized around a family, but their interests spread across industries and national borders. The emerging, competing Chinese business networks will be major transnational actors in East Asia. The tycoons cannot avoid being drawn into the world of political power; indeed, their ability to mediate between the worlds of commerce and government helps explain their success. A few of the Chinese commercial networks have links to secret societies and are involved in various rackets, just as the *yakuza* in Japan or the American mafia have spawned commercial empires that transcend the legal and nether worlds.

And finally, each of the different macro-regions of China— Guangzhou, Hong Kong, and the south; the lower Yangtze from Nanjing to Shanghai; the north China plain; the Manchurian corridor from Harbin to Dalian; etc.—will be differentially linked to the outside world and will pursue somewhat different development strategies. The south will have stronger links to Taiwan, Hong Kong, and Southeast Asia, while the northeast will be more tied to Japan, Korea, and Russia, and the northwest will have contacts with the central Asian republics of the former Soviet Union.

The Net Assessment

When one pieces together the predictable and the uncertain dimensions, the overall picture is not particularly attractive or comforting. China is likely to be in the throes of massive change for the foreseeable future. While the economy is likely to prosper and offer attractive investment opportunities, the mainland political system is likely to be somewhat corrupt, oppressive, and fragmented. The military will play an important role, and nationalism could well be part of the state's message. The military strength of China will grow, although at what pace is uncertain. The regulatory capability of the central state apparatus in many spheres will be low. Beijing will undertake international commitments that it lacks the capacity to enforce or monitor. Indeed, entering the agreement will be part of its strategy for accruing the capacity to implement the agreement. The rise of highly personalistic Chinese business networks will blur the boundary between the mainland and non-mainland Chinese worlds, and the absorption of Hong Kong under mainland rule will intensify the process. Japan and the United States, in short, will have to deal with a sprawling, territorially amorphous, culturally confident, socially undisciplined, economically vibrant, and politically messy China. Neither Tokyo nor Washington should harbor any illusions about this China. It will be a difficult neighbor, but its cooperation is necessary for regional and global stability and prosperity.

The Japanese and American Response

How should Tokyo and Washington respond to China? At stake are matters of strategy and style, security, economic problems and new issues arising from global interdependence, and human rights.

Our cursory review of history identified the broad objective: Tokyo and Washington must manage their relations with Beijing in ways that help solidify rather than weaken the Japanese-American alliance and that facilitate China's constructive involvement in the Asian-Pacific region. This requires constant consultation between Washington and Tokyo about China. It also requires extensive dialogue with Beijing so that China's leaders understand that the Japanese-American partnership is intended to assist rather than harm China. If the Chinese perceive that the intent of Washington and Tokyo is to isolate or weaken them, their natural response would be obstreperousness and a turn to other countries such as Russia—to help them meet their needs.

The implicit existing division of labor makes sense but merits some adjustment. The American military presence in Asia elicits Chinese respect and establishes a propitious context for China's involvement in regional affairs. The United States provides the largest market for Chinese exports, and Chinese dependence on the American market has been growing. Meanwhile, Japan's developmental assistance and loans to China at concessional interest rates are helping Japanese firms to secure significant market shares in many key areas. Over the long run, it would be unfortunate if Japan came to dominate the China market while the United States maintained the security environment for this to happen. Tokyo and Washington share an enlightened long-term interest in Japan absorbing a greater portion of Chinese exports and in the United States acquiring a greater portion of the China market.

In the security realm, both the United States and Japan need an enhanced understanding of China's military strategy and its policies on weapons acquisition and deployment. Washington should not bear the burden alone to deter provocative Chinese arms sales or purchases. In bilateral forms and in multilateral forms, Japanese and Americans should seek greater information about China's defense planning. In private dialogue, Japanese leaders must also express their concerns about Chinese military expenditures. And both must point out the risks of a regional arms race if the Chinese modernize their military forces rapidly and assert territorial claims in disputed areas. Such multilateral fora as the ASEAN Post-Ministerial Conference and the APEC process offer excellent opportunities to pursue this agenda.

Extensive dialogue with China is urgently needed concerning the dangers posed by North Korea's possible acquisition of nuclear weapons. Cooperation among Beijing, Washington, and Tokyo—as well as Seoul—is likely to be necessary to maintain stability on the peninsula in the post–Kim Il-sung era. Economically, continued economic reform, increased transparency, enforcement of a nationally uniform tariff system, protection of intellectual property, removal of internal nontariff barriers to trade, continued development of the legal system, and eventual convertibility of the *renminbi* are objectives both countries share and can help support through bilateral and multilateral assistance.

Perhaps the most neglected set of issues pertains to environmental concerns, population growth and migration, narcotics, and the spread of AIDS. China is a major factor in addressing these global problems, and the Chinese would welcome Japanese and American contributions to their own efforts in these areas. For example, China seeks Japanese and American assistance to improve its efficiency in the use of energy and dissemination of clean coal technologies.

Human rights and democratization merit inclusion in the Japanese and American agendas toward China. Continual dialogue is necessary, and the glare of publicity is necessary. The private sector—foundations, journalists, academics, nongovernmental organizations—has a major role to play. But as we noted earlier, expectations must be kept realistic. It is reasonable to expect the leaders of China to undertake efforts to prevent abuses of basic human rights. Japan and the United States should press the Chinese in this area. Japan should not let the burden fall entirely on the United States.

Finally, both Japan and the United States have a great stake in the future of Taiwan and Hong Kong. Either locale could present thorny policy problems to Tokyo and Washington. The transition from British to Chinese rule may prove more difficult than is currently anticipated. How would the United States and Japan react if Hong Kong is unable to survive as a free and separate entity? Would Japan and the United States adopt similar stances? In Taiwan, in response to the ascent of the Democratic Progressive party, the ruling Kuomintang has muted its previous claim that there is one China and Taiwan is part of it. Slowly Taiwan is drifting toward making explicit and seeking recognition of its status as a separate entity in world affairs. If Taiwan were to proclaim its independence or to step up its efforts to gain entry into the

United Nations, Tokyo and Washington conceivably could respond to Taiwan's initiative in divergent ways. Beijing is likely to press Washington and Tokyo to thwart Taiwan's effort. Japan is probably more susceptible than is the United States to efforts from Beijing to keep both countries firmly committed to a "one China" policy. Both countries would be deeply torn, but the ideological proclivities of the United States would tug in Taiwan's direction, while Japan's economic priorities probably would propel it in the mainland's direction.

This exploration of the Japanese-American-Chinese triangle ends on a guardedly optimistic note. The current approaches of Tokyo and Washington toward Beijing differ in degree but not in kind. History teaches that Japan and the United States can find themselves in conflict over China. An assessment of the Chinese future reveals it is going to be a difficult partner in world affairs. But the basis exists for cooperation among Beijing, Tokyo, and Washington in the realms of security, economics, and issues of interdependence. What are required are consultation, extensive and high-level dialogue with Beijing, coordination between Japan and China on the Taiwan and Hong Kong issues, realism, patience, and firmness.

4

Asian Regionalism and U.S. Interests

BRUCE STOKES AND
C. MICHAEL AHO

The Asian-Pacific region is the black hole of the international economic system.[1] The region represents an enormous concentration of economic energy that promises untold benefits if somehow the rest of the world can tap into it.

But unlike black holes in the solar system, developments in China, Hong Kong, Indonesia, Japan, Korea, Malaysia, the Phil-

---

BRUCE STOKES is the international economics correspondent for the *National Journal*, a weekly public policy magazine published in Washington, D.C. A member of the Council on Foreign Relations, he is the coauthor, with C. Michael Aho, of the forthcoming book *The European Challenge*. His work has appeared in *Foreign Affairs, Foreign Policy*, the *New York Times*, the *Washington Post*, and other U.S. publications. He is a regular contributor to the Japanese magazine *Foresight*.

C. MICHAEL AHO is the senior international economist and vice president at Prudential Securities, Inc. in New York. Previously he was director of economic studies and director of the International Trade Project at the Council on Foreign Relations and an adjunct professor at Columbia University in the School of International and Public Affairs. Dr. Aho was the economic policy adviser to Senator Bill Bradley (1983–84); director of the Office of Foreign Economic Research at the U.S. Department of Labor (1978–82); and U.S. representative to the Man-

ippines, Singapore, Taiwan, and Thailand—the nations that constitute the Asian-Pacific world—have real world implications for the United States. Unfortunately, like black holes, this concentration of energy sheds little light on what can or should be done about the Asian-Pacific's potentially destabilizing force in the economic cosmos.

In the past decade, while Europe was attempting to unify its internal market and the United States was laying the groundwork for a North American free trade area, a de facto economic bloc was also emerging along the western edge of the Pacific. No formal institutional structure or body of international rules defines this new economic space. It has been shaped by market based trade and investment relationships that have grown up in a remarkably short period of time. Initially, this economic pump was primed by direct Japanese investment and large dollops of foreign aid from Tokyo. Increasingly, this economic dynamism has taken on a self-sustaining character of its own, as investment from Korea, Taiwan, Hong Kong, and other overseas Chinese, supplemented by internally generated investment, has driven trade and growth in the region.

During the same period, America's economic importance in the Asian-Pacific region has declined relative to Japan, whether measured by investment or trade. Washington's foreign assistance to the region has been far outstripped by that from Tokyo. U.S. policy toward the Asian-Pacific, once driven largely by security concerns, has more and more been dominated by economic interests that have focused almost exclusively on relations with Japan. Successive U.S. administrations have pursued those interests in an aggressive, unilateral fashion that has often achieved short-term goals at the long-term risk of alienating the world's most vibrant economies.

U.S. failure to adequately attend to its economic interests in the

power and Social Affairs Committee of the OECD (1981–82). He directed the President's Report on U.S. Competitiveness in 1980, has published widely on trade and labor adjustment issues, and is a frequent contributor to the media, both print and broadcast. His most recent books include *Trade Talks: America Better Listen!* and *After Reagan: Confronting the Changed World Economy*.

Asian-Pacific, coupled with Washington's proclivity toward tactical, rather than strategic geoeconomic thinking toward the region, looms as the next "crisis" in U.S. external economic relations.

The Asian-Pacific is the single fastest growing region in the world economy, and promises to remain so for years to come. Moreover, Asian-Pacific laboratories, factories, and markets are the breeding ground of the next generation of both consumer and advanced technologies. If Asian nations—particularly Japan—monopolize the benefits of the region's technological and economic dynamism, the competitiveness of American businesses and the U.S. trade balance will suffer, sowing new seeds of trans-Pacific tension. Moreover, unless U.S. business, in cooperation with the U.S. government, moves quickly to enlarge its foothold in the region, U.S. companies may find their access to those economies hindered or even effectively blocked by the myriad formal and informal commercial ties that are rapidly emerging in the region, and that increasingly bind the region unto itself.

On July 7, 1993, in a speech at Waseda University in Tokyo, President Clinton pledged that "our nation is ready to be a full partner in Asian growth." He said it was time to create a new Pacific community, and he suggested that the forum for that cooperation be the organization for Asia-Pacific Economic Cooperation (APEC), founded in 1989 and made up of fifteen countries on the eastern and western shores of the Pacific.

As President Clinton noted, the foundation of this new alliance will be the continued presence of U.S. military forces in the region. Moreover, he concluded, "The new Pacific community will rest on a revived partnership between the United States and Japan." President Clinton and other Asian-Pacific leaders began the process of putting some meat on the bare-bones APEC structure at the APEC ministerial meeting in Seattle in November 1993, and its accompanying meeting of the leaders of most of the nations in the region. It will be a complicated and diplomatically touchy exercise.

The creation of an Asian common market or a free trade area that spans the Pacific is not in the cards any time soon. Diverse ethnic, political, and economic differences make Asia a far more complicated political and economic terrain than Europe. Moreover, U.S. security and trade relations with Japan, China, and to a certain extent with Korea will always require special attention. China is the new wild card. Its economic potential and military presence ensure that Beijing's relations with Washington and its ties with Tokyo will help shape developments in the region. Balancing these bilateral relations in a new multilateral context will be fraught with pitfalls.

The temptation is for Washington to go slow in developing its new relationship with the Asian-Pacific, but given the pace of economic transformation in the region, time may be the one commodity policy makers lack. Especially for the United States, the window of opportunity is closing in the Asian-Pacific. If a concerted effort is not made soon by Washington to more actively engage the U.S. business community in the region, the opportunity to tap into the Asian economic dynamo may have been lost and the advantage may pass to Japan and others.

Unparalleled Economic Dynamism

The economic dynamism of the Asian-Pacific region is by now the stuff of legend. While the global recession sent the Japanese economy into a tailspin, it knocked a mere percentage point off of real economic growth rates in other Asian countries. East Asia, excluding China, grew by 5.5 percent in 1992 in real terms and China grew at a 12.8 percent rate, according to estimates by Japan's Nomura Research Institute. In the future, real growth is expected to rebound in East Asia and be even more robust in China.

As the world's fastest growing region, the Asian-Pacific is of increasing economic significance to the United States. Singapore now buys more American exports than Italy or Spain, and Malaysia imports more U.S. products than the Soviet Union. Only a quarter of a century ago, total U.S. trade with all of East Asia was less than that with Latin America. In 1992 U.S. commerce across the Pacific was triple that with Latin America and almost 50 percent more than that with Western Europe, according to U.S. Commerce Department data.

Overall, more than 40 percent of U.S. trade is now with Asia.

Asian consumers bought $120 billion of U.S. exports in 1992, supporting 23 million U.S. jobs. Unfortunately, this commerce has become increasingly unbalanced. In 1992 the United States ran trade deficits with Japan ($49.5 billion), China ($18 billion), Taiwan ($9.5 billion), and South Korea ($2 billion).

But the Asian-Pacific region is more than a business opportunity for the United States. It represents a new arena in which Japan and the United States will continue their economic rivalry, and the economies of the region themselves increasingly pose a direct competitive challenge to the United States comparable to that posed by Japan's emergence onto the world economic stage in the 1970s.

At the beginning of the 1980s, U.S. economic involvement in the Asian-Pacific region, whether measured by investment, aid, or trade, was roughly comparable to that of Japan. Today, Japan has clearly emerged as the predominant economic force in the region. While U.S. cumulative direct investment in the East Asian economies more than doubled, growing from $16.7 billion in 1980 to $36.7 billion in 1989, cumulative Japanese investment increased more than fivefold, from $9.8 billion to $54.4 billion. U.S. exports to the region grew from $32.3 billion in 1980 to $66.8 billion in 1989. But Japanese exports to the region grew from $40.8 billion to $92.4 billion.

Japanese investment was triggered by *endaka*—the appreciation of the yen—first in 1985 and then again in 1993. Much manufacturing in Japan, especially of labor-intensive goods such as consumer electronics, has been priced out of world markets. To survive, Japanese firms have had to move their production facilities offshore. At the same time, the yen's greater purchasing power has made overseas investment relatively cheap. Southeast Asia, with its low wage rates and proximity to Japan, has become a natural fit for many companies. It is little wonder that in 1992 Japanese direct investment in Asia rose 8.2 percent.

Such capital flows have built up whole new industries almost overnight. Of the 340 Japanese owned electronics companies in Southeast Asia, 241 of them—including all of those in Thailand, Malaysia, and the Philippines, half of those in Singapore, and a third of those in Taiwan—were built between 1985 and 1990. These Japanese companies have become offshore export platforms targeted on the United States and other markets. The consequences for the U.S. electronics trade balance sheet are now apparent. In 1988 America imported only $7 million in consumer electronics from Thailand. In 1990 America imported $310 million of Thai produced consumer electronics.

By the year 2000, according to estimates by Marcus Noland, an international economist with the president's Council of Economic Advisers, the eight principal East Asian nations, excluding China and Japan, could account for 17.7 percent of U.S. iron and steel consumption, up from 1.3 percent in 1988; 15.1 percent of the fabricated metal products used in the United States, up from 1.9 percent in 1988; and 17 percent of the radio, television, and telecommunications equipment sold in the United States, up from 7.6 percent in 1988. Noland estimates that by the end of the decade, overall U.S. imports from East Asia could result in a net loss of more than 700,000 potential jobs.

Increasing U.S. imports from the Asian-Pacific are, in part, offset by growing U.S. exports to the region. But the continuing, and in some cases growing, U.S. trade deficit with individual countries underscores that this trade remains unbalanced. Moreover, in some countries, despite growing U.S. exports, the United States is losing market share to Japan, whose exports are growing even faster.

In fact, economic projections into the early part of the next century suggest a growing U.S. economic disengagement from the region. America provided 12.4 percent of Association of Southeast Asian Nations (ASEAN) imports in 1990, according to data compiled by DRI/McGraw Hill, and bought 20 percent of their exports. By 2010 the United States is expected to supply only 9 percent of ASEAN imports and buy 12.9 percent of its exports.

Japan, on the other hand, is expected to have the best of both worlds, selling more to the region and buying less. DRI projects Japan, which sold ASEAN 22.8 percent of its imports in 1990, will provide 33 percent by 2010. And while the Japanese bought 19.6 percent of ASEAN exports in 1990, they will buy only 13.5 percent in 2010.

As a result of Japan's growing trade and investment involvement in the Asian-Pacific, the region has also become a battleground for supremacy between the yen and the dollar. Economic growth rates in Asia's newly industrialized economies now track more closely the value of the yen than they do the U.S. economic growth rate, according to studies by Nomura Research. The boom in most Asian economies following the 1985 Plaza Accord that doubled the yen's value suggests the overall effect of the yen's recent appreciation is positive for the region.

The yen's importance in exchange rate policies and the invoicing of trade and finance in the region is increasing, if somewhat erratically. From 1980 to 1987 Asian central banks increased their holdings of yen from 13.9 percent of official reserves to 30 percent. By 1990 those yen holdings had slid to 17.5 percent. The share of the debts of Asia's newly industrialized countries denominated in yen nearly doubled between 1980 and 1988 and then decreased a bit by 1990, according to data compiled by the International Monetary Fund.

While no currencies are yet pegged to the yen, Malaysia and Thailand tie their monies to a basket of funds, heavily weighted toward the yen. Jeffrey A. Frankel of the University of California at Berkeley has estimated that developments in the Tokyo financial market are now the dominant external factor influencing interest rates in Taiwan and Singapore, and are equal to New York's influence in Korea's financial market.

As this mixed picture indicates, the yen has not supplanted the dollar in Asia, but it has eroded the dollar's influence. Since all manufacturers prefer to carry out transactions in their own currency, the rising share of Japan's own imports now denominated in yen suggests that the yen is likely to become even more dominant in Asia as Japan's trade within the region increases.

An Industrial Challenge

These developments are not theoretical concerns of macro economists and currency speculators, but real life challenges for major American industries. The situation facing the U.S. auto industry in the Asian-Pacific region is a case in point.

The East and Southeast Asian vehicle market is small by global standards. In 1990 little more than 2 million cars, trucks, and buses were sold in China, Indonesia, Malaysia, the Philippines, Taiwan, and Thailand combined. That same year 13.9 million cars and trucks were sold in the United States.

But Asian markets are relatively unsaturated, and recent rapid economic growth has sparked unprecedented demand. Already, Thailand, with a quarter of the U.S. population, has become the second largest market in the world for pickup trucks, trailing only the United States. Japanese auto analysts estimate that the Asian vehicle market could grow 25 to 30 percent per year through the middle of the decade, making it the fastest growing in the world.

To date, Japanese automakers have had the stage almost all to themselves, controlling 94 percent of the Thai market, 68 percent of sales in Indonesia, and 40 percent of the market in Malaysia. Moreover, Japanese companies are also minority partners in many of the local auto producing firms. Only in Taiwan, where Ford's joint venture partner has a quarter of the market, have U.S. automakers made major inroads.

Detroit is conscious of the need to broaden its Asian base. General Motors plans a small joint venture in Indonesia and hopes to build at least one manufacturing facility in the region. But Japanese auto industry experts predict twelve to sixteen new auto plants are likely to be built in the region by the year 2000, and they expect that U.S. automakers will build no more than two or three of them.

The cost of Detroit's caution will be paid both by the Big Three—Chrysler, Ford, and General Motors—and the U.S. economy. Automakers participating in the rapidly growing East Asian car market in the years ahead will realize tremendous increases in sales volumes that will, in turn, allow them to slide down the cost curve faster than the competition. Companies shut out of Asia will not be forced to adapt to rapidly changing consumer preferences and technological developments likely to occur there. As a result, they will lack a competitive edge in other markets.

Moreover, without a presence in the Asian market, the Big Three will be stuck in North America with all the cyclical business problems dependence upon a single market brings. Meanwhile, Japanese companies will be able to hedge themselves against downturns with markets all over the world. Once the East Asian market takes off, Mitsubishi, Nissan, and Toyota can use their near-monopoly positions there to squeeze vast profits out of the region, much as they have done for years in their home market. If Japanese automakers can create an East Asian cash cow for themselves, they will have the deep pockets to undercut the Big Three in the U.S. market and elsewhere around the world. The consequences for the U.S. trade balance and manufacturing employment in the United States could be severe.

By the end of the decade, U.S. car companies that have as their strategic ambition to be global players will not remain so unless they are major players in the marketplace of Asia.

American Complacency

For too many years Americans have ignored these business opportunities in the Asian-Pacific economies and disregarded the competitive threat posed by the Asian nations and Japan's growing presence in the region. Economic problems at home have preoccupied decision makers. Companies have pursued a shortsighted, bottom-line mentality in which they have been satisfied to reap large profits on small volumes of exports to the Asian-Pacific rather than make costly long-term investments in building up manufacturing and distribution capacity in the region. At the same time, Americans have had a false sense of complacency about Japan's economic penetration of Asia.

For years, U.S. officials have consoled themselves that people in East and Southeast Asia would never allow Japan to dominate the region because of the animosity other Asians bear toward Japan as a result of Japanese atrocities during World War II. At one time the war's legacy was undoubtedly a barrier limiting Japanese business and policy interests in the region. But time heals even the deepest wounds.

To most individuals in the region, World War II is now ancient history. More than four out of five people in Indonesia, Thailand, Malaysia, the Philippines, and Singapore were born after the war. Nearly one out of two is under the age of twenty. To these Asian yuppies, who will run Asian-Pacific governments and companies, and whose thickening wallets will drive Asian consumer markets in the twenty-first century, Japan is Asia's economic *wunderkind*. A generation raised on high-quality Japanese cars and compact discs will look to Tokyo, not New York, as a model for the future. Recent apologies by Japanese prime ministers for Japanese wartime actions have begun to finally close the book on Japan's wartime record. Complaints about Japanese investment emanating from the region are quite muted compared with what is heard about Japanese firms in some parts of the United States and Europe. The United States can no longer depend on bitter Asian memories of World War II, now two generations old, to defend its interests in the region. Nor can the United States continue to rely on its military presence in the region to secure it a seat at the head of the Asian-Pacific economic table.

Thanks to the Seventh Fleet and American bases in Japan, Korea, and the Philippines, the United States long had unparalleled geopolitical influence in Asia. If Washington had a market access problem with Korea, the implicit threat to withdraw U.S. troops from that country, however unlikely Washington was to carry out that threat, ensured that Korea would never openly defy U.S. economic interests for long. The Clinton administration has pledged not to reduce U.S. forces in either Korea or Japan, but the withdrawal of U.S. forces from the Philippines and the ongoing budgetary squeeze in Washington that could force further downsizing of the military sent ominous warning signals. The postwar security-economic equation has been reversed. Where once America's role as the security guarantor of the region ensured certain derivative economic benefits, now that the United States has become a secondary economic presence in Asia, there is no reason to believe that Americans will continue to support a big security presence there unless the economic tide can be stemmed.

What Then Must We Do?

Despite growing trans-Pacific trade volumes, U.S. trade and economic policy toward the Asian-Pacific—manifested in recent years by discriminatory bilateral and aggressive unilateral trade actions—has been inconsistent, incoherent, and incomprehensible to the countries of the region.

The U.S.–Japan Semiconductor Agreement, the Structural Impediments Initiative talks, and the current Framework discussions with Japan have reinforced fears in the region that all Washington cares about is its relationship with Tokyo, and that the United States has no compunction about settling bilateral trade disputes without regard to how the outcomes affect other countries in the region. The fact that many of the deals struck in these talks open Japan's market to all comers—whatever their nationality—is somehow lost on critics within the region. Perception is more important diplomatically than reality.

Recent U.S. threats of trade sanctions against Korea, Thailand, and Indonesia to force changes in their behavior have proven effective in opening their markets for American insurance companies and in increased protection of U.S. intellectual property, but at a cost of reinforcing paranoia in the region.

Washington's decision to negotiate a North American Free Trade Agreement (NAFTA) with Canada and Mexico set off alarm bells throughout the Asian-Pacific. Business leaders and policy makers in the region saw NAFTA as symbolic evidence that the United States planned to turn its back on Asia and retreat within a Western Hemispheric cocoon. NAFTA promised special access to the U.S. market through lower tariffs for products that meet certain rules or origin. East Asians feared, not unreasonably, that the Japanese and other investors who once sank money into their economies would shift their attention to Mexico, and that Asian-Pacific export markets in the United States would dry up. In fact, public opinion polling in the United States shows that building a Western Hemisphere "trading bloc" in order to engage in global economic combat with Japan has great resonance with U.S. voters.

In part, all these problems reflect the absence of formal alliance structures and institutional arrangements to bind the United States to the Asian-Pacific region. Unlike relations across the Atlantic, there is no North Atlantic Treaty Organization or Organization for Economic Cooperation and Development to use as a forum to iron out disagreements, to allay suspicions, and to coordinate policies between major countries. From an Asian perspective, there is no institution in the Pacific comparable to the European

Community, to present a coordinated front in dealing with the United States.

Until recently, Washington has been unconscionably slow in responding to commercial opportunities in the Asian-Pacific. In the last year of the Bush administration, for example, the Commerce Department's Foreign and Commercial Service wanted to send one of its officers to Vietnamese language school to ensure that it had someone ready to hit the ground running, promoting U.S. exports to Vietnam once commercial relations are restored. For months the State Department blocked the assignment, arguing that such a move might suggest that normalization of relations between Washington and Hanoi was imminent.

Such considerations have in no way impaired Japanese government actions in the region. For some time now, the best and the brightest graduating from Tokyo's Todai University—the equivalent of Harvard, Yale, and Princeton rolled into one—who join Japan's foreign service have chosen to work on Asian affairs. Their predecessors always built their careers working on North American affairs.

Japan's Ministry of International Trade and Industry and its Economic Planning Agency have also upgraded the caliber of staff they send to Bangkok, Jakarta, and other capitals in the region. Their task is to monitor economic developments, collect information, and act as marriage brokers between local governments and Japanese companies. Many officials in East Asian governments now say Japan has better information about their economies than they do.

In recent years, Tokyo has given the region far more foreign aid than has Washington. Moreover, half of this assistance goes to infrastructure and industrial projects (only one-twentieth of U.S. assistance is so targeted). Such emphasis puts Japanese industrialists in direct contact with the economic elites of the region, building ties that can only help future Japanese trade and investment.

The need to develop closer economic and political ties across the Pacific was an idea first suggested by Australia, but U.S. leaders were slow to pick up the ball. In the 1980s Secretary of State George Shultz and later Secretary of State James Baker called for formation of a Pacific Community, but gave the idea little of their time or energy. APEC was finally formed in 1989, but it was slow to come together as an institution and formed a small secretariat only in 1992. Finally, during the 1992 presidential campaign, George Bush proposed signing a free trade agreement with Southeast Asia. The idea was dismissed as mere election year rhetoric and not taken seriously by trade policy makers in Washington. But in retrospect, that proposal and the tentative efforts that preceded it reflected a growing recognition in Washington that the United States could no longer afford to remain a spectator while American business continues to sit on the Asian sidelines.

It is the Clinton administration's task to build on this groundwork. Philosophically, an Asian initiative should marry well with President Clinton's broader thinking on foreign policy and economics issues. Decrying past administrations' compartmentalization of international and domestic policies, Clinton promised to "make the economic security of our own nation a primary goal of our foreign policy," in a speech he gave to the diplomatic corps at Georgetown University on January 19, 1993, the day before his inauguration.

Since his inauguration President Clinton has waxed eloquent about the conjunction of corporate and national self-interest and the merits of greater partnership between business and government. He has promised greater coordination of corporate and national competitive strategies to maximize U.S. interests in Asia and elsewhere.

For U.S. economic policy makers mired in a slow economic recovery, the Asian-Pacific holds out the prospect of a quick fix. By tapping into the region's economic dynamism, the United States may be able to increase exports and improve the competitiveness of its major industries, spurring domestic economic growth in the process.

The initial challenge in that scenario is convincing U.S. business leaders that Asia represents an important future economic partner. Of course, there is little Washington can do to better integrate the U.S. economy with the Asian-Pacific, or to checkmate Japan's growing influence in the region and moderate its adverse impact on the United States, unless U.S. companies are willing to beef up their investment and trade ties in the region and go head-to-head with their Asian rivals. Many American firms say that is impossible. Overseas investment is too risky and expensive, they say, thanks to the lagging economic recovery and the weak dollar. Corporate America is also preoccupied with continuing to defend its home turf against Japanese and European competition, and in exploring the myriad new market opportunities posed by the impending free trade pact with Mexico.

Turning those attitudes around will be no easy task. To date, Washington has sent conflicting signals to the business community. The very fact of negotiating the NAFTA deal suggested to business leaders that if they had one additional plant to build outside the United States, Mexico was the place to build it. The importance of Asia to America's economic future needs to be underscored in words and actions.

Macroeconomic initiatives—national health care reform or long-term equity investment incentives—would go a long way toward improving corporate bottom lines and increasing the availability of capital for companies to invest in Asia. But such proposals have been advocated in the past to no avail, or could take years to come to fruition. The window of competitive opportunity in Asia will begin to close by the end of the decade.

Options for more targeted public policy initiatives focusing on economic relations with the Asian-Pacific are unfortunately limited. Creation of an Asian-Pacific free trade area is an alluring project, but economists note that such an endeavor would bring limited immediate economic benefits to the United States. In addition, the public concerns stirred up by the NAFTA debate in the United States suggest that any attempt to unite markets of such disparate size, wealth, and cultural background is a prescription for political trouble. Nevertheless, on a less ambitious scale there are initiatives that could begin to build a Pacific economic community.

At the macroeconomic level, a number of Asian-Pacific nations have periodically manipulated their currencies to promote exports and curtail imports. Through restrictive fiscal policies they have constrained domestic consumption at times when they could afford more imports and when the world economy would have benefited mightily from their increased consumption. Creation of better consultative mechanisms between finance ministries and central banks in the region would deepen understanding of the international consequences of domestic economic policies and avoid fractious finger pointing in the future.

At the microeconomic level, there are opportunities for initiatives to spur both trade and investment. Regardless of the outcome of the Uruguay Round of multilateral trade negotiations, multilateral rules are likely to trail developments in the real world of commerce. To avoid new trade friction, it will be necessary for the players in the most rapidly growing region of the world economy to impose upon themselves a higher standard than that finally agreed to under the General Agreement on Tariffs and Trade (GATT). These efforts—be they new codes on subsidies or intellectual property—should be in the context of GATT rules and obligations. Moreover, they should not be discriminatory, and should be open to all countries willing to incur the same obligations. But they should set a higher standard of economic liberalization and deregulation wherever feasible.

To encourage exports to the Asian-Pacific region and elsewhere, the Clinton administration has launched a concerted export promotion program, including new advisory services and financing opportunities for small and medium-sized businesses, and relaxation of some export controls on high-tech products much in demand in the newly industrialized nations of Asia. But without adequate funding, always a difficulty in budget cutting times, these initiatives may fall flat.

Public procurement presents a particularly promising export market in the region. The Asian-Pacific governments have embarked on one of the most massive public infrastructure spending campaigns in human history. Tens of billions of dollars will be spent in the region in the next decade building roads, airports, telecommunications links, harbors, and mass transit lines. In the past such contracts have often been reserved solely for national companies, and there is some concern that Japan's substantial program of foreign aid for infrastructure projects will give its firms a leg up in supplying the equipment and expertise for these endeavors. It would be useful to have a joint approach to financing new infrastructure projects in the region, involving increased U.S.

aid and nondiscriminatory bidding on contracts. Tokyo is likely to resist such a proposal, for the obvious reason that its firms have most to gain from the status quo. But resolute pursuit of this advantage will only lead to discord and trade confrontations.

Countries in the region have different standards for telecommunications and other big-ticket items. As new telecommunications networks are constructed, common standards would facilitate trade. APEC advisory groups are working on these issues. But as recent standard-setting exercises within the European Community have demonstrated, this process is fraught with controversy.

Since trade follows investment, impediments that impair companies setting up shop in the region need to be eliminated. All East and Southeast Asian governments impose local content and other investment restrictions on foreign automakers, for example. To make that investment environment more competitive, those requirements have to be eliminated.

A regional investment agreement assuring the right of establishment, transparent regulations and dispute settlement procedures, and a code of conduct for multinational corporations would go a long way toward leveling the investment playing field. The Clinton administration hopes to negotiate just such a region-wide agreement under APEC auspices.

Politics may prove the biggest challenge facing Washington in its efforts to tap into Asian-Pacific dynamism. Recent U.S. public opinion polling and focus groups suggest that Americans are increasingly wary of trade. Where once international commerce was seen as an unalloyed good, now it is viewed as a net negative. Trade is seen as costing jobs, not creating them. Contrary to evidence of mounting U.S. exports, many people think there is nothing the United States makes that foreigners want to buy, and that there is little Americans make that foreigners can't make more cheaply and more efficiently. Further integration into the world economy is seen as a net negative. These sentiments manifested themselves in the opposition to NAFTA and could reemerge if there is any serious effort to bring the U.S. economy closer to Asia's.

Even limited initiatives could face opposition. For example, during the presidential campaign candidate Bill Clinton hammered the U.S. Agency for International Development, the foreign aid arm of the U.S. government, for encouraging relatively minor U.S. investment in Central America. Any concerted effort to promote deeper economic integration with the Asian-Pacific is bound to lead to headlines spurred on by Ross Perot and others, alleging that the White House is intent on exporting U.S. jobs.

One trump card the Clinton administration can play in crafting an Asian-Pacific policy is the American public's abiding concern about Japan. Contrary to the widespread perception of American parochialism, polling data suggest many Americans have begun to think in geoeconomic terms. For example, public opposition to NAFTA is transformed into support if free trade with Mexico is posed as a means of building an "economic bloc" to better compete with Japan.

An Asian-Pacific region without a formal set of multilateral trade and investment rules and institutions will be dominated by informal bilateral relations between Tokyo and the various capitals of the region. This unequal relationship is clearly not in the U.S. interest, nor is it likely to be in the interest of the countries involved. It may not even be in Japan's long-term self-interest, because it will eventually sow new seeds of distrust and frustration with Tokyo.

APEC provides an opportunity to embed Japan in an institutional relationship with Asia, much as Germany was embedded in Europe through the creation of the European Community. Such a regional approach will in no way supplant U.S. bilateral relations with Japan. The bilateral economic and security issues that engage Washington and Tokyo are clearly of such importance to both parties that the current "special relationship" between the United States and Japan is likely to continue for the foreseeable future. But some of the tension that has developed around these issues may be defused if they are folded into a multilateral context. Washington may gain some leverage with Tokyo if other Asian governments join it in pressing Japan to open its markets to more imports. At the same time, Tokyo may see an advantage in presenting a common Asian front against unilateral U.S. trade sanctions.

It will only be through close cooperation between Washington and Tokyo that a strong APEC may be possible, because only these two economic powers have the broad range of economic and security interests, and the diplomatic and business clout, to overcome individual country or industrial sector objections to reduction of regional trade and investment barriers.

In the end, further economic integration of the United States into the Asian-Pacific region is inevitable. The dynamic of the global economy is rapidly building bridges across the Pacific, as evidenced by growing U.S. imports from the region. The challenge facing policy makers is how to ensure that this economic integration is balanced, that the United States is both a market of and a supplier to the rapidly growing economies of the Asian-Pacific.

An even tougher task faces the American public. The economic challenge posed by the Asian-Pacific region will only intensify in the years ahead. Competing with that region will be a difficult and often painful task. It will involve sacrifice and an acceptance that the United States is no longer in an economic league of its own. But failure to rise to the challenge will be even more painful and could sentence this generation's children and grandchildren to a secondary role in the global economy.

Notes

[1] Our thanks to Ernest H. Preeg, an economist with the Center for Strategic and International Studies (CSIS), a Washington think tank, for the characterization of the Asian-Pacific region as a black hole.

5

Southeast Asia and U.S.–Japan Relations

CHARLES E. MORRISON

J apan's role in, and relations with, Southeast Asia have changed dramatically and positively over the past quarter-century. In the 1960s Southeast Asians frequently expressed concern about Japan as a security threat; indeed one 1969 survey of the Indonesian elite found that 84 percent thought Japan was a threat, compared to 67 percent for China, a country widely believed to have been behind a 1965 coup attempt. Resentments over alleged Japanese economic exploitation boiled over into riots in two Southeast

CHARLES E. MORRISON is director of the Program on International Economics and Politics at the East-West Center. He is also an affiliate research associate at the Japan Center for International Exchange in Tokyo. From 1972–80 he worked as a legislative assistant to Senator William V. Roth, Jr., and during part of this time he also taught Southeast Asian politics and international relations at the Johns Hopkins School of Advanced International Studies. He has served as a research adviser to the Japan–United States Economic Relations ("Wisemen's") Group and the U.S.–Japan Advisory Commission. Dr. Morrison is the author or editor of numerous books, including most recently *Japan, China, and the Newly Industrialized Economies of East Asia* and *The Pacific Islands— Politics, Economics and International Relations*.

Asian cities, Jakarta and Bangkok, when former Prime Minister Kakuei Tanaka visited the region in January 1974.

Two recent developments illustrate the changed tone of the relationship. In December 1990 Malaysian Prime Minister Mohamad Mahathir, an unabashed admirer of the Japanese economic model, proposed the creation of an East Asian Economic Group (later "caucus" in place of "group"), or EAEC. This, warned some Americans, could be tantamount to a new Japanese dominated "Coprosperity Sphere." Although the EAEC was received with mixed feelings in Asia, there is little evidence that the evocation of anti-Japanese fears or the negative image of the prewar Coprosperity Sphere found much resonance in the region.

Perhaps even more dramatic was the reappearance of Japanese troops in Southeast Asia for the first time since World War II, this time under the banner of the United Nations forces in Cambodia. Although cautiously accepted in the region, they were positively welcomed by the Cambodians and their immediate neighbors, and the strictures placed upon them through the political process in Japan reassured the other countries. As they left in September 1993, it was with the reported goodwill of their local hosts. According to one Khmer teacher, "It's very different from 1945. This time they came to rehabilitate Cambodia. The Japanese soldiers of 1992–93 are very good."

This chapter addresses two principal issues. First, it looks at the change in attitude in Southeast Asia. What political and economic factors have caused this change? Is it likely to be permanent? Second, it addresses the implications for the United States. Do improving Japanese–Southeast Asian relations negatively affect the United States?

Some Basic Points

In addressing the interactions among Japan, Southeast Asia, and the United States, it is useful to begin with some fundamentals.

First, while the United States and Japan are countries, Southeast Asia is a large geographical region of some ten nations and 435 million people. Within this region, there is tremendous variation in historical experiences and in the cultures, economies, and political systems. Variation occurs not only across countries, but also within countries. Although this chapter frequently refers to Southeast Asia and Southeast Asians, it should be kept in mind that these terms are generalizations and can be misleading. Most of the focus here is on Japan's relations with the Association of Southeast Asian Nations (ASEAN) countries, which have integrated themselves into the global economy and maintained close relations with Japan and the West. The poorest of these countries, Indonesia, now has a per capita income of almost $600 (see Table 1). However, more than 120 million Southeast Asians are in Vietnam, Cambodia, Laos, and Burma (renamed "Myanmar" by its military government), which are among the poorest and most desperate countries in the world.

Second, by virtue of its geography, Southeast Asia traditionally has been a meeting place of peoples and cultures, and an avenue for navigation and commerce. Sixty percent of its population lives on islands, and much of the remainder lives within easy access to the sea. From precolonial times, the Southeast Asian societies were subject to outside influences, first from the Indian and Chinese civilizations (taking much more from the former than the latter), and later from Europe and the United States. At some historical period or another, China, Portugal, Spain, Holland, Britain, France, the United States, and briefly Japan have all occupied and ruled territory in the region.

The overall impact of this historical experience has been both to internationalize much of Southeast Asia (where international languages are spoken with much more fluency than in other parts of East Asia) and to make its societies very jealous of their sovereignty. In the postcolonial period, some Southeast Asia countries sought to strengthen themselves through extensive outside contacts, and others—Burma is the most extreme case—sought to protect their independence through isolation.

Third, there are vast asymmetries of power between the United States and Japan as developed countries on the one hand, and Southeast Asia as a region of developing or newly industrialized countries on the other. Southeast Asia, however, should not be regarded as simply an arena for competition or cooperation

TABLE 1. Macroeconomic Statistics: Southeast Asia

Country	Population		GNP			Direction of Exports				Direction of Imports			
	Mns. 1990	Growth (%) 1988–2000	Bns. 1990	Per Cap. 1990	Growth (%) 1980–90	% to Japan 1970	1991	% to U.S. 1970	1991	% from Japan 1970	1991	% from U.S. 1970	1991
Brunei	0.3	na	na	na	na	0.5	53.8	0.0	1.0	13.7	8.0	0.0	10.0
Indonesia	178.2	1.6	107.3	570	5.5	40.8	37.0	13.0	12.0	29.4	24.5	17.8	13.1
Malaysia	17.9	2.3	42.4	2320	5.2	18.3	15.9	13.0	16.9	17.5	26.1	8.6	15.3
Philippines	61.5	2.4	43.9	730	0.9	40.1	20.0	41.6	35.7	30.6	19.4	29.4	20.2
Singapore	3.0	1.2	34.6	11160	6.4	7.4	8.7	10.7	19.7	18.0	21.3	10.1	15.6
Thailand	55.8	1.4	80.2	1420	7.6	25.5	17.8	13.4	21.1	37.4	29.1	14.9	10.5
ASEAN	316.4	na	308.4	975	na	23.7	18.2	17.0	18.6	24.7	24.1	14.6	14.5
Burma	41.6	2.0	na	na	na	na	8.4	na	5.0	na	8.5	na	2.5
Cambodia	8.5	1.9	na	na	na	na	na	na	na	na	na	na	na
Laos	4.1	3.2	0.9	200	na	na	5.1	na	2.5	na	15.5	na	0.6
Vietnam	66.3	2.1	na	na	na	na	37.9	na	na	27.1	14.3	na	na

Sources: The World Bank, *World Development Report 1993*; East-West Center Program on International Politics and Economics Data Base.

among outside powers. The countries of the region are increasingly becoming the arbiters of the international order within their region, and are also having an impact beyond it. They operate in complex ways with Americans, Japanese, and others, and usually on issues of their own region as the dominant powers.

This leads to a final, derivative point. It is increasingly less accurate to think of Japan, the United States, and Southeast Asia as a triangle. The relations among the three take place in a broader regional and global context. In particular, the three Chinas (mainland China, Taiwan, and Hong Kong) and South Korea are increasingly relevant actors that must be taken into account in any analysis of Japanese–Southeast Asian, U.S.–Southeast Asian, or, indeed, U.S.–Japan relations. A number of other regions or countries—Western Europe, Australia, and India—are also important, although less so.

Japanese–Southeast Asian Relations in Historical Perspective

One of the most striking aspects of Japanese–Southeast Asian relations is their comparative lack of historical and cultural depth. Both Japan and the Southeast Asian societies drew on some of the same Chinese and Indian religious and philosophical traditions, but the direct contact between them was limited even before the Tokugawa shogunate at the beginning of the seventeenth century initiated a two-and-a-half century period of Japanese isolation. Southeast Asian contact with other countries in Asia and the West was much greater than with Japan. The period of European and American colonialism witnessed a large immigration of Chinese from southern coastal areas, who later became the commercial elites of the region. Because of their controversial position in many Southeast Asian societies, these Chinese have often been a liability in China's relations with Southeast Asia, but today they are a strong force for economic linkages. Western colonialism had a strong and lasting cultural impact, providing the basis for sustained cultural linkages with Europe and America. No comparable ties connect Southeast Asia with Japan.

Japan is the only power ever to have controlled the entire

Southeast Asia region, but this was for a period of less than four years. It was long enough to leave a legacy of Southeast Asian bitterness and wariness toward Japan, although certainly not so deep or lasting as in the Korean Peninsula or China. But it was not long enough to establish any kind of positive Japanese cultural orientation among the Southeast Asian elites, or to create a Japanese community with deep experience in or affinity for Southeast Asia. In building a new relationship with Southeast Asia following World War II, therefore, Japan faced a hostile environment with few assets on which to draw.

Aside from the World War II legacy, another negative was the early cold war economic interaction between Japan and Southeast Asia. From the late 1950s, Japan was a large aid provider to the region (its bilateral aid currently is more than ten times that of the United States), and the Southeast Asian region traditionally had trade surpluses with Japan, for most countries their largest or second largest market. However, the pattern of economic interaction was regarded in Southeast Asia as "colonial" in nature. For postwar Japan, Southeast Asia was to some extent the economic equivalent of prewar Korea and China. The Japanese purchased Southeast Asia's fuels, minerals, and other primary products, and sold manufactured goods. They invested in resource exploration and extraction activities and in distribution networks for their products. In the process, they were said to corrupt local administrators and politicians.

A Turning Point in Relations

The 1974 Tanaka trip to the ASEAN countries marked the high point in post–World War II Southeast Asian resentments. Domestic politics having little to do with Japan played an important role in the demonstrations occasioned by the former prime minister's stops in Jakarta and Bangkok, but it was no coincidence that antigovernment demonstrators in these two capitals picked Japan as their ostensible target and rallying point. They could appeal to real resentments that made it difficult for governments to oppose them.

The 1974 events had a sobering impact both in Tokyo and in the ASEAN capitals. As Yoshihide Soeya points out, the trip reflected a Japanese perception in the 1970s that Japan could develop a more autonomous approach to Southeast Asia in the wake of a reduced U.S. presence in the region.[1] This appealed to a sense of nationalism, but was also compatible with a close relationship with the United States, as it was interpreted as "burden sharing." The Jakarta and Bangkok demonstrations, however, challenged some early Japanese optimism and cherished notions that, for example, Japan could serve as a bridge between Southeast Asia and the West, and Japanese economic activities could be separated from political relations.

The Japanese foreign policy establishment was galvanized to give more attention to the political and cultural aspects of Japan's relations with Southeast Asia, and to take other steps to moderate tensions associated with economic relations. Three years later, Prime Minister Takeo Fukuda outlined a new approach based on "heart-to-heart" diplomacy. This included a strong renunciation of a military role, increased economic assistance, and support for the ASEAN organization. Very significantly, the 1977 Fukuda "doctrine" also suggested a political role for Japan in promoting reconciliation between the ASEAN and Indochinese countries. This was abandoned following Vietnam's intervention in Cambodia, but has been revived more recently. The key points of the approach associated with Fukuda have been periodically reaffirmed, including during the January 1993 trip to the region of Prime Minister Kiichi Miyazawa. Japan continues to hope to play an integrating and stabilizing role in Southeast Asia, and again in a context of apparent lack of a prominent U.S. interest in the region.

The events of 1974 also caused a reevaluation of the Japanese relationship in the ASEAN countries. The ASEAN governmental elites had come to depend on Japanese aid, trade, investment, and technology, but were not fully cognizant of the importance of Japan to their own economies and political positions. They had found it easy to criticize Japan with impunity; now they recognized that this could have serious domestic political consequences and potentially a drastic effect on their economies. In the wake of the collapse of the U.S. effort in Vietnam and uncertainty about the future of the U.S. military and economic presence in the region, they needed international friends more than ever, and Japan was the chief source of economic support and of growing importance for diplomatic backing.

If the 1974–77 period marked a major turning point in Japanese–Southeast Asian relations, a number of later developments have reinforced the trend toward strengthened ties. We examine these reinforcing factors in three realms: the international political-security environment, economic relations, and changing attitudes.

The International Environment

The impending end of the cold war created an international political-security environment in Southeast Asia in the late 1980s and early 1990s somewhat analogous to that in the mid-1970s. Although there was no immediate threat to the security of the nations of the region, the winding down of two of the large power geopolitical rivalries (U.S.–Soviet and Sino-Soviet) that played an important role in the balances of power in Southeast Asia created considerable anxiety among Southeast Asia's basically status quo oriented governments. The termination of U.S.–Soviet rivalry removed what had come to be considered a distant and unlikely threat (the Soviet Union), but also called into question the continuation of what the ASEAN countries regarded as the reassuring presence of the United States. Would there be sufficient reason for the United States to maintain its military presence following the collapse of the Soviet Union? The 1991 Gulf War sent an ambiguous signal; the United States committed itself to the survival of a small country, but this was where oil was at stake, and it seemed to require the financial support of others. The equanimity, or enthusiasm, with which the United States ultimately abandoned its bases in the Philippines sent another, and to many Southeast Asians, more disturbing signal.

The end of Sino-Soviet rivalry was of equal significance in Southeast Asia. This rivalry seemed to be the main active check on Asia's largest indigenous military power; it was the card that Vietnam had played, although not entirely successfully. With its collapse, Vietnam was forced to make its accommodation with the

Chinese, withdrawing its forces from Cambodia in 1989 and later sacrificing its anti-Chinese foreign minister.

China, until recently regarded in the ASEAN region as a strategic ally against Vietnam, is now clearly seen as the region's most likely potential security threat. The rapid growth of Chinese defense spending, China's publicized acquisitions of or interest in purchases of Russian equipment and military technology, its use of political and military pressure in dealing with Vietnam, and its continued pressing of its claims to the Spratly islets and reefs in the South China Sea hundreds of miles south of the Chinese mainland and overlapping several Southeast Asian claims are all suggestive of a country dissatisfied with the current regional order. China's rapid economic expansion further fuels apprehensions, not only providing the base for a strong and more technologically capable military, but increased economic competition. Added to this is the uncertainty about the nature of China's future political leadership.

In this context, a status quo oriented Japan in alliance with the United States is seen as a supporter and counterweight, not in a traditional balance of power sense, but for its political and diplomatic support and the stabilizing influence of its economic presence. From the ASEAN governments' perspectives, Japan is the large country most likely to share a similar perspective with themselves on regional political and security issues, and the most likely to listen to ASEAN government positions. Although the Japanese are less vocal than the Southeast Asians, they are known to share the similar concerns about China's future role, and therefore are a natural "ally." They are seen to some extent as a substitute for a more active U.S. presence, but also key to keeping the United States engaged in the region. Without Japan as a strategic base and partner, the U.S. presence would lose its credibility. Finally, ASEAN governments regard Japan as potentially a moderating influence on what they regard as too assertive a U.S. policy on human rights and other political issues.

The 1993 decision to establish an ASEAN Regional Forum (ARF) for intergovernmental dialogue is the outstanding example of Japan–ASEAN political-security cooperation. First mooted by strategic studies institutes in Southeast Asia, the idea was modified and made a formal proposal in 1991 at the ASEAN Post-Ministerial Conference by former Japanese Foreign Minister Taro Nakayama. Like the Fukuda approach of the late 1970s, the Nakayama proposal represented a modest Japanese effort to push out the envelope of Japanese political involvement in Southeast Asia, without overtly threatening the U.S. position. Although not opposing it outright, as it had other proposals for multilateral regional security cooperation, the Bush administration had reservations. But the Clinton administration was in wholehearted agreement with supplementing U.S. bilateral security cooperation in Asia with a multilateral dialogue, and agreement to move forward with the ARF dialogue was achieved at the ASEAN Post-Ministerial Conference in July 1993. For the ASEAN countries, the forum will be a means of keeping outside large powers involved on a multilateral basis in the region, reducing the likelihood that they will have to face a specific threat on their own. For Japan also, the forum helps assure a dialogue with the Chinese on regional issues, but one that includes Japan's major security ally, the United States. It continues a process of diversifying Japan's political-security connections in Asia and the Pacific, but still within the context of close U.S.–Japan security relations.

The desire for a Japanese political and economic presence is probably felt even more keenly in Indochina than among the ASEAN governments. Japan is the largest donor of assistance to Cambodia and Laos, and will be again to Vietnam. Since the Japanese foreign policy is dominated by the bureaucracy and prefers to work with existing governments rather than press for internal political reforms or rapid privatization outside governmental control, the noneconomic "strings" on assistance are relatively few. While there is tremendous interest in Indochina in developing ties with the United States, the United States is seen as having less intrinsic interest in the region and a more ideological approach. Thus from a strictly pragmatic perspective, Japan becomes key in these governments' fight for survival.

Changing Economic Patterns

Changes in the economic circumstances of Japan and the Southeast Asian countries and in their economic relations have been gradually modifying the perceptions in Southeast Asia of one-sided exploitation. Several features stand out: growing economic confidence in Southeast Asia, the alteration of the "colonial" pattern of economic interaction, and the augmented economic role of the newly industrialized economies (NIEs).

The sustained growth of most of the ASEAN countries has given their governments and business communities increased confidence that they can deal with Japanese and other foreign counterparts on a more equal basis. Southeast Asia increasingly has its own large and prosperous businesses, capable of contributing to joint venture arrangements, and less vulnerable to any partner. Adding to Southeast Asian confidence has been the experience of the years 1991–93, as growth in Southeast Asia continued despite the recession in Japan and the United States.

Changes in Japan's economic and demographic profile support the continuing of a trend toward Japanese investment in Southeast Asian manufacturing facilities and exports to third countries or back to Japan. The appreciation of the yen, the increase in wage rates in Japan associated with the tightening labor market, and other cost factors have made the Southeast Asian economies increasingly attractive as locations for production and exporting. Much of the ASEAN region experienced a wave of Japanese investment following sharp appreciation of the yen in 1985–86. This has tapered off with the collapse of the bubble economy in the 1990s, but there continues to be a strong Japanese interest in Southeast Asia. The 1993 yen appreciation will further encourage investment, while increased competition tends to shift this investment interest from the higher-cost Southeast Asian countries (such as Malaysia and Thailand) toward lower-cost countries such as Indonesia and Vietnam.

In contrast to earlier investment, the new Japanese investment is much more associated with manufactured production than with raw material exploitation, and with exporting rather than with domestic marketing. It is the kind of investment that is appreciated in Southeast Asia. While third markets such as the United States remain the most important final destination, Japan is an increasingly important market for ASEAN manufactures. Japanese imports of primary products (particularly in value terms) have declined, and with them Southeast Asian trade surpluses with Japan and Japan's share in Southeast Asia's global exports. However, the proportion of manufactured goods in Japan's imports from ASEAN rose dramatically from 6.1 percent in 1980 to 9.2 percent in 1985, and to 27.3 percent in 1990. The decline in Indonesian and Malaysian oil and gas prices is an important factor in this shift, but not the whole story. The absolute value of manufactured goods exports from ASEAN to Japan increased by over 40 percent annually in the 1986–88 period. Since all of the ASEAN governments place a high value on the growth of labor-absorbing manufacturing production and exports, such figures have contributed to the sense that Southeast Asia increasingly benefits from its trade with Japan.

The growth of a more multilateral Asian-Pacific economy with the rise of the newly industrialized economies, South Korea, and China as major trade, investment, and technological powers is diluting the former prominence of both Japan and the United States as economic partners of the Southeast Asian countries. Overseas Chinese and South Korean investment, in fact, has grown even more rapidly than Japanese investment in Southeast Asia. In 1990, for example, new foreign investment from the newly industrialized economies (including Singapore) accounted for 48 percent of investment in Malaysia (compared to 29 percent for Japanese investment). The comparable figures for the Philippines were 40 percent (compared to 32 percent), and for Indonesia were 30 percent (compared to 26 percent). In Thailand, NIE and Japanese investment each accounted for about 34 percent of new investment.

NIE investment has been even more prominent in areas of higher risk. In Vietnam, the Japanese government delayed the resumption of its bilateral aid program until after the 1992 U.S. presidential election for fear of U.S. reaction, and this and the similar constraints on Japanese companies restrained Japanese investment. According to Vietnamese statistics, during the 1988–92 period, the largest overseas investment came from Taiwan ($789 million), followed by Hong Kong ($606 million). The Japanese with $305 million were the sixth largest source of direct foreign investment, although the pace of Japanese investment appears to have increased.

The nature of NIE investment also affects the relative reputation of the Japanese as investors in Southeast Asia. The NIE investors tend to be smaller and medium-sized companies, more likely to compete with local industries and less responsible with respect to working conditions, the environment, and corporate contributions to communities. They are also perceived as less willing to transfer technology or engage in training of the labor force. Although smaller Japanese firms have also been investing in Southeast Asia, the large-scale investments by established Japanese firms have been more prominent, and have generally looked good to Southeast Asian governments and media in comparison with NIE investments.

There are still many sources of tensions in Japanese–Southeast Asian economic relations. Southeast Asians complain that the Japanese continue to invest far more in the United States and even Europe than in Asia. They worry about investment diversion from Southeast Asia to other areas—Mexico, China, and South Asia. Like other foreigners, the region's manufacturers find it very difficult to break into Japanese markets except under conditions controlled by Japanese partners. There are constant complaints that Japanese firms are reluctant to transfer technologies. Perhaps more galling has been the reluctance of the Japanese to use Southeast Asians in key management positions, because this contrasts sharply with the Japanese practice in North America and Western Europe and is suggestive of cultural prejudice. Specific disputes can become heavily politicized, as in a current controversy between the Japanese builders of a Bangkok expressway and the Thai government authorities.

Despite such complaints and controversies, the complementarity of the Japanese and the Southeast Asian economies and the dynamic interaction between them suggest an evolving, mutually beneficial economic relationship. If there are political challenges to this relationship from Southeast Asians, they are more likely to evolve as a broad challenge to the integration of their economies into the global economic system as a whole, rather than targeted toward their economic interaction with Japan as a specific country.

Changing Perceptions

The changes in political-security environment and economic relations contribute to changes in Southeast Asian perceptions of Japan's regional role. Other factors also contribute. One is the fading of World War II memories. Another is a still weak but growing cultural dimension to Japanese–Southeast Asian ties. The negative legacy of World War II is stronger in some countries (for example, the Philippines) and among some groups (ethnic Chinese in Malaysia and Singapore) than in other countries (Thailand, Burma) or communities (Malays in Malaysia and Singapore). Even among the most affected countries and ethnic groups, however, the impact of Japanese aggression was less than in the Korean Peninsula and China, and the salience of this historical era is gradually receding with generational change and more recent images of modern Japan. Recent controversies regarding Japan's wartime role, such as the treatment of the war in Japanese school textbooks and the "comfort women" issue, have their echoes in Southeast Asia, but without the same intensity of feelings that is found in Northeast Asia. There is no doubt of the strong feeling throughout the region that Japan not become a military power, but as indicated in the preceding discussions of political and economic issues, historically based emotions have generally given way to pragmatism in the way Southeast Asian elites approach the Japanese.

Growing positive cultural contacts have contributed to this picture. As referred to earlier, Japan has relatively few cultural assets compared to the West or China. But since the mid-1970s, it has invested in strengthening the cultural dimensions of the relationships with the ASEAN countries. New programs, such as the Japanese funded ASEAN Cultural Fund and the ASEAN Youth Scholarship, were established. Research and exchange programs proliferated, and there has been a boom in Japanese language and area studies in Southeast Asia. The Japanese business and tourist presence in the region has grown enormously, while the legal presence of Southeast Asians in Japan has also expanded (not to mention the larger illegal populations). Between 1986 and 1991, for example, the Filipino population in Japan tripled, from 19,000 to 62,000, exceeding the number of Americans. In 1990 Thailand hosted 14,000 Japanese residents. This was the largest Japanese presence anywhere in Asia (just above Hong Kong and Singapore), but only the eighth largest Japanese presence worldwide.

All these factors create more familiarity, although certainly not all positive in nature. On the cultural dimension, however, Japan continues to lag behind many Western societies. For example, despite a campaign to increase foreign students in Japan, the number is still small by American, Australian, or Western European standards. In 1990 the largest Southeast Asian groups were 1,544 Malaysians and 948 Indonesians, including vocational students. The West, especially the United States, remains by far the preferred destination for Southeast Asian students. At the same time, Southeast Asian studies and languages remain esoteric in Japan, and Japanese interest in the area seems to lag far behind its interest in the United States, Western Europe, and Northeast Asia.

Implications for U.S.–Japanese Relations

How do improved Japanese–Southeast Asian relations affect the United States? Until the mid-1970s the United States unequivocally supported closer political and economic relations among its friends in Northeast and Southeast Asia, regarding them as a form of burden sharing. It cheered, for example, the creation in 1966 of the short-lived Asia-Pacific Council (ASPAC) linking a reluctant Japan with South Korea, Taiwan, and a number of countries in Southeast Asia and the Southwest Pacific, a grouping that, except for the exclusion of China and inclusion of Taiwan, Australia, and New Zealand, does not look all that different from the more contemporary East Asian Economic Caucus proposal. In the same year, Japan initiated a series of ministerial conferences on the economic development of Southeast Asia. Once again, this was with Washington's blessing, even though the United States was not included.

But as the United States began to see Japan more and more as a challenger to the U.S. position in the region, and as U.S.–Japanese economic relations deteriorated, Americans became more wary of the evolving Japanese regional role in Southeast Asia. Among the concerns and charges are these:

- Japan has used its massive bilateral aid programs and dominant position in the Asian Development Bank and other regional institutions to promote its own exports and increasingly cut Americans out of booming Southeast Asian markets.
- Japanese firms have strengthened their competitive positions in the United States and circumvented U.S. import controls by making use of Southeast Asian (and other) economies as export platforms to penetrate the U.S. market.
- Japanese economic links with Southeast Asia are of an exclusivist nature, mirroring discriminatory business practices and government-business relationships in Japan itself. The interconnected groupings of Japanese companies (*keiretsu* system) and other anticompetitive Japanese business practices are being diffused throughout Asia.
- Japan may be building an East Asian economic bloc. Such a bloc not only would threaten U.S. access to Asian markets, but could challenge the U.S. global leadership position as Japan takes more independent political positions. Japan sees an alternative to the United States in its economic relations with other Asian countries, and the availability of this option will lessen its willingness to accommodate the United States on a variety of economic and political issues.

Behind these concerns lies a more general ambivalence about East Asian growth and the U.S. position in the region. Some Americans regard Asian economic development as a success story for U.S. policy objectives in the region, and see U.S.–Asian-Pacific interaction as economically beneficial to Americans. But many others see past U.S. support for that development more as instrumental in achieving a no longer relevant cold war containment goal rather than as highly desirable in itself. This view stresses that the economic growth of Asia, with Japan in the lead, dilutes U.S. political and economic power, and establishes formidable economic competitors. Even if the United States may benefit in absolute terms from its economic interaction with Asia, its lower relative growth changes the relative weight of the United States vis-à-vis other countries, and creates an environment less controllable by the United States itself.

The more specific fears about Japan's economic role should certainly not be entirely discounted, but they are exaggerated. In trade terms, Japan has replaced the United States in Southeast Asia only marginally. In recent years its share of ASEAN imports has remained nearly constant at about 25 percent, and so has the U.S. share at about 13 to 14 percent. Investment statistics are notoriously difficult to compare, and current U.S. and Japanese means of counting data tend to magnify Japan's investments. Clearly companies of both countries use Southeast Asia as a manufacturing and exporting platform. Electronic firms from both, for example, have made Malaysia the world's largest exporter of semiconductor chips. It is true that Japanese affiliates tend to export more to third countries (including the United States) than do U.S. firms, whose production tends to be directed toward the home market. But it is not clear that distinctive Japanese business practices and government-business relationships are being replicated in Southeast Asia to the disadvantage of Americans. In a 1993 survey, Wendy Dobson concludes that Japanese firms are less open than American firms to outside suppliers (both prefer Japanese suppliers), but that in the electrical/electronics industries there is a tendency toward convergence. U.S. firms increasingly invest in long-term supplier relationships, while Japanese firms are accommodating to ASEAN government pressures to use local suppliers.[2] However, analysis of private sector relationships and their implications remains incomplete.

The expansion of Japan's diplomatic and political role in Southeast Asia will continue, based on the complementary interests of Japanese and Southeast Asia referred to earlier in this chapter. This expansion is not mediated by the United States, but represents a broadening of independent contacts by Japanese and Southeast Asians with each other and other countries in an environment in which the United States is less the dominant power. But while pushed by both domestic and international factors toward fashioning independent contacts, positions, and initiatives in the region, the Japanese government remains highly concerned about the impact of its diplomacy in Washington, still its key foreign policy and economic partner. Therefore, Japan today is both moving ahead with its own relationships and encouraging the United States to remain engaged. This is a difficult balancing act, threatened both by U.S. misunderstanding of Japan's intentions and by Japanese miscalculation of its policy space.

Ironically, while some Americans worry about a concerted Japanese effort to establish Japan as a hegemonial power in East Asia, Southeast Asians frequently complain that Japan is still overly deferential to U.S. policies in the region, and that it should strike a more independent stance on some political and economic matters. Mr. Mahathir, for example, was disappointed by Japan's unwillingness to defy Washington's opposition to the EAEC, especially when there appeared to be significant unofficial Japanese sympathy and support for the idea. The Vietnamese government found frustrating Japan's extreme reluctance to move ahead with its bilateral aid program or push for a resumption of World Bank and International Monetary Fund loans and credits to Vietnam until it was confident that its policies would not provoke Washington. In this case, it was much more clear that without the U.S. constraint, Japanese policy would have shifted much earlier.

These views are very natural. Although few Southeast Asians would like to see an independent Japanese defense posture, in most other respects they complain that both Japan and the United States give greater priority to their ties with each other than either of them gives to Southeast Asia. While they appreciate that close U.S.–Japanese ties contribute to East Asian stability, such ties also can deprive Southeast Asians of bargaining leverage with these much larger powers.

Even were Japan not so deferential to U.S. leadership, the very existence of China in the region makes the notion of a Japanese dominated bloc almost fatuous. China would surely oppose any Japanese led regional institution or Japanese regional role that did not take Chinese interests into sufficient account. Unless there were a real breakup of China, Japan could afford neither to exclude nor to ignore China. But neither could it truly dominate a grouping that included China.

Japan has become a key economy in Southeast Asia and in East Asia as a whole. Its political-security role is growing. But the principal trend in the region is not that Japanese economic interests or political influence are displacing the U.S. roles, or that Japan appears to be seeking to develop a sphere to be dominated by itself. Rather, it is that an increasingly multilateral regional order and economy are emerging in which the individual roles of both Japan and the United States are being gradually diluted by such factors as the rise of other countries and the multinationalization of firms and production networks. This does indeed pose a challenge for Americans, but the challenge is not so much one of "containing" Japanese presence as one of ensuring an appropriate and consistent level of U.S. engagement in the region, and developing realistic expectations about the U.S. role and a style of U.S. involvement to accompany them.

With respect to Southeast Asia, the United States has many assets on which to draw. These include the familiarity with the United States engendered by its education each year of tens of thousands of Southeast Asians, the presence in the United States of large Southeast Asian minorities with ties to their homelands, the continued U.S. military presence in the region, and the widespread use of English by the government and business elites in the region. In many aspects, the playing field favors the United States. The question in the minds of many of the region is whether the United States is willing to play.

Notes

[1] Soeya (1993), pp. 99–100.
[2] Dobson (1993), pp. 68–69.

6

Japan as Number One in Asia

EZRA F. VOGEL

B y many measures Japan had already surpassed the United States as the leading economic power in Asia by the 1970s, but by the late 1980s Japan's lead was indisputable (see Table 1). In 1986 the United States had approximately $10 billion of investment in the Association of Southeast Asian Nations (ASEAN) countries. In 1989 the United States still had roughly $10 billion of investment in these countries, but Japanese investment had increased in the same period from $15 billion to $25 billion. By the early 1990s Japan and the United States were dispensing about the same amount of overseas development assistance worldwide, but only 15 percent of U.S. aid was going to Asia compared with about 60 percent of Japanese aid. In the late 1980s giant Japanese retail-

EZRA F. VOGEL is national intelligence officer for East Asia and the Pacific at the National Intelligence Agency. He is on leave from Harvard University where he is Henry Ford II Professor of the Social Sciences. Dr. Vogel is the author of several books, including *Japan as Number One: Lessons for America*, the all time best seller in Japan of nonfiction by a Western author, and most recently his Reischauer lectures, published as *The Four Little Dragons: The Spread of Industrialization in East Asia*.

ers expanded rapidly into East and Southeast Asia, but shortages of capital prevented their American counterparts from responding in a similar way.

How did Japan regain and expand its preeminence in Asia despite Asian memories of Japanese cruelty in World War II? What is the nature and significance of Japanese preeminence?

After World War II Japan built up its relations in Asia first with Southeast Asia and Taiwan, then with South Korea, and after 1979 with mainland China. After tracing these developments, I would like to consider the overall nature of Japan's role in Asia and the implications this has for its relations with the United States.

Reparations and Reentry

Immediately after World War II, officials of the allied occupation of Japan planned to require Japan to pay very large reparations to Asian countries for wartime damages. However, after China began to go Communist and Japan became an ally against communism, the occupation officials greatly reduced the reparations Japan was to pay. Yet several years later Japan, aware of wartime memories in Asia, voluntarily offered compensation to Asian countries, thus paving the way for reopening markets to their goods.

After 1952, when Japan regained the right to carry on its own foreign relations, a key task of Japanese foreign policy was to negotiate voluntary reparations to Asian countries, far beyond those required by the occupation. Various Japanese missions, public and private, were sent to other Asian countries to explore market opportunities and to bring the requests of Asian nations down to a scale that the Japanese found reasonable. Once agreements were worked out for Asian project proposals that the Japanese would support, Japanese goods began to flow into the countries. The aid that Japan offered through the reparations program had a clear commercial goal. Japanese aid for transport infrastructure projects, for example, not only helped local countries but made it possible for Japanese goods to be transported to consumer markets. But in the case of the Philippines in particular, the United States wanted Japan to help share the burden for rebuilding the

TABLE 1 Japan's Overseas Investment

Investment in ASEAN (1989)
(Billions of U.S. Dollars)

	Japan	U.S.
Brunei	0.03	n/a
Indonesia	10.4	3.7
Malaysia	2.5	1.1
Philippines	1.3	1.7
Singapore	5.7	2.2
Thailand	3.3	1.3
	23.3	10.0

Trade with ASEAN (1989)
(Billions of U.S. Dollars)

	Japan		U.S.	
	Exports	Imports	Exports	Imports
Brunei	na	na	0.1	0.1
Indonesia	3.3	11.0	1.2	3.5
Malaysia	4.1	5.1	2.9	4.7
Philippines	2.4	2.1	2.2	3.1
Singapore	9.2	2.9	7.4	8.9
Thailand	6.8	3.6	2.3	4.4
	25.8	24.7	16.1	24.7

Aid to ASEAN—Disbursements
(Millions of U.S. Dollars)

	Japan (FY 1988 net)	U.S. (FY 1989)
Brunei	—	—
Indonesia	985	72
Malaysia	25	1
Philippines	535	494
Singapore	11	1
Thailand	361	52
	1,917	620

Sources: Dept. of State; Congressional Research Service; U.S.–ASEAN Business Report, December 1990

economy, and Japan therefore gave more generously than they would have for commercial considerations alone.

The aid given by the Japanese through reparations programs became the basis of Japanese aid programs in general. In Indonesia, for example, reparation payments continued for twelve years beginning in 1958. Thus Japanese aid was from the beginning far more focused on Asia than on other parts of the world.

Third World Markets, Resources,
and Import Substitution (1950s–1970s)

In the 1950s Japanese manufacturers did not yet have the confidence that their goods were of sufficiently high quality that they could compete in the well-developed markets of Europe and North America. Export promotion efforts at the time, therefore, focused on the Third World. Japanese business organizations not only sent missions to Asia, but to South America and to Africa. Caravans of Japan External Trade Organization (JETRO) officials, for example, traveled by truck with merchandise to small towns in many parts of Africa, displaying wares that Japanese manufacturers produced, in hopes of building up regular market outlets.

Japanese officials felt that within the Third World, the countries with the largest population had the largest potential markets. They regretted that China was not open, but they made special efforts to establish good relations with India, Brazil, and Indonesia. They realized that these countries were poor, but they felt that Japan could sell textiles, clothing, radios, sewing machines, and simple machinery. JETRO played a critical role in undertaking market research and in trade promotion for Japanese manufacturers.

As Japan made the decision to move from coal to oil in the late 1950s, Japanese planners turned their attention not only to the Middle East but to Indonesia, which had been their primary source of oil before World War II. Given the key role of Indonesia as potentially one of the largest consumer markets in the region and as a source for the most needed energy resource, it is easy to see why, after 1958 when the reparations issue was finally settled and relations normalized, Indonesia should have become the largest recipient of Japanese aid. Some Japanese were wary about large investments during the Sukarno years, but Sukarno's Japanese wife Dewi played a role in keeping good relations with Japan. By 1966 Suharto's new economic policy seemed sufficiently stable and attractive that Japanese were prepared to make significant investments in Indonesian infrastructure.

During World War II the Japanese had perhaps more allies in Indonesia than in many countries in Southeast Asia. Unlike the Dutch, the Japanese occupiers during World War II allowed the Indonesians to use their native language, and they could achieve some success in making use of anti-Dutch sentiment. Some Indonesians were prescient enough to believe that the Japanese would not be able to fight many years against the West but that the Japanese would be useful in the anticolonial struggle against the Dutch. Indeed, many of the leading Indonesian nationalists who came to power after independence, including Sukarno and Suharto, had worked closely with the Japanese during World War II. Several hundred Japanese remained after World War II to work with the Indonesians in their colonial struggle against the Dutch, and after independence a substantial number of them stayed on to work for Japanese trading companies or other Japanese businesses.[1]

The oil shock of 1973 strengthened Japan's interest in resources in Southeast Asia. It occurred just as Japan had made the transition from light to heavy industry, which caused Japanese demand for energy supplies to continue to increase rapidly in the 1970s. In Indonesia, most of the oil prospecting had been done by Western countries, but Japan strengthened its long-term contracts to purchase the oil. The Japanese greatly expanded their interest in liquified natural gas (LNG) from Indonesia so that by the 1980s the total energy supplies (petroleum and LNG) coming from Indonesia were greater than from any other country in the world, including Saudi Arabia. The Japanese also made substantial oil purchases from Malaysia and Brunei, and even some from China.

In their effort to rationalize energy costs after the oil shock, the Japanese decided to move aluminum smelting overseas because the process drew heavily on electricity, and electricity costs were much higher in Japan than elsewhere. By far the largest Japanese project in Indonesia, the Aswan Dam, drew on a $2.2 billion loan from Japan's Export-Import Bank. The dam was used to build a large hydroelectric power plant, and a key part of the project was a large aluminum smelting plant.

The two long-time Japanese colonies, Taiwan and South Korea, presented special problems and opportunities. Given the colonial history, political populists in those localities found it easy to rouse anti-Japanese attitudes. Yet in both colonies, a substantial percentage of the population had learned Japanese in schools, was familiar with Japanese ways of doing business, and was ready to work with Japanese businesspeople as they came to their countries. Because workers there had high educational levels and were highly disciplined, Japanese manufacturers found these localities very attractive. Anti-Japanese feelings were particularly virulent in Korea, but President Park Chung Hee realized that industrial development required Japanese cooperation, and therefore, despite popular protests, normalized relations with Japan in 1965.[2]

Taiwan and South Korea, observing how the Japanese government did things, were wary of foreign capital dominating their economy, and therefore restricted the flow of foreign investments. Yet they did purchase machinery from Japan to use in their own production facilities, and a significant amount of Japanese consumer goods also made their way into these countries.

As Japanese salaries went up in the 1960s, some large Japanese corporations realized that it would be cheaper to move production facilities requiring labor-intensive inputs to Taiwan and South Korea. A favorite industry was textiles. Large Japanese textile firms like Teijin, Kuraray, and Toray made synthetic fibers in Japan, but produced synthetic textiles in Taiwan and South Korea. As much as some in Taiwan and South Korea had hoped to produce things locally, they were not yet able to make chemical fibers, so they purchased them from Japan for their own budding textile industries. In electronics also, in the 1960s and 1970s, many of the more complex electronic processes could be done only in Japan. Therefore, as Taiwan and South Korea began to assemble electronic machinery, some of the inputs had to come from Japan. The simpler parts and assembly work could be done elsewhere, but some of the high-level electronic fibers could only be produced in Japan. In short, as Taiwan and South Korea began to produce their own goods, Japanese firms were often able to use their technological leverage to gain significant control over their industries. Until 1965 Japan suffered chronic trade deficits, and controls on the export of capital were very tight. By the late 1960s, as trade balances became favorable and foreign currency shortages ended, the Japanese government began to relax restrictions on the export of capital, and Japanese companies began to move facilities not only to Taiwan and South Korea but to Southeast Asia.

In Southeast Asia the rapid growth of Japanese investment in the late 1960s and the early 1970s created great problems for local businesses. When Japanese firms first began selling goods, they often used local agents to market them, but as they gained experience and confidence, many believed they could expand their sales and reduce costs by handling the marketing themselves. Some therefore eliminated local agents. Local people felt that the Japanese contributed little positively to the economy. They were extracting resources—oil, lumber, rubber, and agricultural goods—in a neocolonial relationship, but not helping to build up local industry. Instead, the import of Japanese goods was cutting into local industry. They hired few local people, and all the top positions were filled by Japanese. By the early 1970s, the rapid increase of Japanese in Southeast Asian countries was very noticeable. Japanese congregated at the best restaurants, and bid up the cost of property in some of the finest retail areas. They dominated the golf courses.

By the early 1970s, some Asians believed that the Japanese were beginning to behave like the arrogant Japanese soldiers of the 1930s and early 1940s. In Thailand, Indonesia, Malaysia, and the Philippines, it was widely believed that Japanese businesses had bribed officials in those countries to win governmental contracts and to gain whatever permissions were necessary to operate their businesses and to get approval of the necessary infrastructure projects to service their businesses.[3]

In 1974 when Prime Minister Tanaka visited Southeast Asia, anti-Japanese riots broke out. To be sure, some domestic groups used the issue to embarrass their opponents, but whatever the motivations, the anti-Japanese demonstrations surprised the Japanese, and the Japanese business communities in Southeast Asian countries as well as business associations in Tokyo began concerted efforts to reduce the causes of friction. They began to make themselves less conspicuous in prominent public restaurants and golf courses, sometimes setting up their own facilities. They began campaigns to train their employees to treat local people with more courtesy, and they began to study local customs more carefully so as to avoid unnecessary friction. Guidebooks for Japanese tourists to these areas pointed out things to avoid in order not to annoy the local people. Japanese aid programs to Southeast Asia were increased.

By the time Prime Minister Fukuda traveled to ASEAN countries in August 1977, Japanese had made great progress in reducing some of the greatest local irritations toward their activities. The preparations for this visit were undertaken with much greater care than three years before. He offered assurance that Japan had renounced military intentions and supported closer heart-to-heart talks between Japan and Southeast Asian countries. He promised to contribute to ASEAN's Common Fund, and he announced a grant totaling $1 billion for five large industrial projects, one in each of the five ASEAN countries (Malaysia, Thailand, Indonesia, Singapore, and the Philippines). Each of the projects was to enable one country to produce all the requirements for ASEAN in a particular sector.

The Japanese were concerned with the difficulties of penetrating fragmented markets in Southeast Asia with barriers between them. Before they actually committed funds, they wanted to make sure, through feasibility studies, that all the infrastructure and planning were in place. In fact, many Southeast Asian countries did not satisfy Japanese requirements, and the projects were slow in developing. Not all the funds committed were finally used.[4] As a result of the Fukuda visit, an ASEAN-Japan Forum was established to promote further cooperation and to monitor difficulties in the relationship.

Investment in Export Oriented Production

In the late 1980s Japanese investment expanded greatly in Southeast Asian countries, especially in Thailand, Malaysia, and Indonesia. Until then Japanese industrial investments in Southeast Asia had been overwhelmingly for the domestic market, but in the late 1980s Japanese investment in Southeast Asia became oriented more toward export.

By the late 1980s, outside investors were impressed that politics had been stable for two decades, that local governments had expanded their infrastructure, and that bureaucrats were more familiar with the realities of world markets. Local officials had developed working relationships with Japanese businesses and understood how to do business with the Japanese. Except for Singapore and Malaysia, for a brief period after 1981 when it announced a "Look East Policy," Southeast Asian countries did not go out of their way to attract foreign businesses.

What made the Southeast Asian countries receptive to industrial investment from abroad in the mid-1980s were their economic difficulties that resulted from the collapse of the commodity markets. Oil prices fell, rubber prices fell, the prices for agricultural products in Southeast Asia fell, and domestic industries had not been successful in meeting international competition. In the mid-1980s, therefore, Southeast Asian governments eagerly sought foreign industrial plants and were prepared to make investment attractive.

On the Japanese side, the rise of wages since the 1960s had led Japanese companies to move some of their labor-intensive industrial production abroad. In the 1960s and 1970s many Japanese companies chose to locate their offshore production in Taiwan and South Korea. But in the 1980s, as salaries in Taiwan and South Korea rose, Japanese factories seeking to go overseas needed a new location with low-cost labor.

The trend of Japanese industries seeking foreign production sites was greatly accelerated by the Plaza Accord of 1985 and the rapid rise in the value of the yen in the following eighteen months. Factories in Japan, facing labor costs that had almost doubled against the dollar countries, eagerly sought factories abroad. The timing of Southeast Asian countries seeking foreign industrial investment and of Japanese firms seeking to move offshore coincided precisely. As a result, in the late 1980s Japanese industrial companies moved quickly to set up factories in Southeast Asia, especially in Thailand, Malaysia, and Indonesia.[5]

In earlier rounds of industrial investment in Southeast Asia, Japanese firms produced primarily for local markets where competition was not very keen. In the late 1980s, however, Japanese needed to relocate factories producing for the world market. Southeast Asian labor was still cheap, the governments were stable and prepared to cooperate with the Japanese, infrastructure was adequate, and supply lines to Japan were relatively short.

Waves of Japanese companies in consumer electronics, semiconductors, computer peripherals, and auto parts moved to Southeast Asia. Once a leading Japanese manufacturer locates in a certain place, competitors, afraid of being left behind, often follow immediately. Once some firms in a given sector relocate, Japanese suppliers and service organizations follow, making it easy for firms in that sector to operate. Goods can be repaired, and supplies and parts can be brought in quickly and reliably. When a critical mass of Japanese people is reached, Japanese schools, restaurants, food supplies, and golf clubs also follow.

The wave of export oriented Japanese factories established in Thailand, Malaysia, and Indonesia in the late 1980s did far more for the host countries than the earlier factories aimed at import substitution. Producing for competition in world markets requires far higher standards of quality control than producing for closed domestic markets. The Japanese therefore brought in far more modern production equipment, and exercised higher levels of control in the production process.

American firms setting up in Southeast Asia often hired a local manager who had attended an American business school and was familiar with American practices. The company commonly established certain procedures to follow and gave some training in the home company, but then allowed the local manager considerable leeway in hiring local people and running local operations. A comparable Japanese firm at a minimum brought in a Japanese manager, an accountant, and a chief engineer, and often brought in more technical people to guide the production in great detail. The American firm might attract the best local managerial talent. But the team of Japanese leaders who supervised the Japanese owned factory often was able to provide training for supervisors and workers that was far more detailed than their American owned counterparts. The close supervision greatly increased the technical capacity of Southeast Asian workers and gave them, within limits, promising career opportunities.

The wave of Japanese industrial investment for exports was therefore far more welcome than earlier waves of investments. Local government officials realized that it greatly increased their foreign exchange earnings and that it upgraded local technology and the quality of the local labor force, and Japanese investment gave a great spurt to the local economies. In their expansion in the late 1980s, the Japanese, profiting from their experience that began in the late 1960s, avoided serious outbreaks of anti-Japanese activity. The number of Japanese in Southeast Asia greatly increased, but local reaction was on balance generally positive.

Just as small Japanese retailers had worried about an invasion of large department stores and mass marketing outlets in their vicinity, so Southeast Asian retailers worried about the invasion of modern large-scale retailing. Yet even the large wave of Japanese department stores and mass marketing operations like Yaohan, Sogo, Isetan, and Daiei that swept into Southeast Asia in the late 1980s and displaced local retailers failed to mobilize strong anti-Japanese reactions. As in Taiwan a decade earlier, the Japanese could see that a rise in the standard of living and the emergence of a middle class in these countries created a new level of consumption. Japanese department stores positioned themselves initially at the high end of the market, and then, as the middle class in these countries grew and could afford products in the Japanese department stores, sales took off, including the sale of goods made in Japan or in Southeast Asia by Japanese owned companies.

Japanese Breakthroughs in the China Market

Although Japanese tried to keep trading channels with China open even during the peak of the cold war period, economic relations with China were very minimal before 1972 when Prime Minister Tanaka flew to Beijing and established diplomatic relations with China. Japanese businesspeople rushed to China and explored possible business opportunities. Japanese aid programs helped to pave the way for Japanese businesses. Although some investment followed, Japanese businesses found too many difficulties in the China market, and their enthusiasm cooled until Chinese economic reforms and further opening of their economy began in 1979.

After 1979 Chinese economic reforms set off a new round of Japanese enthusiasm for the potential of the China market. New credits and new investment followed. By far the largest project was Baoshan Steel, near Shanghai, the first large-scale, up-to-date steel plant in China. Many major Japanese manufacturers and financial institutions were involved in the construction and supplying of the project, which encountered numerous problems, resulting in mutual recriminations. The Chinese complained that the Japanese had not been honest with them when they submitted a lower bid than their European competitors, and then added many hidden costs. The Japanese had not explained, for example, that the plant required a high grade of coal that was not available in China. The Japanese complained that the Chinese had made their decisions too hastily, did not live up to their bargains to supply materials and infrastructure in a timely fashion, kept adding on costs, and made it impossible for the Japanese to repatriate profits. Several years of production delays followed, and discouraged the Japanese business community from investing in China until the late 1980s. Japanese businesses were happy to continue exporting products to China, but they were very cautious about investment except in Dalian (Liaoning Province), where they found cooperative partners who, as in Taiwan and South Korea, had long years of experience working with Japanese in the colonial period.

In the late 1980s Chinese economic growth and liberalization began to revive Japanese interest, but this was constrained after the 1989 Tiananmen incident, not only because of American pressure, but because of Japanese doubts about basic political stability. Small and middle-sized entrepreneurs from Taiwan and Hong Kong established low-cost, labor-intensive industrial processing activities within China, but Japanese companies, with far higher long-term fixed costs for modern equipment, were far more cautious about establishing plants in China.

Deng Xiaoping's trip to southern China in early 1992 affirmed China's intentions to continue reforms and opening to the outside, and this further reassured foreign businesspeople about the stability of Chinese politics. Japanese could see that China's rapid growth and increasing openness to foreign imports created opportunities for selling Japanese consumer goods as well as intermediate goods. A substantial number of Japanese firms expanded sales outlets in China. After Deng's trip south, China made it easier for foreign subsidiaries in China to sell to the domestic Chinese market, and this attracted Japanese industries. Japanese continued to locate many of their factories in the northeast, near Dalian, but they also expanded into Tianjin, Shandong, Shanghai, and other locations on the east coast.

From 1990 to 1992, after the bubble burst in the Japanese economy, Japanese slowed down their rate of new investment in industrial plant, both within Japan and overseas. By the 1990s the economic boom in Thailand and Malaysia began to drive up wages in those countries, for with small populations they had a limited labor supply. Japanese companies there did not pull out, and in some cases expanded their facilities with internally generated funds, but firms planning to invest in new low-cost labor supplies focused on Indonesia and China. The visit by the Japanese emperor to China in 1992 for the first time in history reflected China's desire to strengthen ties to Japan, and the general climate made it easier for Japanese firms in China.

In 1992 the World Bank and the International Monetary Fund began using purchasing power parity rather than the value of exchange rates to estimate the gross national product of China. Using such data it is possible to conclude that China's gross national product is already in Japan's league, and that within a decade or two, at present growth rates, Chinese GNP might surpass that of Japan and the United States. Yet with almost 1.2 billion consumers, China has few economic resources left after domestic consumption to project onto the world stage. China remains behind the four little dragons (South Korea, Taiwan, Hong Kong, and Singapore) in manufacturing technology and physical infrastructure. Its information about global developments is far behind that of Japan. Other Asian countries are beginning to recognize that China will be a major Asian power in the next decade or two, but they also recognize that in the meantime, Japan remains the unrivaled economic power in Asia.

Japanese Organizations Active in Asia

Japan's basic commercial linkages in Asia, as elsewhere in the world, are through the *sogo shoosha,* the general trading companies, the largest of which are Ito Chu, Mitsubishi Trading, Mitsui Bussan, Sumitomo Trading, Marubeni, and Nissho Iwai. They have substantial offices in each of the other Asian countries, and several offices in large countries. In China they have as many as eight to ten branches, located in each major region. Each branch has local employees who collect detailed information about economic developments in the region or country. When general trading companies find opportunities, where appropriate they notify even small and middle-sized firms in Japan that can make use of the trading company infrastructure to arrange for visits and for servicing local needs. Trading companies can also provide financing and can be involved in transactions all the way downstream from resource extraction through production, marketing, and sales to after-service.

Although many commercial Japanese banks are involved in business in Asia, the Bank of Tokyo plays a special role. Its predecessor before 1945, the Yokohama Specie Bank, was the only bank allowed to engage in foreign exchange at the time. After 1952, when Japan resumed foreign financial activities, for several years the Bank of Tokyo was the only bank allowed to engage in foreign financial transactions. Although other banks acquired these rights in later years, the fact that the Bank of Tokyo has no special ties to any of the financial groups makes it a favorite for government activities abroad and for groups looking for a second bank for larger projects. Because the Bank of Tokyo has ties with many local businesses and governments, going back to the period before World War II, and has great depth of information, it plays a very critical role in the Japanese business community abroad. In each foreign country where Japanese businesses are active, there is typically a Japanese Chamber of Commerce that also serves a representative role for the Japanese business community as a whole. There is also usually a social organization of Japanese residents living in a particular city, and additional specialized organizations. In a large Japanese community, one of the key institutions is the Japanese school, certified by the Japanese Ministry of Education, which offers classes to Japanese youth and typically has a board composed of prominent leaders in the local Japanese business community. The Japanese embassies in national capitals and consulates in important regional cities represent various agencies of the Japanese government and provide further linkages for the various private Japanese organizations, as well as with the host government.

When concessionary loans are provided to host governments for carrying on various developmental projects, they are commonly provided through the Japanese Export-Import Bank. In 1993, for example, Japan's Ex-Im Bank had outstanding approximately $8 billion in loans to Indonesia and a comparable amount to China.

The Overseas Economic Cooperation Fund (OECF), under the supervision of the Ministry of Finance, was originally established under the leadership of Export-Import Bank in 1961. After 1975, as overseas development assistance expanded, it began to have independent authority to give government loans to foreign governments and to corporations undertaking development in the host country. The Japan International Cooperation Agency (JICA), established in 1974 under the supervision of Japan's Ministry of Foreign Affairs, provides for technology assistance and training programs.

Foreign Relations: Economics and Beyond

Japanese businesspeople or government officials commonly have good working relationships with their counterparts in Asian countries. Local people in various countries who have worked for Japanese for a long period of time often develop close personal relationships with their Japanese associates. Japanese communities and youth groups often have sister city and prefecture programs with counterparts in other Asian countries. Far more Japanese tourists travel to Asian countries than tourists from any Western country. Since the mid-1980s, when Japan set the goal of 100,000 foreign students in Japan by 2000, the number of foreign students in Japan has greatly increased, especially from China, South Korea, Taiwan, and to a lesser extent from other Southeast Asian countries. After graduating from Japanese universities, colleges, and technical schools, many Asian foreign students take employment in Japanese companies or work in companies doing business with Japan.

Japanese organizations, with great continuity and long-range planning, have by now often dealt with their Asian counterparts over many years. There is a feeling of reliability in these relationships, and often a positive personal connection as well. The relationships with Japan have achieved sufficient predictability that many Asian leaders are prepared to discuss security issues with Japan. Among smaller countries there is a recognition that if the United States were to withdraw, the Chinese might try to move in to fill a military vacuum, and if so, Japan might become an ally against China.

Yet at deeper levels, there is a lack of trust in the relationships with Japan. Some of the doubts are related to World War II. Most Asians who remember or are concerned about World War II feel that the Japanese have given perfunctory, carefully worded apologies, but that they have not engaged in an open examination of all the atrocities of World War II, nor undertaken a thoroughgoing repudiation of their behavior. Many are not confident that the Japanese would behave differently given a new opportunity.

As Masahide Shibusawa and others have pointed out, in fact many Japanese do look down on Southeast Asians. Within the prestige hierarchy of Japanese companies and the Japanese bureaucracy, the people who have served in Southeast Asia are generally not ranked as high as those who served in the United States and Europe. Southeast Asians in Japan have difficulty affording decent housing, and often feel that they are not accepted into inner circles nor treated as equals.

Furthermore, many Asians feel that Japanese officials and businesspeople are not fully open with them. They acknowledge that most Japanese are very polite and considerate in personal relations, but many suspect that the politeness continues only as long as the relationships are useful to the Japanese. Since the late 1980s Japanese leaders have indicated a desire to play a role beyond a strictly economic one. Ministry of Foreign Affairs officials in particular have indicated a desire to support pollution control, arms control, democracy, and human rights, and to consider these issues in their aid and commercial relationships. Yet economic purposes have remained central to Japanese efforts, and Asian leaders believe that the calculus of Japanese political behavior in Asia can be understood by an economic logic. Japan has looked for markets to sell goods, and it has sought raw materials that it can use for manufacturing. Toward this end Japanese have been interested in maintaining good relationships, but they have been single-minded in their pursuit of economic information and the use of economic leverage.

Since 1952, when Japan resumed control over its foreign policy, the role of the Japanese government has been primarily to promote good will with other countries and to gain access for Japanese private companies. Negotiations with various Asian countries, as with other foreign countries, have been designed to gain access for the firms for sales and investment and to acquire access to resources.

Japanese aid programs have been criticized by other countries for being so closely linked with Japanese businesses. When the Japanese first began their programs of assistance to Asian countries, officials were quite forthright about their desire to promote Japanese business. Since the aid programs have been under criticism of other countries for promoting only the interests of Japanese companies, the Japanese government has increased the proportion of funds earmarked for grants, and imposes no formal requirement that contracts go to Japanese firms. Japanese aid agencies point out that in their contracts and grants, no special preference is given to Japanese firms. In fact, a high proportion of Japanese aid money given to host countries is later used to purchase equipment or services from Japanese companies. One mechanism by which this takes place derives from the special role of Japanese trading companies or other Japanese firms. Often officials in the host country have little understanding of how to write grant proposals that are likely to pass the approval of the Japanese government. A Japanese trading company may give advice on how to get a grant approved in the home office in Tokyo, and it is understandable that in the course of discussions, one or two projects of special interest to the trading company are incorporated into the proposal. Since Japanese trading firms often have advance notice of contracts to be given out by Japanese government agencies, they are in a good position to pass on the information to appropriate Japanese firms in a timely fashion. Japanese aid agencies talk of the increasing proportion of their contracts awarded to companies in the host countries, but the statistics do not necessarily distinguish between local companies with local ownership and those with Japanese ownership, allowing some Japanese firms or joint ventures to count as local.

While pursuing stable relationships that undergird business opportunities, Japanese have in the last two decades shown an interest in regional as well as bilateral relationships. When ASEAN was initially established, Japanese officials had low expectations for what it might accomplish, but after Prime Minister Fukuda's visit to ASEAN in 1977, Japan began to take a more forward role in promoting ASEAN cooperation. One of the goals of Japanese aid to ASEAN since 1977 has been to break down barriers to interregional trade. Japanese companies find the individual national markets in Southeast Asia to be relatively small, and therefore Japan has encouraged ASEAN to develop regional projects and to reduce the barriers to free trade within Southeast Asia.

Since World War II, Japan has not taken an active role in providing political leadership in Asia. Japanese prime ministers consistently travel to Asian countries and welcome Asian leaders to Tokyo, but rarely do they take important political initiatives in these meetings. Yet as the cold war winds down in Asia, most countries are far more concerned with economic growth than with security, and in this arena, Japan's leadership is very broadly based. When countries of Asia look for capital, manufacturing know-how, and technology, they now look overwhelmingly to Japan. Asian countries know that no important issues in Asia can be resolved without the cooperation of Japan.

Regional Preeminence and Global Priorities

Before 1945 Japan was a regional power, with its economic interests and military strength concentrated in East and Southeast Asia. In the 1950s, as it revived its relationships in Asia, it again became a regional Asian power. However, in the 1960s, as its economy grew and its world trade expanded, Japan became for the first time in its history a global economic power.

In the 1980s some Japanese leaders, observing continued Asian growth, Western economic slowdown, and signs of Western economic protectionism, began to talk of tilting to Asia rather than the West. In the early Meiji period, Fukuzawa Yukichi advocated *datsu A,* forgetting about Asia to catch up with the civilized West. Now, some argue that Japan should return to its Asian roots. Study groups on Asia have recently expanded, and Asian specialists within the government have begun to challenge the dominance of the Western specialists. Many Japanese business leaders now feel more comfortable dealing with Asians than with Westerners. When Europe or America show signs of protectionism, Japanese leaders seek to ally with Asian leaders against their Western counterparts. When Westerners talk of European and North American economic blocs, some Japanese talk of Asian blocs. When the United States begins imposing its version of human rights on Asian nations, Japanese find kindred souls among other Asian leaders who have a different set of priorities. Japanese leaders are more prepared to work with other Asian nations with which the United States has human rights quarrels: China, Vietnam, and even Myanmar.

Yet the reality is that Japan's primary economic interests lie with North America and Europe (see Table 2), and even more rapid growth in Asia is not likely to change this fundamentally in the foreseeable future. Even after the cold war ended, Japanese leaders recognized that their security interests lay in cooperating with the United States. Other Asian nations would not feel secure with Japan as a major military power, and Japanese leaders realize that militarization would affect their ability to pursue their interests in Asia. Japanese leaders who become frustrated with American economic pressures occasionally talk of the possibility of forming an Asian economic bloc. It is likely that Asia will become

TABLE 2 Direct Overseas Investment by Country and Region

FISCAL YEAR	1988			1989			1990			Cumulative Total for FY 1951–1990		
Country of Region	Number of Cases	Amount ($ mill.)	Share %	Number of Cases	Amount ($ mill.)	Share %	Number of Cases	Amount ($ mill.)	Share %	Number of Cases	Amount ($ mill.)	Share %
USA	2,434	21,701	46.2	2,668	32,540	48.2	2,269	26,128	45.9	22,944	130,529	42.0
Canada	109	626	1.3	180	1,362	2.0	157	1,064	1.9	1,281	5,656	1.8
North America Total	2,543	22,328	47.5	2,848	33,902	50.2	2,426	27,192	47.8	24,225	136,185	43.8
Panama	327	1,712	3.6	263	2,044	3.0	206	1,342	2.4	3,855	16,244	5.2
Brazil	48	510	1.1	39	349	0.5	15	615	1.1	1,461	6,560	2.1
Cayman	53	2,609	5.5	41	1,658	2.5	34	588	1.0	261	7,332	2.4
Bahamas	12	737	1.6	14	620	0.9	4	121	0.2	110	3,459	1.1
Mexico	1	87	0.2	9	36	0.1	14	168	0.3	274	1,874	0.6
Bermuda	9	337	0.7	11	228	0.3	17	360	0.6	136	1,578	0.5
Antilles	10	172	0.4	8	38	0.1	7	9	0.0	64	795	0.3
Peru	—	—	0.0	—	—	0.0	—	—	—	96	696	0.2
Chile	13	46	0.1	10	47	0.1	11	30	0.1	99	311	0.1
Argentina	5	24	0.1	1	3	0.0	4	213	0.4	131	431	0.1
Venezuela	5	51	0.1	4	75	0.1	9	77	0.1	113	341	0.1
Virgin Islands	6	133	0.3	4	118	0.2	4	15	0.0	17	305	0.1
Puerto Rico	—	0	0.0	—	3	0.0	2	23	0.0	41	167	0.1
Colombia	3	6	0.2	2	4	0.0	3	59	0.1	65	131	0.0
Others	18	9	0.0	17	19	0.9	9	8	0.0	474	259	0.1

TABLE 2 *(Continued)*

FISCAL YEAR	1988			1989			1990			Cumulative Total for FY 1951–1990		
Country of Region	Number of Cases	Amount ($ mill.)	Share %	Number of Cases	Amount ($ mill.)	Share %	Number of Cases	Amount ($ mill.)	Share %	Number of Cases	Amount ($ mill.)	Share %
Latin America Total	507	6,428	13.7	421	5,238	7.8	339	3,628	6.4	7,197	40,483	13.0
Indonesia	84	586	1.2	140	631	0.9	155	1,105	1.9	1,873	11,540	3.7
Hong Kong	335	1,662	3.5	335	1,898	2.8	244	1,785	3.1	3,743	9,850	3.2
Singapore	197	747	1.6	181	1,902	2.8	139	840	1.5	2,559	6,555	2.1
South Korea	153	483	1.0	81	606	0.9	54	284	0.5	1,847	4,138	1.3
China	171	296	0.6	126	438	0.6	165	349	0.6	859	2,823	0.9
Thailand	382	859	1.8	403	1,276	1.9	377	1,154	2.0	2,465	4,422	1.4
Malaysia	108	387	0.8	159	673	1.0	169	725	1.3	1,509	3,231	1.0
Taiwan	234	372	0.8	165	494	0.7	102	446	0.8	2,400	2,731	0.9
Philippines	54	134	0.3	87	202	0.3	58	258	0.5	850	1,580	0.5
India	6	24	0.1	9	18	0.0	7	30	0.1	167	196	0.1
Brunei	—	0	0.0	—	0	0.0	—	—	—	31	109	0.0
Pakistan	1	2	0.0	5	83	0.1	3	9	0.0	58	110	0.0
Others	12	15	0.0	16	17	0.0	26	69	0.1	273	234	0.1
Asia Total	1,737	5,569	11.8	1,707	8,238	12.2	1,499	7,054	12.4	18,634	47,519	15.3
Saudi Arabia-Kuwait	—	20	0.0	—	32	0.0	—	26	0.0	4	1,441	0.5
Iran	—	1	0.0	—	1	0.0	—	—	—	108	1,006	0.3

TABLE 2 (Continued)

FISCAL YEAR	1988			1989			1990			Cumulative Total for FY 1951–1990		
Country of Region	Number of Cases	Amount ($ mill.)	Share %	Number of Cases	Amount ($ mill.)	Share %	Number of Cases	Amount ($ mill.)	Share %	Number of Cases	Amount ($ mill.)	Share %
United Arab Emirates	2	194	0.4	2	6	0.0	—	—	—	47	441	0.1
Saudi Arabia	2	8	0.0	—	—	0.0	—	—	—	101	369	0.1
Bahrain	3	31	0.1	1	24	0.0	—	—	—	23	129	0.0
Other	3	4	0.0	2	3	0.0	1	1	0.0	57	45	0.0
Middle East Total	10	259	0.6	5	66	0.1	1	27	0.0	340	3,431	1.1
U.K.	211	3,956	8.4	285	5,239	7.8	270	6,806	12.0	2,134	22,598	7.3
Netherlands	105	2,359	5.0	112	4,547	6.7	138	2,744	4.8	780	12,816	4.1
Luxemburg	13	657	1.4	13	654	1.0	7	224	0.4	150	5,607	1.8
West Germany	67	409	0.9	119	1,083	1.6	134	1,242	2.2	1,187	4,689	1.5
France	148	463	1.0	168	1,136	1.7	171	1,257	2.2	1,328	4,156	1.3
Switzerland	27	454	1.0	19	397	0.6	16	666	1.2	304	2,495	0.8
Spain	32	161	0.3	58	501	0.7	43	320	0.6	320	1,867	0.6
Belgium	13	164	0.3	23	326	0.5	39	367	0.6	336	1,720	0.6
Ireland	12	42	0.1	11	133	0.2	10	49	0.1	100	614	0.2
Italy	26	108	0.2	47	314	0.5	52	217	0.4	307	900	0.3
Norway	4	186	0.4	12	280	0.4	19	138	0.2	71	648	0.2
U.S.S.R.	8	9	0.0	12	19	0.0	15	25	0.0	43	247	0.1
Turkey	4	110	0.2	4	40	0.1	6	58	0.1	34	224	0.1

TABLE 2 *(Continued)*

FISCAL YEAR	1988			1989			1990			Cumulative Total for FY 1951–1990		
Country of Region	Number of Cases	Amount ($ mill.)	Share %	Number of Cases	Amount ($ mill.)	Share %	Number of Cases	Amount ($ mill.)	Share %	Number of Cases	Amount ($ mill.)	Share %
Austria	9	22	0.0	7	18	0.0	11	38	0.1	74	164	0.1
Portugal	4	7	0.0	10	74	0.1	3	68	0.1	47	182	0.1
Greece	1	1	0.0	—	—	—	1	4	0.0	18	101	0.0
Others	9	9	0.0	16	48	0.1	21	71	0.1	192	237	0.1
Europe Total	692	9,116	19.4	916	14,808	21.9	956	14,294	25.1	7,425	59,265	19.1
Liberia	68	648	1.4	72	643	1.0	50	531	0.9	930	4,832	1.6
Zaire	—	—	0.0	—	—	0.0	—	—	—	56	282	0.1
Nigeria	1	0	0.0	1	1	0.0	2	1	0.0	93	159	0.1
Zambia	—	—	0.0	—	—	0.0	—	—	—	17	142	0.0
Others	5	5	0.0	15	27	0.0	18	19	0.1	362	411	0.1
Africa Total	74	653	1.4	88	671	1.0	70	551	1.0	1,458	5,826	1.9
Australia	357	2,413	5.1	448	4,256	6.3	407	3,669	6.4	2,760	16,063	5.2
New Zealand	32	117	0.2	47	101	0.2	46	231	0.4	371	925	0.3
Papua New Guinea	7	2	0.0	6	10	0.0	4	9	0.0	213	226	0.1
Northern Marianas	91	88	0.2	62	124	0.2	48	134	0.2	328	456	0.1
Vanuatu	1	14	0.0	8	40	0.1	3	4	0.0	60	108	0.0
Fiji	—	—	0.0	—	—	0.0	26	47	0.1	97	108	0.0

TABLE 2 *(Continued)*

FISCAL YEAR	1988			1989			1990			Cumulative Total for FY 1951–1990		
Country of Region	Number of Cases	Amount ($ mill.)	Share %	Number of Cases	Amount ($ mill.)	Share %	Number of Cases	Amount ($ mill.)	Share %	Number of Cases	Amount ($ mill.)	Share %
Other	26	34	0.1	33	86	0.1	38	72	0.1	128	212	0.1
Oceania Total	514	2,669	5.7	604	4,618	6.8	572	4,166	7.3	3,957	18,098	5.8
Grand Total	6,077	47,022	100.0	6,589	67,540	100.0	5,863	56,911	100.0	63,236	310,808	100.0

Note: The table only includes countries whose cumulative totals for FY 1951–1990 exceeded $100 million.
Source: Japanese Ministry of Finance, May 1991

relatively more important to Japan, and that there may be distinct moves to strengthen its alliances with Asia. But Japanese business leaders and government officials know that their major economic and security interests lie with the United States. Despite emotional frustrations in working with the United States, they realize that while Japan is number one in Asia, Japan's number one priorities still lie with the West.

Notes

[1] See Nishihara (1975).

[2] For an account of Japan's relations with South Korea see Tanino (1988).

[3] For an account of Southeast Asia attitudes toward Japanese businesses in their countries see Thom and McCauley (1992).

[4] For accounts of Japan's relations with ASEAN countries see Shibusawa (1984) and Sait (1991).

[5] Detailed data on Japanese investment by firm and company is published periodically by Toyo Keizai Shiposha. See, for example, *Japanese Overseas Investment: A Complete Listing by Firms and Countries, 1986–1987*. For an account of the strategies of Japanese firms in Asia, see Tokunaga (1992).

7

U.S. Military Forces
in East Asia:
The Case for
Long-Term Engagement

THOMAS L. McNAUGHER

I t is difficult to find a region more important to the United
States yet more enigmatic and uncertain to U.S. strategists
than East Asia. The region is home to the world's fastest growing
economies and supplier of ever-larger portions of world product. It
has become America's most important trading partner, at a time
when the importance of trade to the U.S. economy, while still
relatively small, is twice what it was only two decades ago. Particularly in an era of slow growth in the domestic U.S. economy,
growth in U.S. trade generally, and especially with East Asia, has
become vital to overall U.S. economic performance.[1]

THOMAS L. McNAUGHER is a senior fellow in the Foreign Policy
Studies Program at the Brookings Institution and a professorial lecturer at
the Johns Hopkins School of Advanced International Studies. As an ac-
tive duty Army officer from 1968 through 1975, Dr. McNaugher served in
the Republic of Vietnam from 1970 to 1971, and taught army ROTC at
Syracuse University from 1972 to 1975. Dr. McNaugher's books include
The M16 Controversies: Military Organizations and Weapons Acquisition (1984),
Arms and Oil: U.S. Military Strategy and the Persian Gulf (1985), and *New
Weapons, Old Politics: America's Military Procurement Muddle* (1989).

The region's importance extends well beyond the narrow confines of U.S. economic interest. It is becoming increasingly realistic to think in terms of a "Pacific technology basin," over which the U.S. has less and less control. While this has positive benefits for economic growth, the ability of East Asian states to buy, develop, deploy, and above all export key military technologies portends less beneficial effects for world order. Meanwhile, rapid economic growth has already linked East Asia to such global concerns as energy use and pollution, and such links are likely to grow much stronger in the future. Even if the world subdivides into three major regions, as some economists argue, the spillover effects of rapid growth will have global effects demanding global attention.

These arguments suggest a vital U.S. interest in an East Asia that is stable and increasingly open to U.S. investment and trade. Ideally, its member states should be more concerned with economic growth than with preparing for war, and they should be willing to engage responsibly in the institutions and discussions that are emerging to handle global issues.

Unfortunately, the strategy—especially the military strategy—best able to move East Asia in these directions is a good deal less obvious than the interests themselves. The future of major regional powers is remarkably difficult to predict. The Soviet Union has collapsed, and Moscow is too distracted by domestic political problems and security challenges in Ukraine and Central Asia to define a new Russian role in the Far East. China, the world's fastest growing economy in recent years, could achieve enormous economic and military clout in the decades ahead, but could also fracture, or at least decentralize, under the strain of rapid growth. Japan is still struggling to define a global political role to match its enormous economic clout. The Koreas may be headed toward accommodation, but it is difficult to discount the possibility of war or a North Korean nuclear capability, either of which would severely strain the regional security situation.

A much broader uncertainty arises from the increasingly global economic activity that has gripped the world over the past two decades. Although trade has increased substantially, the more important trends spring from dramatic increases in the efficiency of information processing, which have hastened the emergence of truly global firms and financial markets. States no longer control what were once the key instruments of "domestic" economic policy; indeed, the distinction between "domestic" and "foreign" has grown murkier, whether it refers to firms, products, or technology. Some argue that globalizing economic trends discourage war and encourage cooperation, but there is considerable debate about the ultimate inevitability of such trends as well as their pacifying effects on international relations. Strategists are left to wonder about the status of states and power, the basic "stuff" of national strategy.

These uncertainties leave the United States military "all dressed up," as they say, but with no clear idea where to go. Roughly 103,000 U.S. military personnel remain deployed to bases in South Korea, Japan (including Okinawa), and Guam. Behind these stand five carrier battle groups based in Hawaii and on the West Coast, plus ground and air forces based in the United States, able to swing to the Western Pacific when needed.[2] Although these forces remain a visible symbol of continuing U.S. interest and involvement in East Asian affairs, their principal military role disappeared with the collapse of the Soviet Union. They remain crucial to the defense of South Korea and Japan, and they help defend sea lanes that are all important to trade through this region. But the first two of these look like cold war hangovers, while the last doesn't require a large forward presence, especially of U.S. ground forces. No one has a clear idea of what military missions these forces should perform in the long run, or whether they will even be needed.

Perhaps—indeed, hopefully—they will not be needed. Current economic trends can be spun into scenarios of a much more pacific Pacific. But the validity of such projections remains much more a matter of faith than of evidence, and military strategists are and should be agnostic. So are most East Asians, and for good reason—key structural and historical features of their region create serious obstacles to the pacifying effects of economic trends. Near-term U.S. military missions flow from the region's history, in which the U.S. has been deeply involved, militarily, since 1941. Longer-term missions flow from the region's structure more than from its history, and center on the formidable challenge of accommodating China, with its enormous power potential, into regional and global security frameworks. U.S. forces have a role to play in encouraging China's cooperative engagement with its neighbors. They are also better positioned than any in the region to hedge against less benign outcomes.

Global Trends, Regional Problems

The past two decades have seen a dramatic expansion in global trade and investment. The value of global trade rose from $312 billion to $4,340 billion between 1970 and 1990, from 11.2 percent to 20.6 percent of global product over that same period. Roughly 40 percent of that trade is among subcomponents of the same firms, testament to the importance of multinational firms, and also to the work of increasingly global financial markets, which have vastly improved capital flows across borders.

These trends would seem to bode well for countries interested in stability and economic growth. Globalizing economic forces have already begun to constrain state power and encourage international cooperation. The traditional tools of state fiscal policy have acquired perverse international consequences. Deficit spending, once a means to stimulate the domestic economy, now may stimulate imports instead, as happened to the United States in the 1980s. And interest rate adjustments, once a tool for controlling the domestic economy, now interact with international exchange rates, often with perverse consequences for the local and global economies.[3] These interactions have already encouraged the formation of the G-7, in which leaders of the seven major industrialized states seek to coordinate fiscal policies and exchange rates.

The benefits of economic growth and the desire for more of it have also spawned an interest among states in stability and good neighborliness. East Asia offers some of the best cases in point. China, once a source of support to insurgencies across Southeast Asia, has become increasingly interested in regional stability and good relations as its economy has benefited from trade and investment.[4] Thailand, albeit still deeply suspicious of Vietnam, now talks of "turning battlefields into markets." Meanwhile, Vietnam and North Korea highlight the costs of remaining outside the growing global economic network. Intense, region-wide enthusiasm for expanding economic and security cooperation bears witness to a near-universal desire among East Asians to head off security problems and get on with the creation of wealth. Optimists can spin this evidence into a vision of a richer, more humane, and less violent world. Conflict will persist, since increasingly interdependent states will have much to argue about. But they will have considerably less reason to attack each other, since the creation of wealth no longer depends on things military forces can seize, while the costs of rupturing complex economic and business links is growing all the time. Indeed, "power" among states will grow less and less usable as these linkages grow, since the well-being of each state will depend increasingly on the well-being of others.[5] By the same token, an expanding economic pie creates conditions for positive outcomes for all parties to conflict—so-called win-win situations that make war unattractive by comparison.

This is an attractive vision, perhaps realizable. Yet the evidence thus far is far too scanty and ambiguous to make policy on the basis of beneficial economic trends alone. Political realists raise questions, for example, about the sustainability of globalizing economic trends as well as their beneficial effects. Such global integration as has occurred over the past two decades, they argue, owes largely to the peculiar stability of the bipolar cold war world, and to U.S. economic dominance, which allowed the U.S. to impose reasonably stable rules on the free-world economy. With cold war bipolarity gone and U.S. economic hegemony eroded, these thinkers expect global *dis*integration rather than integration.[6] Some see the reemergence of the traditional anarchic state pattern. But others see the world dividing into three regions—East Asia, Europe, and the Western Hemisphere—within which economic activity is increasingly integrated, but among which economic links erode.[7]

Realists also highlight the negative effects of economic growth. Richer states are also more powerful states. Most obviously, states can convert growing wealth into military power. True, military force isn't what it once was. The presence of nuclear weapons makes war less likely between states that possess them, and the proliferation of nuclear weapons to other states will create dynamics that, while hard to predict, will surely differ from the security dynamics of the nonnuclear past. Meanwhile, the complacent indigenous populations easily subjugated by imperialist powers a century ago have been mobilized and armed, often with sophisticated weaponry, making subjugation by force costly, if not impossible. Still, military force remains the last bastion of state security, and ways will be found to use it.

In any case, economic power is itself still power. Realists would argue that states are far from helpless in the face of advancing globalization:

> Although [global] economic interconnections have grown, so has the capacity of national governments and industries to respond. . . . Governments can reshape the structure of global competition and global industry to the benefit of national welfare.[8]

Technology, in this view, is localized in the skills of people and the capital of plants and communities.[9] It can be encouraged by government policy, and the rents thus won can be used to generate a "technology trajectory" that puts successful states ahead of their competitors. States on the most advanced technology trajectory get the best jobs and the highest incomes, while setting themselves up for more of the same down the road.[10] The most advanced states, of course, can also field the most advanced weapons, giving them the advantage should economic competition give way to violent conflict. Japan's technological prowess and relatively closed economy make it the realists' favorite case in point.

The continuing potency of states makes their leaders deeply ambivalent about the purported benefits of spreading economic growth. Yes, they enjoy the pleasures of their own expanding wealth, and they may recognize that this depends on the well-being of at least some of their neighbors. Insofar as wealth creates power, however, they have to worry about who is getting richer. The distribution of *relative* gains from economic growth is thus more important than *absolute* gains accruing to all,[11] and the "fundamental problem of international relations in the contemporary world is the problem of peaceful adjustment to the consequences of the uneven growth of power among states. . . ."[12]

Sadly, for all the optimism generated by its economic dynamism, East Asia is plagued by historical and structural problems that provide grist for the realists' mill. This is, to begin with, a region of strong states with no long history of economic or security cooperation. There is no NATO in East Asia, no Western European Union, no Conference on Security and Cooperation in Europe; East Asia's only equivalent is the Association of Southeast Asian Nations (ASEAN), created in 1967 with a charter that avoided any reference to security (although the organization has performed important security functions). East Asians talk frequently of the need for security cooperation largely because they have so little of it.

They also talk about expanding economic cooperation, and have begun to create institutions for this purpose. Yet the East Asian economic miracle has thus far depended much more on *global* than on *regional* economic linkages, and especially on trade with the United States.[13] Meanwhile, cynics could justifiably argue that in key cases East Asian economies actually benefited from regional instability. The Korean War gave Japan's ailing postwar economy its initial boost. U.S. involvement in the Vietnam War brought plenty of dollars and U.S. demand to the ASEAN states. And Thailand's businesses, as well as its army, have been able to exploit Cambodia's resources despite, indeed partly because of, that country's civil war. Not surprisingly, organizations like the Asia-Pacific Economic Cooperation (APEC) forum are new and still searching for missions.

East Asia, in short, is neither institutionally nor experientially prepared to handle serious security challenges cooperatively. Yet challenges there are, in the form of historical and structural problems that could all too easily disrupt the region's current stability. They center, respectively, on Japan and China.

History and the Problem of Japan

Despite their common interest in economic growth, the states of East Asia remain deeply suspicious of each other. Such suspicions can be found at every level and between virtually every state in the region. But Japan's conduct before and during World War II clearly makes it the principal focus of concern—concern that Japan's behavior in the postwar era has not fully allayed. Only reluctantly and very recently has Japan confronted and apologized for its past behavior. And while it left much of its external security during the cold war to the United States, it nonetheless rearmed, even acquiring components and technologies for a nuclear arsenal. All the while Japan has acquired enormous economic power—its GNP is many times those of all neighbors save China—while showing the same resistance to the imports and investments of neighbors as it has shown toward those of the United States. Despite a region-wide economic presence, Japan remains culturally and to a great extent politically apart from the region around it.

The burden of this history falls especially hard on Japan's relations with its nearest neighbors, China and Korea. Japan's colonial efforts to transform Korean culture, its brutality to Koreans during World War II, and a lingering perception of racial arrogance and exclusiveness on both sides add a special dimension of bitterness and suspicion to Japan's relations with the Koreas. South Korea and Japan took fifteen years to normalize relations after the Korean War, despite common hostility to the Soviet Union and common relations with the United States. With the Soviet threat gone, each has begun to focus on the other as a potential threat. Although North Korea's purported nuclear program has added genuine substance to Japan's threat perception, suspicions run much wider and deeper than this.

Sino-Japanese relations are slightly warmer than Japan's relations with the Koreas, partly because Japanese are much more favorably disposed to the Chinese than they are to Koreans. But Japan behaved as abominably in China after 1931 as it did in Korea, leaving Chinese as suspicious as Koreans of Japan's intentions, and as concerned as the Koreans about Japan's penchant for rewriting or ignoring this phase of its history. No country reacts more quickly than China to expansions in Japan's military forces or their missions. Having been the dominant civilizing force in Asia for centuries—indeed, having given Japan among others its alphabet and religion—China also resents Japan's current power and its tendency to tutor China on the intricacies of economic growth.[14]

Among Southeast Asians, attitudes toward Japan vary. All

Southeast Asians worry about Japanese rearmament. But Singapore is the most strident in expressing its concerns, while Thailand, perhaps because it was not invaded by Japan during World War II, tends to be positive about Japan and its growing economic presence in Southeast Asia. For most Indonesians, China is the bigger worry, the result of Chinese support to Indonesia's domestic problems in the early 1960s.

The United States buffers East Asia from this history. It handles Japan's external security, allowing Japan to maintain large forces that do not directly threaten neighbors. The U.S. also mediates diplomatically between Japan and its neighbors; in the complex negotiations surrounding South Korea's efforts to reach an accommodation with North Korea, for example, Japan has tended to follow the U.S. lead in dealing with both Seoul and Pyongyang. Finally, U.S. economic strength tends to be seen as a balance to Japan's growing economic power, especially among the smaller states of Southeast Asia. All of this lends credence to the statement of Singapore's former president, Lee Kuan Yew, that a break in the U.S.–Japan relationship would create "a disastrously unstable state of affairs."[15]

That instability would register inside as well as around Japan, since the U.S. buffers Japan itself from this history. The U.S. nuclear umbrella has allowed Japan to maintain its nuclear allergy despite being surrounded by nuclear powers. The U.S. military presence has also allowed Japan to build relatively large and sophisticated armed forces despite widespread antimilitarism among the population. This has stunted the development of institutions of civil-military relations, institutions conspicuously missing in the years before World War II. An abrupt break in the U.S.–Japan relation would be as wrenching to the Japanese themselves as for many of their neighbors.

This is not to say that Japanese ignore security issues. The security debate in Japan has grown increasingly serious over the past decade, and especially since the cold war ended. Virtually all Japanese realize that a country with Japan's economic clout cannot remain a political pygmy forever. Many share with their regional neighbors a nagging uncertainty about U.S. staying power in the absence of the Soviet threat, and thus contemplate a time when

Japan will operate globally and regionally with much more independence than it did during the cold war.[16] In 1993 North Korea's refusal to allow full international inspections of its nuclear facilities, combined with its provocative testing of long-range missiles in May 1993, have added urgency to the nuclear debate in Japan as well.[17]

Although some Japanese would like to see Japan acquire greater independence from the U.S. in the security realm, most realize that for the foreseeable future neither the Japanese nor their neighbors are prepared for a rupture in the U.S.–Japan relationship. Many are as concerned with encouraging continued U.S. internationalism as they are with defining a wider role for Japan in regional affairs. And even those Japanese officials who want their country to focus more on its Asian links are unanxious to sacrifice Japan's underlying ties to the United States.[18]

East Asia's "Japan problem" is thus also a U.S. problem. In the absence of a Soviet threat, and in the presence of continuing trade friction with Japan, will the United States nonetheless remain committed to the region and to its relationship with Japan? President Clinton's embrace of the region has been reassuring thus far. But it remains to be seen whether Japan can move fast enough to a more balanced economic relationship with the United States to placate American frustrations. If it does not, the region may yet be forced to test the truth of Lee Kuan Yew's comments about instability.

Shifting Power and the
Challenge of China

Historically derived suspicions are reinforced by the vast disparities in power and power potential that mark East Asia's strategic landscape. Suspicions of Japan, for example, are aggravated by Japan's enormous economic clout relative to its neighbors. Although Japan has invested its wealth widely and to positive benefit around the region, neighbors remain suspicious that Japanese economic cooperation is merely a prelude to Japanese domination. China, relatively weak but growing fast, could pose the same problem over the long haul.

Indeed, it is China, far more than Japan, whose power potential is likely to pose the greatest challenge to regional security in the years and decades ahead. China's potential is vast, as Americans and Asians are now coming to understand.[19] Its population of 1.2 billion dwarfs that of all neighbors save India. Its resource endowment, though by no means lush, contrasts sharply with Japan's poverty in this area. These natural assets plus its central location already give China substantial leverage along its borders, in Indochina, and in the South China Sea. Although China remains underdeveloped in many ways, its natural potential and the incredibly rapid pace of its development since 1978 suggest that China's sophistication may slowly come into line with its size.

China's emergence casts a sharp light on the underlying ambiguity of East Asia's situation, the tension between liberal economic optimism and realist political pessimism. Unquestionably, China's economic growth and further growth potential constitute a regional and global asset, already being exploited to produce a bigger economic pie for all participants. Indeed, China's immediate neighbors have been able to avoid the economic slowdown that currently grips Japan, the United States, and Western Europe largely by redirecting their trade and investment to China.[20] U.S. and Asian businesspeople see nearly endless potential in China's market and a relatively skilled and disciplined labor force.

Moreover, an overriding interest in economic growth and the end of cold war hostilities have produced substantial improvements in China's relations with neighbors who were once bitter enemies. Russia and China have settled some 90 percent of the border disputes that almost took them to war in 1969. They have also agreed in principle to deploy their forces no closer than 100 km to that border.[21] In August 1993 India and China signed a "Peace and Tranquillity" agreement that shelved (but did not solve) border disputes that took these two countries to war in 1962.[22] China and Vietnam renewed normal diplomatic relations in 1991, and in 1993 signed an agreement "to shun the use of force over border disputes on land and at sea."[23]

Yet while China's neighbors bask in the absolute gains afforded by China's rapid growth, they worry about the long-term effects of the relative gains accruing to China. If China successfully exploits

its economic potential, after all, its huge economy is at least as likely to be independent as interdependent with those of its neighbors. It will also have the potential to dominate the region militarily. While China's neighbors trade vigorously with it, they wonder whether they are not helping to produce the next regional hegemon.

There is evidence to propel such concerns. If a desire for stability and trade has motivated China's interest in settling land border disputes, for example, it has made Beijing still more assertive about its ownership of offshore territories that lie near important sea lanes and perhaps atop important resources, especially oil.[24] China claims the Spratly and Paracel Islands, and thus virtually all of the South China Sea, rejecting claims by Vietnam, Brunei, Malaysia, and the Philippines. It also claims Diaoyutao, an island group northeast of Taiwan that is claimed by Taiwan (which calls the group Diaoyutai), and that is also both claimed and occupied by Japan (which refers to the islands as Senkaku).[25]

Although they refuse to discuss possession, China's leaders have taken pains in recent years to disavow "hegemonic" intentions in the South China Sea, even offering to codevelop the area's resources with other claimants. Yet China's actions hardly inspire confidence. Its defense budget, like its economy, has experienced double-digit growth over the past few years, and while some of that increase has gone into raising the pay of People's Liberation Army (PLA) soldiers, part has gone to purchase long-range aircraft, aerial refueling capabilities, and the beginnings of a blue-water navy. China is developing military bases on Hainan and Woody Islands in the South China Sea.[26] It has forcibly wrested islands from Vietnam over the past fifteen years, and in a provocative recent move it hired an American firm to explore for oil on islands lying on Vietnam's continental shelf.[27]

Southeast Asian governments understandably tend to see China's codevelopment offer as a thinly veiled scheme to lure them into recognizing Chinese ownership of the islands while forcing them into Chinese dominated economic arrangements. Increasing arms expenditures among the Southeast Asian states owe at least partly to uncertainties about China's intentions. While this has not yet become "the next great arms race," as one scholar recently described it, the wealth and technical sophistication of these states can sustain a grand arms race if their fears warrant it.[28]

Although China and Japan downplay their own island dispute, Japan has also taken note of China's arms purchases. Reportedly Tokyo has warned Moscow not to sell more sophisticated aircraft to China.[29] Japanese diplomats evidently threatened China with a loss of development assistance if they purchased an aircraft carrier from the Ukraine, as they were reportedly interested in doing in 1992. And a well-informed Japanese defense analyst recently suggested that China and North Korea are together becoming the new rationale for producing the expensive FSX fighter/strike aircraft, whose development was initially premised on the Soviet threat.[30]

But it is in the Sino-Russian relationship that the relative gains problem may have its most perverse effect. Russians looking east already see the world's largest country growing rapidly, and increasingly linked to U.S. and Japanese technology through Pacific trade. Chinese growth confronts Russia in its huge but relatively weak and inaccessible eastern region, where the Russian population is little more than 10 million and logistics difficulties still hamper military operations. Chinese growth also confronts Russia at a time when its own economy and polity are in disarray. Despite border agreements and burgeoning trade with China, and even as they sell China a sizable cache of arms, Russian strategists have begun to see China as a major long-term threat.[31]

Russian concern at the moment focuses on the revival of dormant Sino-Russian border disputes, but this understates the implications of Sino-Russian hostility, should it reemerge. These are nuclear powers; Russia's nuclear forces are constrained by the Strategic Arms Reduction Treaty (START) agreements, while China remains conspicuously aloof from nuclear arms control agreements. And while Russia finds it difficult if not impossible to afford the force posture it needs to defend its huge expanse, China continues to convert its army from an infantry-heavy force trained for "people's war" to an armor-heavy force that, while geared for mobile defense, is inherently offensive in character. It is partly with this contrast in mind that Russia's new military doctrine, leaked to the Western press, reportedly disavows the Soviet Union's no-first-use pledge.[32] The consequences of increasing Sino-Russian animosity go well beyond East Asia.

Such Russian concerns, although low key at the moment, go to the heart of the challenge China poses not just to East Asia or the United States, but to the world. China is not a threat, at least yet. But thus far its power has grown without discipline, outside any of the prevailing regimes that might limit or direct its build-up, reassuring its neighbors. The continuation of that trend by a country as large and potentially powerful as China could pose the single most difficult global adjustment of the post–cold war era. The obvious challenge is to test China's willingness to cooperate, not only within multilateral regimes in East Asia, but within global regimes like START and perhaps an extended conventional forces in Europe (CFE) agreement.

All of this may sound like a vast overreaction to short-term growth in a country whose political system could easily buckle under the strains of growth and generational change in its leadership. Yet it makes good sense to handle China as if it were on a long-term growth path whatever path it takes. For one thing, China does not have to realize all of its potential to pose a significant challenge to regional security, since the problem, as Gilpin put it, is not absolute power but relative changes in it. Even such additional power as China has acquired over the past half-decade has set off mild alarms in Southeast Asian capitals as well as in Moscow.

Meanwhile, China's size, location, and increasing importance to the regional and global economy link *any* of its futures to regional and global security, just as the Soviet Union's collapse has raised an array of security issues different from, but only marginally less urgent than, its earlier assertion of power. Indeed, China's slow decay after 1840 was among the most important regional security issues of the previous century. China's future decay, if it occurs, will present different problems, stemming especially from China's nuclear status. But it will be better under almost any circumstances to have invited Chinese participation in some kind of multilateral security frameworks than to have left it to its present outsider's role.

Between the extremes of superpowerhood and fragmentation

lie futures that everyone prefers, in which China grows more democratic and peaceful, or at least deemphasizes force in relations with neighbors, or finds that its huge size is no cure for the constraints of interdependence. These are plausible but very uncertain possibilities. The question for U.S. and regional strategists is whether outsiders, or even the Chinese themselves, can find ways to move China in these directions.

Moving China to the Center

The U.S. role in buffering East Asia from its history is well understood in the United States. Defense Department strategy documents refer frequently to the "stabilizing" role of U.S. forces deployed along the Western Pacific rim.[33] U.S. diplomats never tire of saying that the U.S.–Japan relationship is "the most important bilateral relationship" in the world. While this statement contains an important economic dimension, Japanese and Americans alike understand that for the foreseeable future, a break in their security relationship would serve neither the U.S., Japan, nor East Asia. To the extent that U.S. forces stationed in Japan have become crucial symbols of the U.S.–Japan security relationship, no one is anxious to see them reduced, let alone taken home.

There is considerably less agreement in the United States on China's importance in the region and to U.S. strategy. Having seen China as a strategic counterweight to the Soviet Union over the second half of the cold war, U.S. officials *reduced* China's importance in their strategic calculus as the cold war came to an end, even though the Soviet Union's collapse actually increased Chinese power and independence.[34] The importance of human rights issues in Sino–U.S. relations bears witness to this fact. Representative Barney Frank inadvertently made this point in 1990, stating in hearings that "it is hard today to conjure up a major threat to our national security sufficient . . . to dilute our commitment to human rights."[35] China's growing trade surplus with the United States, now second in size only to Japan's, has also become a bone of contention between the two countries.

Presidents have been more prone than some legislators to see China's importance to an array of U.S. security concerns. Chinese cooperation was and remains essential to resolving Cambodia's civil war and the Korean confrontation. China's arms transfers to volatile regions like South Asia and the Middle East clash with the U.S. interest in stability and nonproliferation. Finally, as a permanent member of the U.N. Security Council China has potential veto power over the growing number of global issues now before that body. These, more than President Bush's personal affinity for China, explain Bush's reluctance to sacrifice links to Beijing on the altar of human rights.

President Clinton has arrived at the same conclusion despite his campaign promise to take a harder line on human rights and trade. Increasingly aware of China's overall importance, he has finessed the human rights issue (at least for 1993) and is now beginning to raise China's place in U.S. foreign policy. Reportedly the Clinton administration is now willing to send still higher-level U.S. officials to Beijing, waive some of the economic sanctions imposed on China in retaliation for its sale of M-11 missiles to Pakistan, and revive military contacts with the PLA.[36] In the policy background lie Clinton's virtual embrace of East Asia, his administration's openness to multilateral dialogue, and his promise of continued U.S. military support to South Korea and the region generally. Clinton's defense budgets support this commitment; the Pentagon's recent "bottom up" review reversed earlier promised cuts in the kind of forces (Marines and Navy) that are deployed to East Asia.

Clinton has thus avoided the collision with China many feared his election would precipitate. Yet the U.S. engagement with China remains wary and troubled.[37] It would be difficult in any case to overcome the unfairness inherent in encounters between the world's most powerful and technologically advanced state and one still suffering from massive underdevelopment despite recent strong growth. Yet U.S. policies toward China often seem designed to reinforce China's post–cold war fear, much enhanced by U.S. military success in the Gulf War, that the U.S. seeks "hegemony."[38] Many in Beijing see U.S. pressure on human rights issues as part of an ideological strategy aimed at making China democratic and capitalist.[39] They see in high-seas U.S. pressure to inspect a Chinese ship suspected of carrying precursor chemicals to

Iran as confirmation of the U.S. desire to be a global police officer. Recent U.S. opposition to China's underground nuclear test looks to Chinese like a bald U.S. effort to sustain its own nuclear superiority. Finally, U.S. opposition to China's arms sales looks steeply one-sided to Chinese in view of the huge size of U.S. arms sales, not to mention the recent U.S. sale of F-16s to Taiwan.

For all the resentment it provokes, U.S. policy still misses the core security issues that surround China's emergence. It deals with the extensions of Chinese power—its seat on the Security Council, its arms transfers, its support to Pyongyang—but not with China itself. It is as if U.S. policy treats what are seen as the "global" manifestations of Chinese activity—proliferation, U.N. activities and the like—without yet recognizing that China's future is itself a global issue. A China that is fully able to exploit its economic and military potential will be a global power. But the challenge of China's emergence is already having perverse security effects, both in prompting Russia to raise the salience of nuclear weapons in its military doctrine and in encouraging Southeast Asians to hedge by purchasing arms. Russia's reaction to China could affect the existing security structure in Europe, while it is hardly in the U.S. interest to see an arms race in a region where so much of its own economic well-being is at stake.

With China potentially a global problem and the U.S. clearly a global as well as regional power, dealing with China should be a principal U.S. strategic concern. In the worst case China is a problem without a *regional* solution. Its economy and military, fully developed, could dwarf those around it. If China is to be interdependent economically, it will be at the global level. And if its military power is to be balanced in some fashion, this too will require global involvement. The challenge China poses is perhaps the most potent argument for long-term U.S. economic and military engagement in East Asia.

How should the U.S. proceed? Political realists would argue that the best the U.S. can hope to do is to balance Chinese power if and as it grows; the anarchic state structure will negate efforts to construct a broader set of cooperative arrangements in the region or across the Pacific. Alliances can serve U.S. interests, but these are likely to be more fluid than those that pertained during the cold war, because China will be more economically integrated into the region and because it is unlikely to pose the stark ideological threat posed by Moscow's communism. Hard-core realists might add that it is in the U.S. interest to seek to weaken China by, for example, withholding trade and technology, or by seeking to weaken or destabilize China's government.[40] From this perspective it makes no sense to aid the development of a competing global power with China's potential.

Yet such policy prescriptions are unworkable and unwise. East Asians see too much to be gained by bringing China into the regional economy, and too much to lose if China's economy turns downward or if China's disintegration floods the surrounding region with millions of refugees. A U.S. strategy aimed at isolating or destabilizing China will thus almost inevitably fail. And it will drive a wedge between the U.S. and regional friends, including Japan and South Korea—hardly a comforting thought for those interested in stability and continued economic growth. Moreover, such an approach prematurely declares China a "threat" when for some time to come it would be more productive to see in China a challenge—that of encouraging or coaxing China into cooperative, constructive regional and global engagement. Given China's current relative weakness and its interest in economic growth and overall friendly relations, there is no better time to start facing this challenge than now.

There is an obvious and crucially important economic dimension to such a strategy. If China is potentially a problem without a regional solution, then the U.S. must remain economically engaged in East Asia, and in China's development. This constitutes yet another argument against curtailing most favored nation status in response to perceived human rights violations in China. It also requires the U.S. to combat latent tendencies toward regionalization of the global economy.[41] U.S. policies must seek to bolster trans-Pacific economic as well as security linkages, while tackling underlying structural problems in the U.S. economy that constrain the global competitiveness of U.S. firms.

But the principal concern here is the role of U.S. military forces in a strategy aimed at engaging China cooperatively, and the next section outlines approaches the U.S. might take in this regard. The chapter then examines U.S. relations with the Koreas and Japan from the perspective of a strategy aimed to engage China. Korea and Japan obviously impose important challenges on U.S. strategy in their own right. Yet they acquire important new dimensions in the context of a long-term focus on China. The U.S.-Japan security relationship is no less important for moving China to the center of U.S. strategy; encouraging Chinese cooperation is in Japan's interest, although managing the U.S.-Japan relationship in light of a strategy toward China is not likely to be easy. Equally important, the Korean situation, which looks now like a bothersome cold war hangover, is already becoming a key focus of U.S.-China interaction, and has the potential to become the energizing issue for a Northeast Asian security dialogue.

The Substance of Military Dialogue

The effort to engage China constructively in the security realm faces two major problems. On the one hand, China's forces are so large that even modest and essentially defensive changes in their size or character are likely to appear threatening to neighbors. To make matters worse, China is so far behind the industrial powers technologically and doctrinally that it understandably feels compelled to take steps that will be far from "modest and essentially defensive" in character. It is unlikely that any outside power can stop China's slow but steady drive to build a "blue-water" navy, for example, or to convert its army to a mobile armored force replete with force projection capabilities. As with China's economy, China's military modernization is apt to be impressive—in this case worrisome—because the potential is so great and the distance to be covered is so large.

On the other hand, arguably China has not in fact shown much interest in compromise. This is most obviously the case in the South China Sea, where Beijing refuses to discuss disputed ownership of the Spratlys and Paracels. It is also the case along the Sino-Russian border, where the emerging border agreement involves Russian concessions, and where troop withdrawals involve only Russian troop movements.[42] Finally, the Chinese seem to be at pains to distance themselves from the established nuclear arms

control regime. During the cold war Beijing promised to participate in nuclear arms control when superpower arsenals had been
cut in half. START promises to do that and more; yet now Beijing
hinges its participation on U.S. and Russian agreement in principal to eliminate the weapons entirely. China's recent nuclear test is
yet another disturbing sign of Chinese independence in this area.

China's intentions need to be tested, but the tests need to be
appropriate to the situation. In the nuclear area, for example,
China's forces are so small and backward that it makes little sense
to seek Chinese force reductions within an expanding START
framework. It would make more sense initially to engage Beijing
on issues like transparency, safety, and crisis stability. The need for
such engagement is likely to arise anyway out of continuing efforts
by the U.S. and Russia to reduce their nuclear arsenals and to
ensure that their nuclear weapons are neither prone to accidents
nor geared for surprise attack. Such measures as taking nuclear
forces off full-time alert and removing warheads have the benefit
of deemphasizing the importance of nuclear weapons and reducing whatever threat China attaches to Russian and U.S. nuclear
arsenals.[43] There should be obvious points in the U.S.–Russian
dialogue on nuclear arms where China's participation can be invited, its willingness to engage tested.

The Chinese would no doubt complain that they have not been
asked to join such key regimes as START. An obvious bargain
would be to invite China to join the nuclear arms control rule-
making club in return for its agreement to live by the rules so
written. The problem with involving China in the START talks,
however, is that doing so will necessitate inclusion of the acknowledged nuclear powers, Britain and France, as well as perhaps
India and Pakistan. Thus it is more practical to engage China on a
bilateral or trilateral basis (with Russia) before seeking formal expansion of START.

Conventional force issues are still less tractable, since much of
China's conventional force posture lies beyond U.S. engagement.
Yet these are the most important issues, since in the end it is
China's conventional forces that tweak neighbors' security con-
cerns, including Russia's. Offshore, at least, U.S. naval power
promises to be more than a match for Chinese projection capabili-

ties for many years to come, assuming the U.S. chooses to remain engaged. The U.S. thus can seek to deter China's use of such forces, but also to trade some of its own capabilities, or freedom of maneuver, in return for constraints on China's forces.

Naval cooperation is a good place to engage China. Whether or not the South China Sea is a Chinese "lake," as Beijing seems to see it, it is a major highway for ships carrying global trade. It is unlikely that China will be free to control that shipping without provoking the concern of countries far beyond those that immediately border the area. Rather, China could reassure global trading interests, as well as its Southeast Asian neighbors, by taking an interest in cooperative measures to ensure the safety of sea lanes.

Although China's ground forces have gotten smaller over the past decade, they are becoming more mobile and capable as Beijing seeks to create forces capable of what the U.S. came to call "airland battle." The Chinese are a long way from having such a force, suggesting that the modernization process will continue. Such structural and technological changes, combined with the relatively greater density of China's infrastructure and population along the Sino-Russian border, are likely to put increasing pressure on strategists in Moscow, who at this point lack the budget to sustain even the reduced forces called for in their planning documents. One alternative in this case would be to encourage Russia and China to locate military logistics facilities well away from their mutual border, a technique that works better with mechanized and sophisticated forces than with infantry. Another, however, would be to embed guarantees concerning the Sino-Russian border in a multilateral security framework of some sort.

Korea as a Zone
of Sino–U.S. Engagement

The Korean Peninsula may offer the best avenue by which to approach the creation of such a framework, for handling nuclear as well as conventional force issues. At the moment the principal concerns on the peninsula are the continuing military stand-off between the two Koreas, the small but still real possibility of war between them, and North Korea's purported nuclear program.

The U.S. and China have been deeply involved in negotiations on these issues, albeit largely in the background. Although they have disagreed on tactics, they have generally agreed on the desirability of ending the military confrontation and bringing North Korea's nuclear program under international control.

Korea's location amid Northeast Asia's larger powers raises the risk, however, that this relatively amicable state of affairs will sour as the Koreas make progress toward unification.[44] In the past Korea's location often made it the victim of larger neighbors seeking either to control Korea or to prevent others from controlling it. In the late nineteenth century, for example, Japan fought China and then Russia to gain position in Korea, which it made a colony in 1910. The imperialist era may be over, but Korea's location is likely still to make its status and loyalties a matter of concern to neighbors. While this is widely understood with respect to another Korean war, it holds true in the event of peace. Progress toward Korean unification will move the locus of the Korea "problem" from the Korean Peninsula to the region around it.

The resulting dynamic could be very disruptive. Presumably a unified Korea, surrounded by nuclear powers and deeply suspicious of Japan, would have to take steps to ensure its own security, and especially to acquire nuclear cover. Would China accept a unified Korea allied to the United States and tucked under the U.S. nuclear umbrella? Would the U.S. or Japan be happy if Korea chose instead to ally with China? Such choices could aggravate underlying tensions and suspicions among these powers. Or Korea might take an independent route, seeking to play neighbors off against each other while acquiring its own nuclear weapons—a move sure to exacerbate regional tension, not least because it would exert enormous pressure on Japan to go nuclear as well.

The linkages between regional security and security on the Korean Peninsula are already evident at the nuclear level, thanks to North Korea's purported nuclear weapons program. Fear that Pyongyang is building a bomb has provoked serious concern in Tokyo, while the Bush administration's decision in the fall of 1991 to withdraw tactical nuclear weapons from seaborne and overseas forces no doubt helped coax Pyongyang into signing a set of relatively far-reaching inter-Korean agreements later that year. Inter-

Korean negotiations reached their present impasse in the spring of 1993, when Pyongyang balked at allowing more intrusive inspections by officials from the International Atomic Energy Agency (IAEA) and threatened to leave the Non-Proliferation Treaty (NPT). These moves, coupled with reluctance in Seoul and Beijing to apply further sanctions, won Pyongyang high-level talks with the United States, but these have yet to produce tangible results. At least some in the United States wish to take a tougher line with Pyongyang. But to do so they need China's cooperation, and Beijing (as well as Seoul) has thus far been reluctant to agree to further sanctions.

Further progress toward bringing North Korea's nuclear program under international supervision may require the elaboration of regional security guarantees, along the lines, perhaps, of various proposals to make the Korean Peninsula a nuclear-free zone. These involve agreement by the surrounding nuclear powers *not* to use nuclear weapons on the peninsula in return for Pyongyang's pledge to give up nuclear aspirations.[45] The need for such an agreement would represent an opportunity to launch a discussion among Northeast Asia's nuclear powers about the future of their nuclear arsenals. Japan-Korean animosity and Japan's ambitious nuclear reprocessing program would probably require Japan's participation in such discussions.

As thorny as the nuclear issue has been thus far, its resolution would open the way to negotiations that are still more complicated, for two reasons. On the one hand, while conventional force reductions among the two Korean militaries may increase their sense of security with relation to each other, they are likely to *increase* their sense of insecurity with relation to their neighbors, whose militaries may not be shrinking at all. On the other, movement toward a Korean accommodation will raise questions about the political alignment of a unified Korea on which the U.S. and China may not agree as easily as they have on the nuclear issue. The process of Korean unification thus could become increasingly divisive for surrounding powers. To the extent that those powers wish to avoid such problems, on the other hand, they will face powerful incentives to open a dialogue on conventional force issues among China, Russia, and the United States.

Much will depend on how the inter-Korean dialogue proceeds, or whether it proceeds—North Korea could block further progress, or it could collapse under the weight of sanctions. Seoul and Beijing are understandably anxious to avoid the latter, since it would present them with a prodigious refugee crisis and a bill for bringing North Korea's economy up to par. In fact, both the crisis and the bill are likely to surpass the financial and administrative capabilities of either China or South Korea. The problem will have to be handled internationally. Thus North Korea's collapse, like more peaceful progress toward a Korean accommodation, will be a regional affair.

The logic of the Korean situation virtually begs for a regional security dialogue. In a sense, it has already prompted dialogue among the surrounding powers, albeit in the form of "multiple-bilateral" discussions that have become common and necessary in the absence of more elaborate discussions. Questions about when to move the bilateral discussions into a more formal multipolar setting must be addressed, but there is less question that the United States is likely to be best positioned to prod such a discussion into existence when the time arrives.

Whether or not the U.S. is able to coax such a forum into existence, clearly the Korea negotiations will bring the U.S. into engagement with China. Moreover, that engagement has the potential to become more adversarial as the Koreas move past the nuclear issue, on which China and the U.S. are in broad agreement, and toward unity, where their interests are more likely to diverge. Indeed, the issue of how to ensure the security of a unified Korea has the potential to be very divisive, especially if it is allowed to develop into a "zero sum" game in which the U.S. and China see themselves competing for the role of Korea's ally. Thus whatever the forum, the U.S. should begin as early as possible to aim U.S.–China negotiations toward a cooperative outcome.

The U.S., Japan, and China

During the cold war, the Soviet threat gave the U.S. and Japan a common strategic purpose that helped sustain their relationship even as their economic differences grew more contentious. Not surprisingly, the absence of such a common strategic purpose has made the U.S.–Japan relationship more difficult to manage, and has raised questions about its future. President Clinton may have allayed fears of an impending divorce somewhat by his embrace of East Asia, but keen observers worry that by rationalizing the embrace largely in economic terms Clinton has focused the U.S. and Japan on the most fractious of the issues between them. Political realists would expect the relationship to erode in any case, since in their view it was primarily a common threat that held it together in the first place. Liberal economists point to the elaborate interdependence that marks these two economies; yet even they worry that these two states might be on "a collision course."[46]

Recognizing the importance of China's emergence and moving it to the center of U.S. strategy has the advantage of giving the U.S. and Japan something else to talk about besides economics. And talk about it they must, for the approach to China must be handled cooperatively if it is to succeed. A common U.S.–Japanese message to Beijing on key security issues would carry substantial weight, while in disagreement Tokyo and Washington could easily undercut one another's leverage with China, especially where economic sanctions are concerned. Meanwhile, given China's lingering fear of Japanese militarism, any erosion of the U.S.–Japan relationship that compels Japan to rearm will almost surely prompt a response from China, leading to a destabilizing arms race.

Still, China is not the Soviet Union; even if China grows more powerful and less cooperative, it is unlikely to provide the kind of "glue" that the Soviet threat provided to the U.S.–Japan relationship. Notwithstanding Japan's treatment of China earlier in this century and China's continuing fear of Japanese militarism, historical and cultural links between these two countries run deep and are generally positive. While Japan and Russia remain wary of each other even today, China and Japan maintained an economic relationship even in the heyday of the cold war.[47] That relationship took off after 1972, and acquired depth and diversity during the 1980s.[48] Though it remains far from an equal and interdependent relationship, it is far more mutually beneficial than anything yet evident in Japan's relationship with Russia. Sino-Japanese relations are likely always to be more complicated and subtle than those that characterized Japan's relations with the Soviet Union.

Managing the U.S.–Japan relationship thus will also be more complicated, even with the help of a common strategic enterprise. China has already been a bone of contention between these two states. Japan was much less anxious than the U.S. to impose sanctions on China after the Tienanmen incident, and it was Japanese Prime Minister Kaifu who announced, at the G-7 conference in Houston in July 1990, that his country was prepared to end China's international isolation by resuming negotiations on a $5.2 billion loan package to Beijing. Japanese are opposed to the notion of curtailing most favored nation treatment for China as punishment for human rights abuses. U.S. adoption of such a policy could provoke a serious crisis in U.S.–Japan relations.

Yet in the broader strategic sense, Japan, China, and the United States would seem to have common interests that could be exploited to encourage cooperation. However much the Chinese resent U.S. "hegemonism," they appreciate the U.S. military presence in East Asia as a lid on Japanese militarism; this concern may be even greater now than it was during the cold war.[49] This sets limits on Beijing's willingness to seek tactical advantage by playing Japan and the U.S. off against each other. Worrying about a breach in U.S.–Japan relations also gives Beijing an interest in constructing multilateral security organizations capable of containing Japanese power.[50]

Meanwhile, Japanese recognize the importance of U.S. forces in covering elements of their security beyond self-defense. More broadly, the Japanese well understand that their freedom of action in East Asia, their interest in regional stability, and perhaps even Japan's internal stability, depend mightily on the health of their security relationship with the United States.[51] Finally, at least some Japanese have concluded that, given Japan's lack of natural resources, its "natural ally should be the power that dominates the seas at any given time."[52] Even in the absence of a Soviet threat Japan has powerful reasons for retaining its security ties to the United States.

Reasons to cooperate can be found on the economic side of the ledger as well. The Chinese remain wary of becoming too dependent on Japan for technology and investment, and thus are not anxious to see intraregional economic linkages grow at the expense of links to the United States. Japan is of course far more heavily invested in the United States than it is in China, and for all the friction in their relationship Japan and the U.S. are deeply interdependent economically. Each of these economies has much to offer the other two, and this too should set limits on how far each capital will let divisiveness go before seeking to rein it in.

This said, the fact remains that unequal trade could disrupt the U.S.–Japan relationship, especially at a time when citizens in the United States are questioning their country's global role and global linkages. Messy "peacekeeping" operations in Somalia and perhaps Bosnia could yet sour Americans' support for international involvement, and in this context Japan's commercial behavior, seen by some Americans as predatory, could yet ignite protectionist and nationalist pressures, prompting a nationalist response from Japan as well. To the extent that this is the case, the top priority of U.S. security policy in East Asia must be economic in nature; there is no viable alternative to U.S. pressure, carefully applied, as a means of further opening Japan's economy.[53]

Conversely, given China's concerns about Japan's intentions and the absence of a compelling threat, it would be counterproductive for the U.S. to pressure Japan to build more forces or to extend the operational perimeter of its forces outside of international control. Japan's peacekeeping operations bill, already responsible for Japan's engagement with U.N. operations in Cambodia and Mozambique, would appear to contain more than enough latitude for exploring Japan's global security role without adding to Japan's existing force posture or suggesting increasing Japanese independence in the security realm.

Ultimately the U.S. and Japan must face the question of Japan's wider involvement in regional security. Japan's navy cannot forever confine itself to the 1000-mile perimeter it agreed to defend in 1981. Nor is it so confined. Japanese minesweepers weathered regional and domestic criticism to journey to the Persian Gulf after Desert Storm. Meanwhile, Japan's peacekeeping operations bill opened the way for Japanese military and civilian participation in United Nations operations in Cambodia and Mozambique. These activities require no additions to Japan's force posture, and certainly do not require the purchase of projection forces. The best area for gradual expansion of Japan's military activity lies in the area of protecting sea lines of communication (SLOCs), where Japan shares an interest with the United States as well as its neighbors. Japanese involvement in such activities would be mediated by the United States quite naturally, since SLOC protection remains one of the U.S. Navy's most common and important missions.

The advisable goal of U.S. strategy should be to extend the U.S.–Japan security relationship over the long term, unless and until the beneficent state of regional relationships makes it unnecessary, at which point the U.S.–Japan economic relationship should be a very productive one. The security relationship makes enormous strategic as well as historic sense. But the political challenge of sustaining support for it among two very different cultures, each with its own isolationist tradition, is formidable.

Conclusions

President Clinton has embraced East Asia for its economic importance. While Europeans may feel slighted as a result, in fact the president has merely brought U.S. policy into accord with economic trends that emerged some years ago and are likely to remain valid for some years to come. Meanwhile, the Clinton embrace has given initial reassurance to regional states worried that the U.S. would depart the region soon after the cold war ended. The danger in Clinton's policies is that their near-exclusive focus on economics will highlight potentially divisive imbalances in U.S. trade relations with several East Asian states—not just Japan— and thus ultimately magnify America's frustrations and protectionist tendencies.

The solution to this dilemma lies in what Clinton thus far has missed, namely that East Asia's importance to the global economy is matched by China's importance to global security. The effects of China's emergence on East Asian security are already apparent in the gentle but clear upswing that marks most defense budgets in the region. Should Chinese military power continue to grow without international discipline, its likely effects on Russia will be felt in Europe and the United States. True, China may not continue to grow. But strategy should worry about worst cases, and China's emergence as an uncooperative and assertive regional and global power is potentially a global worst case.

The goal of U.S. strategy should be to encourage Chinese cooperation in multilateral regional and global security arrangements, to test China's intentions, and hopefully to head off its emergence as a threat. Significantly, the U.S. hedge against the possibility of an emerging Chinese "threat" is also the military desiderata for multilateral security cooperation: continued U.S. military engagement in East Asia. U.S. forces dampen underlying suspicions of Japan and in this sense alone enhance the prospects for regional security cooperation. Meanwhile, U.S. forces will play a major role in balancing China in the worst case that China indeed emerges as a threat to its neighbors. In the best case, on the other hand, U.S. deployments and freedom of military maneuver are likely to be the major pawns in negotiations with China and its neighbors to develop cooperative security arrangements. U.S. forces should remain deployed to the Asian-Pacific rim unless and until such arrangements loom as a real possibility.

Notes

[1] See, for example, C. Fred Bergsten, "The Real Key to U.S. Growth Lies in Europe and Japan," *Washington Post*, (Outlook Section), pp. C1–2. The caveat about sluggish U.S. economic growth is important, however. Roughly 90 percent of the total U.S. GDP is still generated domestically. Thus changes in domestic economic performance remain vastly more important to the welfare of U.S. citizens than changes in trade. Even America's most ardent "Japan bashers" admit that eliminating Japan's one-sided trade patterns will have marginal effects on U.S. welfare in comparison to solving self-inflicted economic ills like the huge federal deficit, problems in the educational system, and so forth.

[2] Department of Defense, *A Strategic Framework for the Asian Pacific Rim: Report to Congress 1992*, pp. 17, 22.

[3] See the discussion in Bosworth (1993), pp. 1–29.

[4] See, for example, Perkins (1986), p. 6.

[5] The best elaboration of these issues is Keohane and Nye (1989).

[6] The classic statement is Mearsheimer (1990), pp. 5–56. See also Waltz (1993), pp. 44–79.

[7] On the possibilities for increasing regionalization, see Sandholtz, et al. (1992), pp. 25ff.

[8] Sandholtz, et al. (1992), pp. 38, 49.

[9] Tyson (1990), pp. 160–161.

[10] Sandholtz, et al. (1992), pp. 25–29 and chapter 6.

[11] On the issue of relative versus absolute gains, see Mastanduno (1991), pp. 73–113; also Grieco (1988), pp. 485–507.

[12] Gilpin (1981), p. 230.

[13] The United States remains Japan's major trading partner, for example. And the six member states of ASEAN trade far more with the world than with one another. Intra-ASEAN trade actually declined in the years after the organization was formed, from 19.1 percent of ASEAN exports to 16.8 percent. Krause (1982), p. 24.

[14] On this and other tensions in Sino-Japanese relations, see Whiting and Jianfei (1990–91), pp. 107–135.

[15] Quoted in Richardson (1992), p. 36.

[16] For an excellent summary, see Brown (1993), pp. 543–559.

[17] North Korea's test of the Rodong I missiles, capable of reaching many targets in Japan, prompted Tokyo to water down language in the final communique of the G-7 conference held in Tokyo in July 1993, as well as to reemphasize the importance of the U.S. nuclear umbrella. See Clayton Jones, "Korea Prompts Japan to Review No-Nukes Policy," *Christian Science Monitor*, August 10, 1993, pp. 1, 14. On Japan's nuclear debate, see Selig Harrison, "Yen for the Bomb," *Washington Post*, October 31, 1993, pp. C1, C2.

[18] Brown (1993), pp. 554–555.

[19] See, for example, Kristof (1993), pp. 59–74.

[20] See, for example, Laurence Zuckerman, "China's Record Expansion Stokes Region's Economy," *Asian Wall Street Journal*, May 10, 1993, pp. 1, 16.

[21] "CIS, China End Talks on Border: Russia to Withdraw Troops," *FBIS-SOV-92-234*, December 4, 1992, p. 2.

[22] The two sides agreed to respect the existing line of military control, which many observers take as "a clear signal that [a final border] settlement is likely to leave the disputed territories in the hands they have been in since 1962." Unable to agree on a formula for cutting forces along the border, the two sides agree to create a hotline between commanders, to provide advance notification of maneuvers along the border, and to take common steps to prevent airspace violations. See "Hands across the Himalayas," *The Economist*, September 11, 1993, pp. 31–32, and Kaye (1993), p. 13.

[23] "Beijing, Hanoi Sign Border Agreement," *South China Morning Post*, October 20, 1993, p. 9. Significantly, the Vietnamese signatory to the agreement, Deputy Foreign Minister Vu Khoan, would say only that the agreement was "better than nothing."

[24] In February 1992 China's People's Assembly passed legislation that asserted Chinese claims to offshore islands more assertively than in the past. In particular, it referred explicitly to Diauyutai rather than using the usual reference to "Taiwan and accessory islands." See "New Law Claims Sovereignty Over Spratly Islands," *FBIS-CHI-92-039*, p. 15.

[25] Despite the 1992 legislation, both China and Japan continue to suppress nationalist sentiments in both countries for the sake of their economic relationship. For background, see Whiting and Jianfei (1990–91), pp. 108–126.

[26] On China's military expenditures, see Shambaugh (1992), pp. 88–106, and Robert S. Greenberger, "China's Neighbors Show Concern Over Beijing's Weapons Shopping," *Asian Wall Street Journal*, October 19, 1992, p. 14.

[27] See Richardson (1991), p. 16; Nicholas D. Kristof, "China Signs U.S. Oil

Deal for Disputed Waters," *New York Times,* June 18, 1992, p. A8; and Joseph A. Reaves, "China's Resurgent Navy Makes Waves in Clash with Vietnam," *Chicago Tribune,* May 8, 1988, p. 7.

[28] Klare (1993), pp. 136–152.

[29] Yu (1993), p. 313.

[30] Interview. Yu (1993) asserts that "the draft of a 1992 Japanese defense White Paper even states that China and North Korea have replaced the former Soviet Union as the major military threat in the Far East."

[31] On Russian concerns about "the shift in power between [Russia and China] as a result of Chinese economic growth," see Allison (1993), p. 7.

[32] On the nuclear issue, see "The Emerging Russian Nuclear Strategy and Doctrine: Where Are the Enemies," Seminar Report (a discussion with Colonel Vladimir Dworkin, head of the Center for Geopolitical and Military Forecasting), Center for Naval Analyses, July 1993, pp. 1–2. On Russia's new military doctrine, see Fred Hiatt, "Russia Shifts Doctrine on Military Use," *Washington Post,* November 4, 1993, pp. A1, A33.

[33] The Bush administration's official Asian-Pacific strategy document, for example, noted that the "continuing U.S. presence in Japan and the strength of the U.S.–Japan security relationship are reassuring to many nations in the region as well as to Japan." Department of Defense, *A Strategic Framework for the Asian Pacific Rim: Report to Congress 1992,* p. 4.

[34] Writing in 1992, Harding could still assert that most U.S. officials "still regarded China as less important, less admirable, and less cooperative than they had in the past," p. 290.

[35] Harding (1992), p. 291.

[36] Jim Mann, "U.S. Moving to Improve Relationship with China," *Los Angeles Times,* September 30, 1993, pp. A1, A4.

[37] For a useful summary, see Jim Mann, "Pressures Build as U.S.–China Ties Turn Sour," *Los Angeles Times,* August 26, 1993, pp. A1, A3.

[38] Jencks (1992), p. 462.

[39] Jin Gan, "China's National Security Environment and Its Perceptions of Threat in the 1990s," unpublished manuscript, Atlantic Council, pp. 1–2.

[40] See, for example, Sullivan (1992), pp. 3–23.

[41] Economists can identify weak trends in this direction, notably in the European Community, where intraregional trade grew markedly over the 1980s. Many East Asians see the North American Free Trade Agreement (NAFTA) as extending a trend begun in Europe to the Western Hemisphere, essentially forcing East Asia into a regional trading pattern. In fact, however, the rapid pace of China's growth, combined with economic slowdowns in the U.S., Europe, and Japan, have probably increased intraregional trade even in East Asia. Meanwhile, some critics of Japan's economic behavior see that country as gradually seeking to create an East Asian trade bloc. See Frankel (1992), and Laurence Zuckerman, "China's Record Expansion Stokes Region's Economy," *Asian Wall Street Journal,* May 10, 1993. For arguments about Japan's long-term goals, see Sandholtz, et al. (1992), pp. 39–42.

[42] In their border negotiations the Soviet/Russian delegation ultimately backed off the longstanding Soviet position, based on a treaty signed in 1860, that gave Russia all the islands in the Amur and Ussuri Rivers up to the Chinese bank. The new agreement respects the Thalweg principle, which places the border at the center of the deep-water channel or the centerline of nonnavigable streams—

meaning Russia has given up roughly half of the territory it once claimed. Russian qualms about the current border settlement are outlined in Ginsburg (1993), pp. 317–320.

[43] For examples of steps toward "responsible nuclear custodianship," see Blair (1993), pp. 271–285.

[44] These issues are developed more extensively in McNaugher (1993), pp. 12–17.

[45] There might appear to be no need for such an agreement in light of U.S. assurances, outlined in the joint U.S.–PDRK statement published at the end of high-level talks in June 1993, "against the threat and use of force, including nuclear weapons." It remains unclear, however, whether this statement goes beyond the standard U.S. assurance not to use nuclear weapons except against a state that has nuclear weapons or is supported by a nuclear weapons state. In this case North Korea's alliance with China, a nuclear weapons state, would mean that the U.S. still reserves the right to use nuclear weapons in Korea. Selig S. Harrison, "Breaking the Nuclear Impasse: Paths to Cooperative Security in Korea," unpublished paper presented at the Conference on Northeast Asian Security, cosponsored by the Brookings Institution and the Institute of Foreign Affairs and National Security, Washington, D.C., November 1–2, 1993, p. 12. For more on the nuclear-free zone proposal, see Harrison (1991), pp. 599–631.

[46] See, for example, Bergsten and Noland (1993), especially chapter 1.

[47] Iriye (1990), pp. 629–634.

[48] See especially Wang (1993), pp. 625–641.

[49] Jonathan Pollack (1990) points out that in the late 1970s and early 1980s the Chinese "openly encouraged Japan to enhance its military power, hoping to complicate Soviet strategic designs further." Chinese observers were considerably less enthusiastic, however, when Japan's defense budget continued to rise in the late 1980s even as U.S.–Soviet relations warmed, pp. 716, 719.

[50] Drawing on extensive interviews in Beijing, Bonnie Glaser (1993) concluded that "if China becomes anxious about a U.S. troop withdrawal from Japan . . . there could be more urgency in Beijing about backing the creation of a framework for multilateral security that could check the growth of Japanese military power," p. 269.

[51] As Yukio Satoh, director-general, North American Affairs Bureau, Ministry of Foreign Affairs, put it, "No country in Asia would want to deal with a Japan that was severed from the U.S." Quoted in Brown (1993), p. 556. For a more comprehensive development of this argument and its effects on Japan's security decision making throughout the cold war, see Green (1993).

[52] Okazaki (1986), p. 48.

[53] See Lincoln (1990), pp. 135–164.

8

Meeting the Challenge of Japan in Asia

GERALD L. CURTIS

Introduction

The end of the cold war and the relative decline in U.S. economic power are forcing a more profound reexamination of U.S. foreign policy goals and strategies than at any time since the days following the end of the Second World War. In this reexamination, no region is more important than Asia, and no single country more crucial than Japan. The United States has vital national interests at stake in its relations with Asia; the challenge for U.S. policy makers is to design strategies that will promote those interests.

In order to do so, careful attention has to be paid to a number of questions about the region and about U.S. policy there. How has the strategic, political, and economic environment for U.S. policy in Asia changed, and what new challenges do these changes pose? Are the objectives of Japanese policy in Asia compatible with American interests in the region? How valid are the underlying assumptions behind the alternative strategies for U.S. policy toward Japan and Asia that are currently vying for acceptance? Finally, what should be the main elements of a new framework for dealing with Japan in the context of a broader U.S. policy in Asia? An emphasis on the need to construct a new framework for U.S. policy does not necessarily mean that past approaches should be scuttled and entirely new policies adopted to replace them. There may be compelling reasons to continue many of the policies of the past. It is necessary, however, to explain why these policies and commitments continue to serve U.S. national interests, now that the conditions that gave rise to them no longer exist. Public support for an active U.S. political and security role in the region, or an understanding of why Asia should be given priority attention in foreign economic policy, will not be forthcoming unless an effort to define what Asia means for the United States in the post–cold war world is successfully undertaken. The momentous changes that have occurred, and that are continuing in Asia and in the world at large, create the need for new concepts, for a new "architecture" for U.S. policy.

The Challenge of Change

To say that we are living in a period of tumultuous change is rapidly becoming a cliche. But it is true, and Asia is no exception. Asia—which for the purposes of our discussion embraces Japan, Korea, China, Taiwan, Hong Kong, the six countries of the Association of Southeast Asian Nations (ASEAN) (Thailand, Indonesia, Malaysia, Philippines, Singapore, and Brunei), and the three countries of Indochina (Vietnam, Cambodia, Laos)—has become the dynamic center of world economic growth. Economic integration is increasing, propelled by aggressive entrepreneurial businesspeople from Taiwan and Korea and Southeast Asia, as well as from Japan.

A sense of optimism, self confidence, and self esteem pervades the region. Many Asian leaders believe the "Asian way" can make a positive contribution to thinking about economic development and political order, even though they do not necessarily agree on what the "Asian way" is. Throughout the region too, one senses a new feeling of excitement that Asia should and can be something more than a geographical expression.

The anxieties that exist tend to reflect mostly domestic concerns: how to resolve the distortions of rapid growth that are manifest in urban congestion, pollution, and income disparities, and that create potentially explosive social tensions. Increasingly also, Asian states are being forced to respond to the demands for greater political representation, democratization, and human rights as their societies develop large, well-educated middle classes.

Concern about international relations in the region has several facets. There is worry that tensions in the U.S.–Japan relationship will have an adverse impact on the economic well-being and the security of other countries in the region. It is doubtful that any country in Asia, including China, believes that its own national interests would be served by a weakening of the U.S.–Japan relationship. Anti-Japanese sentiment in the United States is viewed with alarm because of the danger that it will lead to protectionist policies, which in the end would hurt smaller Asian economies more than Japan itself. There also is concern that further souring of the U.S.–Japan relationship will intensify domestic pressures in the United States to withdraw strategically from Asia or spur changes in Japanese policy that could upset the regional balance of power.

The end of the cold war has not resolved uncertainties about the balance of power in Asia. Even during the cold war years, threat perception in Asia was more complex than in Europe. Asia did not have a clear front line against the Soviet Union comparable to the eastern border of West Germany. The demise of the Soviet Union has reduced the perceived Russian threat, but it has not eliminated other threats that are generated within the region itself by the military confrontation on the Korean Peninsula, and by the possibility that China and Japan would seek or feel forced to fill any vacuum that might be left by the reduction of American power.

Moreover, the Russian threat is viewed, at least in Japan, as being in abeyance rather than having been removed. Russia still has powerful military assets in the Asian theater. It was actively engaged in international politics in the Far East and fought a war with Japan long before the Russian Revolution occurred. In the minds of many strategic thinkers in Japan and elsewhere who are familiar with the history of the Far East, it is only a matter of time before Russia reemerges as a major factor in the geopolitics of the region.

Attitudes toward Japan vary widely within the region. China and the two Korean states, the countries closest to Japan and the ones to suffer the most during Japan's militarist era, are the most suspicious and fearful that Japan will seek to flex its political muscles in the region and once again become a major military power. These concerns are less pervasive in Southeast Asia. Opinion about Japan's future role there is not uniform, but there is considerable optimism that Japan will continue to eschew development of major military force projection capabilities as long as the United States maintains an active military presence in the region and its alliance with Japan. In this part of the world the principal perceived threat to long-term stability is not a remilitarized Japan, but a reinvigorated China seeking to assert a position of dominant regional influence.

Concern over China's intentions and its growing military capabilities is evident throughout Asia, including Japan. Uncertainty and anxieties seem certain to grow stronger as China becomes more powerful economically, as its military modernization program proceeds, and as it continues to develop a navy with the ability to project force far from China's shores and especially into territories in the South China Sea, sovereignty over which is a bone of contention with several other countries.

Having said this, however, the fact remains that the security environment in Asia is more benign today than at any time at least in this century. With the exceptions of South Korea and Taiwan, no country in Asia currently has to confront a major external threat to its security. In this environment, Asian countries continue to press forward with economic development programs that make Asia the fastest growing economic region in the world.

Asia's Economic Record

Asia's economic achievements are impressive by any comparative measure. It has been growing faster than the rest of the world for the past twenty years. The average growth rate of "developing Asia" (i.e., Asia excluding Japan) over this period has been 7 percent a year, compared with 2.5 percent for the advanced industrial world, 3 percent for Latin America, and a little over 2 percent for Africa.[1] During the last half of the 1980s, while the world grew at an average rate of 2.9 percent, gross domestic product growth averaged 8.6 percent in the newly industrialized economies (NIEs) of Singapore, Hong Kong, Taiwan, and Korea, 6.8 percent in the ASEAN four (Indonesia, Malaysia, Thailand, Philippines), and 7.9 percent in China. Double-digit growth in China in the past few years has made it the world's fastest growing economy. In 1992 it registered a growth rate of 12.8 percent.

Asian economic growth is likely to outpace the rest of the world for some time. According to World Bank estimates, developing Asia will grow at least twice as fast as the rest of the world over the next ten years. If this happens, by the end of this decade developing Asia alone will contribute in absolute terms more than twice as much to additional world output as either North America (including Mexico) or the European Community.[2] ASEAN, with more than 300 million people, could be a trillion dollar economy by the end of the decade.[3]

The emphasis on exports in the economic development strategies of many Asian countries, and their success in pursuing these strategies, have sharply expanded Asia's share of world trade. In 1960 Asia accounted for 5.4 percent of world exports; by the end of the 1980s, 27 percent. The dollar value of total Asian trade with the world tripled during the 1980s alone. In 1991 the region's exports totaled $477.8 billion; its imports, $490.2 billion.[4]

In recent years, more and more of this trade has taken place within Asia itself. Trade within the region grew at an annual rate of 40 percent from 1986 through 1990. As a result, intraregional trade, which represented 22 percent of total Asian trade with the world in 1980, accounted for 35 percent in 1991.[5]

While these are surely impressive figures, it is important not to exaggerate their meaning. Economic power is not about to move across the Pacific from the United States to Asia, as earlier in this century it moved across the Atlantic from Europe to the United States. Asia accounted for some 9 percent of world gross national product in 1960 and about 22 percent today. By the end of the decade, it is entirely possible that its share of world output will approach 30 percent. But so will the shares held by North America and by the European Community. The situation today thus is entirely different from what it was at the end of the Second World

War, for example, when Japan's economy was in ruins, Europe was prostrate, and the United States alone accounted for perhaps as much as half of the world's GNP. No economic "power shift" is occurring if by that is meant a shift in the center of gravity of the world economy from North America to Asia. What we are witnessing is a growing equalization of economic power among North America, Western Europe, and Asia.

Moreover, aggregate figures for Asia chosen to show how economically powerful the region has become can obfuscate as well as illuminate reality. Most of Asia is poor. China has huge economic size but not commensurate economic power because of its enormous population and the gross disparities in growth and levels of economic well-being within the country. It will be many years before Chinese per capita GNP approaches the level of Asia's NIEs, much less that of Japan.

Most of Southeast Asia is still part of the developing rather than the developed world. Even an economically successful country such as Korea enjoys a per capita level of output that is less than a quarter that of Japan's. Japan's economic power in fact is a major reason why recitation of aggregate Asian economic data can so easily distort reality. Japan accounts for 16 percent of world GNP, the rest of Asia for 6 percent. While the Asia-Pacific Economic Cooperation organization (APEC)[6] countries produce close to 50 percent of world output, Japan and the United States together account for four-fifths of this figure.

In thinking about the implications of Asia's emergence as a third major center of the world economy, it is important to underscore the fact that economic growth is not a zero sum game—and that Asia is not a unitary actor. Rapid growth in Asia will contribute to growth in the rest of the world.

Japan in Asia

Strategic thinking about U.S. policy in Asia requires making judgments about Japan's position in the region. What is Japan's current role in the region's economy and what is it likely to be in the future? Is there any evidence, for example, that Japanese firms are "crowding out" American business and securing an unchallengeable position of economic dominance for Japan in the Asian region? To what extent are Japanese policies compatible with U.S. interests? What are the dangers of serious political differences arising as both countries pursue their respective interests in the Asian region?

Asia is an area of primary attention to Japanese policy makers, a region where they believe Japan has an important role to play, politically as well as economically. Japan has been particularly keen to strengthen its ties with ASEAN. After Prime Minister Tanaka's visit to Southeast Asia in 1974 sparked anti-Japanese rioting in Jakarta and Bangkok, the Japanese government and business community set about the task of improving relations with Southeast Asian countries with great determination. From the 1977 Fukuda Doctrine's call for "heart-to-heart" relations with ASEAN to the 1993 "Miyazawa Doctrine" advocating enhanced regionalism, Japan has worked to reduce longstanding animosities. Its efforts have paid handsome dividends as attitudes toward Japan have changed for the better to a remarkable degree. The strengthening of Japanese-ASEAN relations is one of the outstanding achievements of postwar Japanese diplomacy.

Japan in the Asian Economy

Asia has become an increasingly important market for Japanese exports over the past decade. By 1992 over 35 percent of Japan's exports went to Asia, up from 26 percent in 1980.[7] The dollar value of Japan's exports to the region in 1992 was about $120 billion. Two-way trade with Asia currently amounts to some 36 percent of Japan's total world trade, compared to 26 percent for trade with the United States. The United States, however, remains Japan's most important single-country market, followed by Germany and then by Korea and Taiwan.

On the import side, Japan draws about 36 percent of its total imports from Asia. The value of Japanese imports from the region roughly doubled between 1980 and 1991. Viewed in terms of the region's exports, however, the share of total Asian exports going to Japan actually declined over the decade, from 22 percent in 1980 to 14 percent in 1991, largely because of rapid growth in Asian intraregional trade. Nonetheless, the sheer size of the Japanese economy makes Japan an important market for Asian exporters.

Japanese trade is supported by Japan's enormous aid program in the region. Today Japanese official development assistance (ODA) is not tied formally any more than other countries', but Japanese companies are major beneficiaries of Japanese ODA spending. About half of the total Japanese aid budget of $11 billion goes to Asia, concentrated now in ASEAN and China. Over the past five years, Indonesia, China, the Philippines, Thailand, and Malaysia have consistently ranked among Japan's top ten foreign aid recipients.

Japanese direct investment in Asia increased dramatically during the 1980s. In yen terms, Japanese foreign direct investment (FDI) increased 3.3 times its 1982 level by 1989, with electrical machinery, chemicals, and metals industries being the top manufacturing sectors in terms of cumulative flows.[8] Investment in ASEAN from 1985-92 was about $20 billion. In the early 1990s investment continued to increase in Asia even though it fell off elsewhere. Worldwide investment by Japanese corporations in the year ending March 1993 amounted to $34.1 billion, barely half of the total four years earlier. In Asia, however, Japanese companies invested $6.4 billion in the year ending March 1993, compared to $5.9 billion the previous year. Asia currently accounts for 19 percent of Japan's outstanding foreign investment, up from 12 percent in 1990.[9]

The recent sharp appreciation of the yen is bound to spark another overseas investment drive by Japanese companies. Japan had only 9 percent of its manufacturing industry's total productive capacity located outside of Japan at the end of 1991, a level a half to a third smaller than for the United States.[10] Thus there is both room to expand its overseas manufacturing production and a strong incentive to move more production offshore, to countries where manufacturing costs are lower. The attractiveness of Asia as a target for Japanese FDI is certain to continue, particularly toward those countries such as China, Indonesia, the Philippines, and increasingly Vietnam, where labor is relatively cheap. Moreover, booming consumer markets throughout the region also are a powerful magnet for Japanese investors. Investment recently has increased even in China where Japanese companies, worried about political stability and the absence of consistent rules and regulations, have hesitated to undertake long-term investments. In the year ending March 1993, Japanese FDI in China nearly doubled, from $579 million to $1.07 billion.

Again, such figures need to be put in perspective. The notion that Japan is shifting its economic focus away from the United States to Asia is not rooted in reality. Japanese FDI in Asia increased substantially in the late 1980s, but it did elsewhere as well. The fact is that the share (not the absolute amount) of FDI going to Asia was generally smaller after 1985 than before. North America has been the favorite destination for Japanese FDI since the historic 1985 Plaza Accord. In 1989, for example, 50 percent of Japan's FDI went to North America, 22 percent to Europe, and 12 percent to Asia. It is true that the momentum of investment in Asia stayed high while it declined in North America after the asset "bubble" burst and Japan's investment boom subsided. In 1991 the Asian share of total Japanese overseas direct investment registered 14.3 percent. The figures were 45 percent for North America and 22.5 percent for Europe.

These figures, however, do not answer the question whether Japanese investment is dominant in Asia. Since the Japanese economy is so large, even a relatively small share of Japan's total overseas direct investment can amount to an enormous influx of capital for a poor Asian country. How dominant are Japanese investors in Asia?

The reality is that Japanese investment in Asia is increasing absolutely and as a share of Japan's total global investment, but it is not increasing as a share of the total flow of investment capital to Asian countries. Along with investments by the United States and by European countries, what is especially remarkable about the Asian regional economy in recent years is the rapid increase in investments by non-Japanese Asian companies in other Asian countries. Taiwan, for example, has become the leading source of FDI in Malaysia and Indonesia. Korea also has begun to export capital in significant amounts. In Southeast Asia, the combined annual investments of the four NIEs—Singapore, Taiwan, Hong Kong, and Korea—now surpass Japan's.

The dynamic quality of these shifts in investment flows is very impressive. As recently as 1987, Japanese investment in the ASEAN four accounted for 35.6 percent of all new foreign investment in these countries; the four NIEs provided 19 percent. Four years later, in 1991, according to data provided by Jardine Fleming,[11] Japan's 15.2 percent share of investment in the ASEAN four was surpassed by Taiwan's 15.4 percent; the four NIEs combined provided 29.5 percent.

Subsequently the situation has changed once again. Since 1990, as labor costs moved upward in the ASEAN four, NIE investment fell off in those countries and shifted to Vietnam, China, and Myanmar. Companies from the ASEAN four themselves have become major investors in other countries in the region: an estimated 10 to 15 percent of foreign capital currently going into China is coming from ASEAN countries.[12]

Some observers of economic trends in Asia now conclude that the future does not lie with Japan after all, but with "Greater China," since so many of the recent investments in the region have been made by Chinese businesspeople in Taiwan and Hong Kong and by overseas Chinese in Southeast Asia. Speculation is rife that by the turn of the century, ethnic Chinese businesspeople linked through region-wide clan networks will rival Japan in terms of economic power and political clout.

Such projections should be treated with great skepticism. For one thing, "overseas Chinese" is a misnomer. Many of these ethnic Chinese businesspeople have been in their adopted countries in Southeast Asia for generations, speak no Chinese, and do not have extensive ties, familial or otherwise, with the mainland. It is not surprising that there should be considerable nervousness among some Southeast Asian Chinese business families that being labeled "overseas Chinese" might undo their efforts to assimilate and threaten their precarious position as an ethnic minority in their respective countries. What makes the emphasis on "Greater China" especially inappropriate, however, is that the reality of Greater China is its deep and possibly growing fragmentation.

Japan's activities, on the other hand, have been anything but fragmented. Japanese business and government have pursued policies that are mutually reinforcing. The government has directed the major share of its overseas development aid to Asia, and Japanese firms have scoured the region for trade and investment opportunities. The result of these efforts has been to give Japan the leading position in the Asian economy.

But it is a mistake to conclude that this has created a situation in which "Japan based firms are moving into strategic control of the world's greatest and fastest growing new markets."[13] There are important industries, such as automobiles, where Japan is dominant, but there are others, such as energy and petrochemicals, where it is not. The communications industry, including international broadcasting, is another example where Japan lacks competitive advantage. NHK's effort to compete for an Asia-wide audience with its own international television broadcasting system against CNN and Hong Kong based Star Television was a failure. In telecommunications and other major industries, Japan faces stiff competition from companies in the United States and Europe, and at the lower end of technological sophistication, it must compete with the products of lower-cost Asian countries. The Asian economy is dynamic and expanding, creating opportunities for businesspeople from many different countries to succeed if they aggressively seek to exploit the opportunities that exist, and if their governments do their part to facilitate access to these markets.

Japan's trade and investment patterns underscore the point that Japan is a global economic power. Its interests are not served by the creation of protectionist regional blocs, nor is there any evidence that Japan is engaged in a kind of "strategic denial" to U.S. firms in the Asian region.[14]

Japan's Economic Power and Political Influence

Japan's economic power in Asia translates into political influence. Although individual Southeast Asian leaders expressed skepticism about the desirability of sending Japanese troops to participate in the U.N. sponsored peacekeeping operation in Cambodia, for example, the official reaction in ASEAN was supportive of Japanese policy. On the issue of Japanese membership on the U.N. Security Council, to take another example, even China has been careful not to openly oppose Japanese aspirations for fear of antagonizing its largest trading partner and largest donor of foreign aid.[15]

As Japan's interests in Asia have grown stronger, Japan has become much less hesitant to take positions different from the United States. Japan was the first country to normalize relations with China after Tiananmen, and it has taken a different and less confrontational line with respect to human rights abuses there. It supported a regional security dialogue when the United States was still resistant to the idea. It has taken a more hardline position toward Russia, partly because of the continuing dispute over contested islands north of Hokkaido, and in part because Japanese strategic thinkers believe that the Russian threat is dormant but not extinguished.

While Japan continues to stress its commitment not to become a military power in the region, it has not cut defense spending. It has slowed the rate of increase—it was lower in the 1993 budget than it had been for twenty-three years. This is true even though China and other countries in the region are increasing their military spending. Nonetheless, Japanese defense spending amounted to $36.5 billion in 1992, which may be two to three times China's military expenditures, even when one factors in off-budget spending by the Chinese military. Japan continues to upgrade its weaponry and to stress domestic production of advanced weapons systems, and it has technologies in place in the nonmilitary sector that could quickly be converted to military use were the need to arise. Given these capabilities and the deep-seated suspicions among its neighbors of its intentions, the Japanese decision to stockpile plutonium as part of a long-term nuclear energy program has created considerable nervousness and criticism in the rest of Asia.

Japan is feeling its way toward a more active political role in Asia, but its actions are constrained by several important factors. Antipathy to the Japanese military is strong both within Japan and in the region. It is particularly powerful in Japan's nearest neighboring countries, Korea and China. Moreover, enduring features of Japanese foreign policy that are not likely to change dramatically unless Japan's own security environment drastically deteriorates also will constrain Japan's role in Asia. These include a risk-minimizing orientation, an emphasis on stability, the lack of a proselytizing attitude about democracy or human rights, and a preoccupation with economic benefits.[16]

The debate about Asia in Japan has undergone an important metamorphosis in recent years. Japanese have been debating for a hundred years whether they should "return" to Asia, or whether they needed to "leave" Asia in order to be accepted as a member of the advanced Western world. Inevitably, when Japan has run into trouble with the West, voices calling for its return to Asia have grown louder. Since this advocacy of return has been part of a reaction against the West, it has tended to be combined with a xenophobic nationalism. The rest of Asia has been understandably wary at the thought that the Japanese might be coming back to Asia as a way to get out of the West.

But there is an important new thrust in the recent Japanese debate about Asia and about Japan's place in the world. It is the view increasingly voiced by intellectuals, politicians, and business leaders that Japan's Asian identity and its "Westernness" are part of a coherent whole. It is the idea that Japan can be Asian without rejecting its ties to the West, and that it can play an important role in Asia without retreating into an anti-Western nationalism. This was the note that former Prime Minister Miyazawa struck when he pronounced his "Miyazawa Doctrine" in Bangkok early in 1993.[17] It also appears to be the sentiment of Prime Minister Hosokawa and many of the key leaders in his coalition. It demonstrates, incidentally, how out of touch with the complexities of the modern day world are predictions that we are entering an era in which conflict will be between what are described as almost hermetically sealed civilizations.[18]

In any event, alliance with the United States continues to be viewed by Japan's leadership as the key to Japan's continued security and prosperity. Japanese differ in their views on tactics and strategies to employ in dealing with the United States. However, no politically significant constituency argues that Japanese interests would be better served by breaking Japan's alliance with the United States. There is no major security issue, regarding Asia or elsewhere, where the two countries have sharply opposing policy positions. Even on issues where Japanese approaches have diverged from U.S. policy, such as human rights issues in China or aid to Vietnam, considerable care has been taken to consult closely with the United States and to take U.S. views into account. There is no reason to believe, in other words, that Japanese and American goals in Asia are incompatible. Quite the contrary, continuation of close bilateral U.S.–Japan relations remains the cornerstone upon which the Asian strategies of both countries are based.

The United States in Asia

The collapse of the Soviet Union, the decline of American economic preeminence, the rise of Japan, and the successful adoption of export led economic growth strategies by most Asian countries have fundamentally altered the dynamics of economic and political interaction among countries in Asia. The end of the cold war broke the link between Asian security concerns and a larger global strategic competition. In an important sense, it has had the effect of throwing Asia back upon itself, producing growing anxiety throughout Asia about the credibility of U.S. security commitments, and prompting a search for new approaches to deal with regional security.

The glue of the Soviet threat no longer binds the United States and Japan, nor do cold war security concerns work any longer to buffer economic tensions between the two countries. The forces of the cold war era that pushed the United States and China into uneasy alignment against a common adversary no longer exist. As the importance of China as an element in U.S. strategy to deal with the Soviet threat has declined, American concerns have risen over China's policies on such issues as human rights, arms sales, trade, and environmental protection.

China's rapid economic growth has increased its importance to the United States as a trading partner and investment target, but in a broader sense China looms smaller on America's global map than it did during the cold war. For Japan, China has only grown in importance, and the belief is widespread and deeply felt that developing close and friendly relations with this huge and increasingly powerful neighbor is in Japan's vital national interests, regardless of what happens in Sino-American relations.

In this post–cold war world, there is a danger of U.S.–Japan conflict erupting over issues related to China policy. Conceivably, this could produce a situation in which U.S. relations deteriorate simultaneously with both Japan and China, a situation that would hardly serve U.S. national interests (or those of Japan, for that matter).

The end of the cold war has sparked new interest in exploring regional approaches to security, and the end of American economic dominance and the rapid deepening of trade and investment ties among Asian countries have intensified efforts within Asia to build regional economic institutions. These developments raise important questions about how the United States should relate to this new regionalism.

President Clinton has responded by offering a somewhat tentative vision of a Pacific community that includes countries in the Western Hemisphere that face the Pacific, as well as countries in East and Southeast Asia.[19] Malaysian Prime Minister Mahathir, on the other hand, has offered a quite different and narrow vision, of an Asian community that excludes not only countries in the West, but "Western" countries in the South Pacific such as Australia and New Zealand, even though they are increasingly being integrated into the Asian regional economy. Japan and other Asian countries have been leery to embrace Mahathir's proposal, but neither have they rejected it.

The United States in the Asian Economy

Determining what policies the United States should pursue toward Japan in Asia requires first of all having a clear understanding of what our interests are in the region. Few Americans seem to be aware of how important Asia is to the U.S. economy. Over 40 percent of U.S. trade is with countries in the Asian-Pacific region. Two-way trade across the Pacific in 1992 totaled $315 billion, one-third more than trade across the Atlantic. Five of the ten largest trading partners of the United States are Asian states.

In recent years, Asia has grown in importance as an export market for U.S. goods. The rate of U.S. export growth to Asia in the 1980s was faster than that of overall American exports. It grew at an especially rapid clip after the 1985 Plaza Accord and the consequent depreciation of the dollar, raising the Asian share of U.S. exports from 11 percent in 1980 to 15 percent in 1991. U.S. exports to Japan, despite the problems of market access there, more than doubled between 1985 and 1990; they now exceed exports to France, Germany, and Italy combined. U.S. exports of $20.6 billion to ASEAN in 1990 exceeded exports to South America or South Asia, the Middle East, or the former Soviet Union and Eastern Europe.[20] Two-way U.S.-ASEAN trade grew at an annual rate of 9.8 percent between 1986 and 1992. This compares to an average 25 percent annual increase in Japan's trade with ASEAN in the same period.[21] These numbers indicate both that the United States is an important player in the Asian regional economy, and that much more needs to be done to improve its performance relative to Japan and other countries in the region.

The United States continues to be the largest export market for most Asian countries. U.S. imports from developing Asia more than tripled from 1980 to 1991, to a $102 billion level. Despite increased Japanese imports of Asian goods during this period, developing Asia continues to send a larger share of its exports to the United States than to Japan. In recent years, however, Asia has expanded exports to other markets faster than to the United States. As a result, the United States' share of total developing Asia's exports has declined from a 1986 peak of 30 percent to a 1991 level of 21 percent, about the same share as at the beginning of the 1980s.

The United States is also a significant investor in Asia. The value of its foreign direct investment in Asia doubled between 1982 and 1991. Hong Kong, Singapore, and Indonesia were the top locations, and oil the dominant sector. The United States holds an especially strong position in refining and petrochemical industries, total investment in this sector in developing Asia in 1991 being an estimated $5 billion (compared to Japanese investment of $1 billion). This is a major potential growth area for the United States since the demand for chemicals is expanding twice as fast in Asia as in North America and Western Europe. By the year 2000 developing Asia's market for chemicals is expected to surpass that of North America in size.[22]

U.S. official development assistance in Asia is nearly insignificant, however, compared to Japan's. In 1990 some 6 percent of total U.S. foreign aid, $560 million, went to Asia and Oceania. Only two Asian countries, the Philippines and Indonesia, are among the top twenty-five recipients of U.S. aid. Indonesia is a good example of how small American aid spending in Asia is compared to Japan's. In Indonesia in 1992 U.S. aid was $43 million, while Japan's was $1.2 billion. Not only was U.S. aid in the region dwarfed by Japan, but when Asia and Oceania (the island states of the South Pacific) are considered together, U.S. aid fell behind Australia ($600 million), France ($1.1 billion), and Germany ($630 million).[23]

It is unrealistic to expect an increase in U.S. aid to Asia. There is almost certain to be congressional pressure to reduce it further. Emphasis in U.S. policy should be put on encouraging the Japanese government to continue to use its influence with aid-recipient countries to increase the share of Japanese ODA funded project contracts that go to non-Japanese companies, and to find innovative ways for the economic aid bureaucracies of both countries to cooperate. The United States has a large number of seasoned development specialists with extensive field experience that Japan generally lacks. Both countries have complementary strengths that can usefully be combined, as is the case with a biotechnology project currently being jointly sponsored in Indonesia.

The Debate over U.S. Strategy

The challenge facing the United States in Asia is clear enough: to design a strategy that minimizes threats to peace and security, promotes economic and political development, and maximizes opportunities for American business to benefit from the region's economic growth. This is no easy task, however, in light of the many remarkable changes that have occurred in Asia and in the global economy and international political system.

Not many Americans think hard about Asian affairs; what is so striking about those who do is how far apart they are both in their analyses of present realities and their prescriptions for American policy. Before presenting my own proposals, it is useful to survey briefly the several distinct conceptions of what an optimal American Asian strategy should entail that are competing for acceptance in the United States.

Integrationist Optimism

Some observers of U.S. relations with Japan and with Asia who take an optimistic view of the future do so out of an idealist or integrationist conception of the international order. According to this school of thought, there is no need for a major rethinking of American policy because the dangers that lie ahead are not very great. The argument essentially is that economic linkages among countries in Asia and between them and the United States, and especially the economic interdependence of the United States and Japan, create such strong vested interests in maintaining stable relationships that tensions and conflicts are bound to be contained. According to this view, while trade negotiators huff and puff and threaten dire action if the other side does not mend its ways, private industry in Japan and the United States and increasingly elsewhere in Asia steadily proceeds to deepen its interdependence. Joint ventures, technology-sharing agreements, and mutual dependence for components and technology create transnational corporate alliances that effectively constrain the policy options of governments. By this reasoning, the frictions in U.S. relations with Japan and other Asian countries are merely part of an elaborate game of winning mostly symbolic political concessions while the fundamental process of economic integration moves relentlessly forward.[24]

There are several problems with this integrationist view. One is that there is no convincing historical evidence that economic integration in and of itself eliminates the potential for conflict among states. Nor is U.S.–Japan friction a "game." In the absence of a common security threat, persistent and serious disagreements over economic policy are almost certain to lead to a deterioration in security and political relationships. Now that the cold war era has ended, progress in resolving trade frictions between the United States and Japan is essential to maintain continued close political and security relations between the two countries.

Integration optimists believe that a kind of economic MAD,

comparable to the Mutual Assured Destruction theory of strategic stability between the United States and the Soviet Union, will work in the economic realm to keep the United States and Japan, and by extension the United States and the rest of Asia, from letting their economic disputes get out of hand. There is good reason to doubt that economic MAD alone is sufficient to prevent serious conflict. Many interests compete for attention and influence in U.S. domestic politics, including those of groups hurt by foreign competition and committed to reversing the trend of growing interdependence. It is not a foregone conclusion which interests will win out.

Revisionist Pessimism

In sharp contrast to the optimists, there is a second school of thought profoundly pessimistic about current U.S. policy toward Japan and Asia. These "revisionist" critics of U.S. policy toward Japan tend to attract the support of traditional international relations "realist" theorists with their emphasis on classic balance of power concepts. At the extreme, the pessimist argument is that postwar U.S. policy toward Japan and toward Asia has proved bankrupt, that alliance with Japan is a mistake, and that the United States should become an outside "balancer" of the regional balance of power not tied formally to any of the regional powers.

Proponents of this line of thought argue that the United States and Japan are economic adversaries, if not enemies, and continuing the current relationship simply provides an American military cover for Japan to win an economic war and establish its hegemony over Asia. Thus, in this view, it hardly serves U.S. interests to maintain a security treaty that provides U.S. Navy protection over what is rapidly becoming a Japanese economic lake. With a new balance of power emerging in Asia, in the revisionist view, it is no longer in the U.S. interest to support Japan's economic success because that success has meant harm to the American economy.

Chalmers Johnson, a noted "revisionist" critic of Japan, puts the argument as follows:

A new policy should be based not on our hegemony but on recognition that there soon will be—perhaps already is—a balance of power in the region. Its main components are Japan, China and the Association of Southeast Asian Nations. Our commitment should not be to any one of them but to maintaining a balance of power among them.[25]

Johnson advises that in addition to ending its commitment to Japan, the United States should take a tougher position toward China by "among other things, recognizing Vietnam and refusing China's claims to sovereignty over the whole South China Sea. To complicate China's decision making, we also ought to continue supporting Taiwan's defenses. . . ." In addition, Johnson maintains, the United States should "strongly support" South Korea but "withdraw U.S. ground forces, which no longer serve a military purpose."

There are many problems with Johnson's prescription for Asian policy. Most important, rather than contributing to a balance of power in the region, his approach would undermine the balance that now exists. Once having ended its commitments in the region, the United States would lack the capability to maintain a balance of power; instead, its influence would rapidly dissipate. One is puzzled by the assumption that by breaking its alliance with Japan, the United States somehow would acquire power resources it does not currently possess to challenge Japan's economic leadership in Asia. Curious, too, is the notion that ASEAN, a rather loose grouping of six mostly developing countries, could balance either China or Japan.

There is a good case to be made for recognizing Vietnam and for giving American companies the opportunity that firms in Japan and other countries already enjoy to invest and trade there. It is also in American interests and in the interests of stability in the region to ensure that Taiwan has the military strength needed to maintain the existing balance in the Taiwan Strait. But regional stability would hardly be served by policies that were intended purposely to "complicate China's decision making." Breaking the U.S. relationship with Japan, antagonizing China, removing troops from South Korea, and as a result provoking an arms race among states suddenly confronting a power vacuum and fearful for their security hardly add up to a recipe for constructive American engagement in the Asian region.

Status Quo Conservatism

There is another conception of how the United States should deal with Japan and Asia in the post–cold war era. It is essentially a status quo approach, and was the one adopted by the Bush administration. It is a view rooted in the conviction that as much as things have changed in the world with the end of the cold war, they have not changed all that much in Asia. From this perspective, only marginal changes in the approach the United States has adopted toward Asia since the end of the Second World War are needed to secure American interests.

In response to those who argue that the U.S. military presence is no longer needed to balance the Soviet Union, advocates of sticking with the tried and true policies of the past nearly half century can point out that balancing the Soviet Union was always only part of the role of the U.S. military presence in Asia. U.S. military power also played a regional role. Asia is a huge expanse of land and water with more than a dozen countries at dramatically different levels of economic development, operating under different types of political systems, embracing different religious and cultural traditions, and only beginning to explore the possibilities of meaningful regional integration.

Given the complex security picture in Asia, the U.S. military presence has been a key stabilizing factor. Any drastic shift in America's role in the region, advocates of the status quo approach argue, would simply create uncertainties and insecurities, unleashing forces that would raise tensions throughout the region.

Support for this position is most strongly heard in Asia itself. Not only is there no pressure from countries in the region for the United States to withdraw, but there is considerable anxiety evident throughout Asia that the United States will retreat from the region despite its protestations to the contrary, and that this will compromise regional stability. Actions taken by several countries in Southeast Asia in the aftermath of the Philippine government's decision to terminate the U.S. naval presence at Subic Bay are indicative of their desire to see the United States remain in the region. Singapore signed an agreement that allows U.S. forces to use military repair facilities for ship visits, repair, resupply, and Air Force training missions. Indonesia and Malaysia agreed to repair U.S. warships on a commercial basis, and other understandings appear to have been quietly arrived at to facilitate American military deployments.

There is much to be said in favor of many of the key components of this status quo perspective on American interests and strategic priorities in Asia: its recognition of the stabilizing role of the United States' military presence in the region, its emphasis on keeping the alliance with Japan as the anchor for U.S. policies in the region, and its understanding of the adverse consequences that would flow from sudden shifts in American policy.

An essentially status quo approach to Asian policy, however, fails to respond to two central realities of the contemporary world. One is the relative decline in U.S. economic power. The end of American dominance of the global economy is as profound in its implications for the distribution of political power as the end of the cold war. There is no longer majority political support in the United States for the argument that U.S. interests are served by making its markets accessible to exports even from countries that are not themselves substantially opening their own markets. Magnanimity in this sense is no longer the hallmark of U.S. international economic policy. In its place we see the rise of economic nationalism in various guises: outright protectionism, demands for unilateral market-opening concessions by others, and the growing popularity of managing trade through voluntary export restraints, market share agreements, and so on. Advocates of a status quo approach to our Asian policy have neither supported nor have they been able to resist the political pressures for such changes in trade policy. The well-known result has been confusion and inconsistency in U.S. policy and heightened political tensions with Japan and other trading partners.

The other reality that this approach fails to take into account is the growing sentiment within Asia in favor of developing multilateral mechanisms to deal with regional economic and security issues. President Bush was slow in throwing his support behind

APEC, and his administration was especially resistant to proposals to establish a region-wide security forum. The administration seemed to fear that regional security arrangements might dilute U.S. influence exerted through its bilateral relationships, or that they would create apprehensions in the region that U.S. support for such fora was a fig leaf to cover a policy of U.S. strategic disengagement from Asia.

Former Secretary of State James Baker captured the essence of Bush administration thinking about the appropriate framework for U.S. policy in Asia in a speech in Tokyo in the autumn of 1991:

> To visualize the structure of U.S. engagement in the Pacific, imagine a fan spread wide, with its base in North America and radiating westward. Its central support is the alliance and partnership between the United States and Japan. To the north, one spoke represents our alliance with the Republic of Korea. To the south, another line extends to our ASEAN colleagues. Further south, a spoke reaches to Australia. . . .[26]

Secretary Baker gave a nod in support of regional economic institutions by adding that "connecting these spokes is the fabric of close economic interests now given form by . . . APEC." But he made it clear that the central thrust of U.S. policy was maintaining multiple and separate spokes into the region.

The concept expressed by Secretary Baker also has been described as a wheel, with the United States being the "hub" and individual Asian countries the "spokes" of the regional regime. The fact is, however, that support within Asia for expanding regional approaches to economic cooperation and security has forced the United States to adjust its "hub and spokes" approach. To its credit, the Clinton administration has recognized these pressures for change and has embraced a policy of both strengthening APEC and establishing a regional security forum.

The U.S. and Japan in Asia

A framework for U.S. policy toward Japan in Asia should consist of several major components: strengthening U.S. economic competitiveness; continuing its alliance with Japan; pursuing improved market access in Japan; encouraging the development of

APEC and reliance on multilateral approaches to deal with economic issues; developing more extensive consultative mechanisms with Japan on key regional issues, especially in regard to Northeast Asia; and promoting new arms control arrangements in the region, including support for regional and subregional security fora. The appropriate imagery for a new architecture for U.S. strategy in Asia is not that of a hub and spokes, but of an intricate web that encompasses economic, political, and security relationships, and that embeds the critical and troubled U.S.-Japan relationship in a larger set of regional dialogues and institutions.

Competitiveness at Home

First and foremost, the U.S. government must do everything in its power to improve the competitiveness of American industry. It is not possible to have a strong U.S.-Japan relationship in the context of a weakening American economy. The United States has to strive to be Japan's toughest competitor in order for their relationship to grow stronger and serve U.S. interests. Improving American competitiveness requires decisive action on two main fronts.

One is putting the U.S. economic house in order by such steps as reducing the budget deficit, designing policies to increase savings and investment, raising the quality of our public schools, and gaining control over spiraling health care costs. Making substantial progress in dealing with these domestic issues is far more important than any export promotion policies the administration might adopt to improve the competitiveness of U.S. business overseas.

As far as Asia-specific policies are concerned, much can be done to strengthen the ability of U.S. government agencies to provide information and various forms of assistance to American companies willing to take the risks of entering the Asian market, or to expand their operations in Asia and elsewhere outside the United States. This involves, for example, strengthening and better coordinating the information-gathering capabilities of the Commerce Department and other agencies in Washington and of the commercial offices of U.S. embassies in the region. Also it means allocating more resources to organizations such as the Export-Import Bank, whose financing activities on behalf of American companies pale into insignificance compared to Japan. In 1993 the Clinton administration announced a number of export promotion measures that may improve the competitive opportunities for U.S. business abroad. The important question is whether American business leaders will take advantage of these and other opportunities or not.

Even the most ambitious government program to strengthen the competitiveness of American firms in the global marketplace will accomplish little if companies themselves do not respond to the challenges that face them. An excellent study of the implications for the United States of Asian economic integration, prepared by the U.S. International Trade Commission, strikes an extraordinarily depressing note in this regard. After making the point referred to above that "unlike the U.S. case, . . . firms in Japan, Germany, France, Italy, and the United Kingdom all have access to significant Government-backed financing programs, and these programs are decisive in some contracts," the report adds, almost as an afterthought, that "price, after-sales service, design flexibility, and local market presence are also reported to be advantages offered by U.S. competitors."[27] The most aggressive proactive government commercial agenda in Asia cannot produce positive results unless American firms take the steps necessary to overcome these disadvantages.

The competitiveness of American industry has improved in recent years, and exports have been the growth sector of the U.S. economy. Nonetheless, American business has not given the sustained attention or invested in the resources, both financial and human, needed to be successful in this, the fastest growing region in the world economy. One can walk around Bangkok's automobile clogged streets and find precious few American-made cars. Their absence from this market cannot be blamed on Japanese import barriers.

Moreover, the American mass media remain largely indifferent to Asia, and thus help keep the public in the dark about what is going on there. Indonesia alone, for example, has nearly twice the population of all of Eastern Europe, and is certain to grow faster and offer more opportunities for entrepreneurial businesspeople for years to come. Yet media attention and business interest tend to gravitate to what is thought to be more familiar European terrain. American efforts to be a bigger part of the Asian economy must begin at home, both in terms of public education about the region and in creating mechanisms to assist American businesspeople prepared to tackle the Asian market.

Alliance with Japan

The anchor for a successful U.S. policy in Asia in the future will remain its alliance with Japan. The alternative of breaking the security treaty relationship, of treating Japan as a kind of economic enemy, and of opting for a policy that tries to make the United States the balancer of twenty-first century Asia in the way that Great Britain played a balancer role in nineteenth century Europe cannot secure U.S. national interests.

Having Japan as the home port for the U.S. Navy's Seventh Fleet is of critical importance in enabling the United States to conduct military operations not only in the Pacific, but into the Indian Ocean and the Middle East as well, and in protecting sea lanes through which so much United States commerce passes. The Marines on Okinawa and the modest Army and Air Force facilities that exist in Japan are critical to the defense of South Korea. It would certainly be more expensive to maintain these capabilities without the military arrangements that currently exist with Japan. More important, a break in the security relationship with Japan, the existence of which is reassuring to nearly every country in Asia including Japan, would provoke a massive and costly arms race and also reduce U.S. influence in the region.

The bilateral security relationship, in contrast to trade relations, is free of serious controversy. Japan has assumed an increasingly large share of U.S. base costs and continues to do more. The missions of Japan's Self Defense Forces are designed in ways that complement and reinforce U.S. military capabilities in the region. There is a high degree of interoperability between the forces of the two countries, and close and smooth working relations between them.

If there is a serious issue in the bilateral military relationship, it is not a strictly military one but an economic one. For many years Japan has insisted on arrangements that enable it to license American military technology for manufacture in Japan instead of making less expensive "off the shelf" purchases of U.S. military hardware. Changing this pattern is no simple matter, especially since Japan can purchase similar technology in many cases from other countries if the United States insists in too rigid a manner on a shift away from excessive emphasis on licensing arrangements in Japan's weapon procurement policies. Nonetheless, a greater effort should be made to shift the balance between licensing and direct purchases, especially in light of Japan's repeated assertions that it is not interested in becoming a military power or in exporting weapons. Continuing attention also needs to be paid to securing U.S. access to Japanese dual-use technologies that have important military as well as civilian applications.

The goals of U.S. policy toward Japan also should include forging closer economic links between the two countries and between both of them and the rest of the regional and world economy. The alternative of somehow "containing" Japan economically and weakening or breaking the U.S.–Japan economic relationship is not a realistic option. Some Japanese are concerned that the United States eventually might try to use accession to NAFTA as a way to draw Asian states one by one away from Japan. Yet an attempt to reduce Japanese economic power by bringing Asian countries into a free trade agreement that excluded Japan is bound to fail. Japan has not only economic power, but political clout in the Asian region that it will use to protect its interests. Policies that would induce Japan to use that political power against U.S. interests make no sense for the United States. The only conceivable consequence would be to push Asian countries toward establishing their own closed regional bloc, and lessen the American presence in the region.

The United States and Japan have a high degree of mutual dependence (which is, after all, what "interdependence" means), and share many common interests in the region and globally. The president and senior administration officials need to hammer this message home to the American people and to the U.S. Congress.

Not only this administration but previous ones as well have failed to explain to the American public adequately and frequently enough why the interests we have at stake in our relations with Japan and with the rest of Asia are so vital.

Pursuing Market Access in Japan

An important element in U.S. policy toward Japan as part of a broader Asian policy, and the one that provokes the most controversy, is a policy to improve market access for American and other foreign firms in Japan. This issue should be treated as distinct from the question of Japan's trade surplus, global or bilateral. It is a mistake to link the two, both because Japan's trade surplus has little to do with market access—Japan ran a large trade deficit in the 1950s when its markets were much more closed than today—and because market access issues should be important to the United States even if the Japanese surplus were to disappear. Firms with competitive products to sell in Japan should be able to sell them, whatever the dimensions of the trade imbalance happen to be.

There should be an emphasis on negotiating better market access in Japan because there is indeed a problem. The common complaints of foreign manufacturing firms and financial institutions, regardless of their nationality, about Japanese market access leave no room for doubt that there is more to the problem than the failure of American businesspeople to try hard enough, as Japanese government spokespersons and business leaders regularly maintain. A combination of tough negotiations to reduce barriers in respect to specific sectoral issues, an emphasis on seeking access for all foreign companies rather than on striking trade-distorting bilateral deals, continued emphasis on removing a variety of non-tariff type trade barriers, and avoidance of solutions that end up strengthening bureaucratic controls on the Japanese economy rather than weakening them should be the key elements of a market access strategy.

Basic conditions for a successful negotiating strategy involve making informed judgments about what is politically possible, devising a strategy to accomplish clearly defined and realistic goals, and having a fallback position in the event one's declared goals are not met. "Feel good" policies that give negotiators a kind of personal satisfaction of knowing they were tough with Japan but that fail to produce results need to be avoided.

By this standard the Clinton administration's initial foray into trade negotiations with Japan was little short of disastrous. Demands that Japan agree to quantifiable targets both on sectoral issues and the overall trade balance created the impression that the administration was in favor of managed trade. As a consequence, the Clinton administration accomplished what most people would have thought to have been the impossible—namely, to put the Japanese government in a position where it could pose as the defender of free trade. The administration apparently was surprised by a Japan that was prepared to "say no" to its demands for "results" and was put on the defensive as it tried to explain that it was not in favor of managed trade.

In the summer of 1993, during the G-7 summit meeting in Tokyo, President Clinton and then Prime Minister Miyazawa concluded a U.S.-Japan Framework for a New Economic Partnership (the so-called Framework agreement). The Framework calls for the United States and Japan to negotiate agreements on five "baskets" of issues. Whether it produces significant results partly depends on whether the Japanese prime minister will be able to deliver significant concessions. But it also is a question of whether the Clinton administration can clearly identify its priorities and whether the president will be strong enough politically to defend agreements that the Congress is likely to criticize for not going far enough.

Soon after coming into office, the Clinton administration decided not to try to revitalize the so-called Structural Impediments Initiative (SII), apparently because senior officials in the administration and perhaps the president himself accepted the popular but specious argument that attempts to change Japanese processes are futile, and that only "results oriented" negotiations work. This was an unfortunate decision. SII in fact ran into increasingly stiff opposition from some elements in the Japanese bureaucracy precisely because it was successful in creating or strengthening domestic Japanese constituencies in favor of government deregulation and market-opening measures. A way should be found to revive it with a different name. Foreign pressure can have a salutary effect when it finds powerful allies inside Japanese society; it is doomed to fail if it is perceived as one-sided, mean-spirited, or humiliating. Yet each U.S. administration seems to have to learn these basic lessons of dealing with Japan all over again.

Emphasizing Multilateralism

Another important element in a strategy for dealing with Japan not only on trade matters, but on other economic issues as well, is an emphasis on multilateral approaches, both global and regional. Strengthening the General Agreement on Tariffs and Trade (GATT) by successfully concluding the Uruguay Round is of central importance. Japan's refusal to take any significant initiative that would have given it a leadership role in pushing these negotiations to a successful conclusion was a major failure of Japanese foreign policy in the last years of Liberal Democratic party (LDP) rule. One would like to believe that Prime Minister Hosokawa and his coalition government recognize the need and the opportunity for Japan to play a global leadership role to strengthen the multilateral trading system, and that they will take concrete measures to do so.

Another multilateral mechanism for dealing with trade, investment, and other economic issues in Asia is APEC. Although an acronym that is still unfamiliar to all but a small group of Americans, this government-level "Asia-Pacific Economic Cooperation" organization created in 1989 has the potential to be an important mechanism for promoting a kind of "open regionalism" in which agreements to lower trade and investment barriers will make the region more accessible to countries both outside as well as inside it.[28]

APEC can provide an arena where coalitions favoring greater liberalization can form and exert more pressure for policy changes than any one country could do on its own. The United States and Japan have common interests in promoting new trade and investment rules to expand access to Asian markets. APEC provides a useful setting for devising such rules and, more generally, for coordinating economic policies at a multinational level.

APEC also is a response to the growing desire in Asia to give institutional expression to the reality of regional economic integration, and it does so in a way that includes rather than excludes the United States. Having APEC heads of state meet in the United States in November 1993 made the existence of this organization better known to the American public. It also induced the media, for a few days at least, to give Asia some attention. APEC's chair rotates annually among its members. Serious thought should be given to having the chair of APEC, when it is not one of the Group of Seven (G-7) countries, attend the G-7 summit, as does the commissioner of the European Community.

Bilateral Consultations on Regional Threats

The United States and Japan engage in a range of bilateral consultations on important regional issues. There is close consultation, for example, on the issue of North Korea's suspected nuclear weapons program. After the Tiananmen incident, there also apparently were considerable consultations between the United States and Japan on China policy, including between President Bush and Prime Minister Kaifu and the others who succeeded Kaifu in that position. Close consultation and coordination of policy where possible will be even more important in the uncertain and fluid international situation in Northeast Asia in the future than they have been in the past. Successful U.S. policy to deal with North Korea, China, and eventually with a Russia active once again in East Asia will depend in considerable measure on the ability of the United States to work closely with Japan.

In regard to North Korea, for example, the United States and Japan, working closely with South Korea, have moved along parallel tracks to encourage North Korea to accept arrangements for inspection of installations suspected to be involved in a program to develop nuclear weapons. Both the United States and Japan have made it clear that finding a resolution to the nuclear issue would lead to expanded contacts, which in the case of Japan in particular would produce needed benefits for the North's strapped economy.

Should these efforts to use positive incentives to dissuade North

Korea from pursuing a nuclear weapons program fail, the issue of sanctions will have to be joined. Having the United Nations Security Council adopt sanctions against North Korea will require the agreement of China. Making sanctions work will require the cooperation of Japan. The annual remittances to North Korea from Korean residents in Japan, for example, are generally estimated to be considerably larger than North Korea's annual government budget. These funds pass through Japanese banks on their way out of the country. It may be impossible for the Japanese government to stop these financial flows completely, but it could make transfers more difficult and substantially reduce the amount going into North Korea. It may be difficult for Japan to undertake such a drastic action in light of its risk-minimizing orientation to foreign affairs. But it is far from impossible, given the real concern that exists about the nuclear issue and about North Korea's recent testing of missiles that are able to reach Japan, and in light of the fact that it would be undertaken at the behest of the United Nations Security Council. What is certain is that close consultation and coordination between the United States and Japan are essential for any sanctions to be effective.

Reference already has been made to the danger that the United States and Japan might pursue different policies toward China, producing a situation in which U.S. relations could deteriorate simultaneously with the two most powerful countries in East Asia. Such an eventuality cannot be forestalled simply by calling on Japan to follow U.S. policy toward China, no matter where it might lead. The United States does not have that kind of leverage over Japan. Even during the height of the cold war, Japan tried to edge away from U.S. efforts to isolate China by adopting a policy of "separating politics and economics," which enabled Japan and China to maintain some trade and contacts. Now Japan is more determined than ever to strengthen Sino-Japanese relations, and to avoid actions that would stir up animosities between the two countries. The United States, on the other hand, no longer constrained by the need to balance Soviet power and influence, is less hesitant than it was during the cold war years to express its outrage over human rights abuses or arms sales that violate international agreements. Accordingly, there is considerable room for differ-

ences over China policy to arise between the United States and
Japan.

Basic U.S. and Japanese objectives in regard to China are compatible. Both support China's economic modernization, and both
want to be active participants in the Chinese economy. Both oppose Chinese sales of missile technology abroad, and both insist
that Chinese government policies should reflect respect for basic
human rights.

They have fundamental disagreements, however, about what
policies offer appropriate means to achieve these ends, particularly
in respect to human rights. There is virtually no support in Japan
for curtailing most favored nation treatment for China to punish it
for human rights abuses. Were the United States to adopt such a
policy, it would result perhaps in the most important schism in
U.S.–Japan relations since the end of the Second World War.
Extensive bilateral consultations concerning China, therefore, are
important both to maximize the leverage the two countries have to
influence Chinese policy, and to minimize the dangers of serious
antagonisms erupting between the United States and Japan over
China.

Preoccupation with bilateral trade frictions, however, is a major
hindrance to establishing such consultative processes, whether in
regard to China or other issues. The effort to give substantive
content to their "global partnership" must come from their leaders, but U.S.–Japan summit meetings increasingly have become
occasions to argue about sectoral trade issues. Among other
things, this pattern has had a perverse impact on public opinion,
convincing many people that U.S.–Japan relations are essentially
antagonistic and that there is little at stake other than access to
Japan's "closed" market. The fact remains, however, that the need
for bilateral consultations on a whole range of regional and global
issues can only grow stronger in the coming years.

Facing the Challenge of Regional Arms Control

A framework for U.S. Asian policy also needs to include new
approaches to arms control. The current relatively benign security
environment in Asia is likely to prove both fragile and transitory. It

is not rooted in the existence of a well-developed regional security regime; it is simply the immediate consequence of the end of the cold war.

This favorable situation will not last for many years. A process of arms modernization is under way in Asia, and the danger of an arms race arising later in this decade is all too real. China's military modernization program is a source of concern throughout the region. Japan too continues to develop its military strength, and it has in place the technology to make a quick jump to a new military posture should it feel the need to do so. Both North and South Korea are heavily armed, and the danger of nuclear proliferation on the peninsula is real and immediate. The "China-Taiwan nexus probably constitutes the most vibrant arms market in the world today," according to one observer,[29] and several countries in the region, especially Japan, China, and both Koreas, possess sophisticated arms manufacturing capabilities. Several states in Asia either already possess chemical and/or nuclear weapons, or have the technological know-how to do so.

The U.S. military presence in the region is reassuring. The Clinton administration has decided on a military strategy that will keep forces in Korea and Japan at current levels, and that reaffirms in unambiguous terms the U.S. commitment to the security of South Korea. Leaving aside the Korean situation, however, the U.S. military presence in Asia is reassuring precisely because threats to security in the region are perceived to be so low. U.S. involvement in another land war in Asia is inconceivable, with the important exception of a North Korean attack on the South. Territorial disputes in the South China Sea and elsewhere are unlikely to engage U.S. naval forces unless free navigation of sea lanes were to be threatened directly. Withdrawal of U.S. forces from Asia would create a dangerous vacuum, but their presence alone cannot provide a sufficient security umbrella for the region.

The remaining years of this decade provide a window of opportunity to establish a new security regime in Asia. If the window closes without the essential elements of this system having been put in place, Asia will emerge early in the next century armed to the teeth, with several countries possessing nuclear and other weapons of mass destruction, with naval forces capable of interfering with

the free flow of maritime commerce, and with a heightening of
suspicions and tensions directly threatening vital U.S. national interests. Moving vigorously to avoid this scenario is a challenge that
will confront the United States for the rest of the 1990s.

The establishment of an ASEAN Regional Forum on security,
agreed upon at the Post-Ministerial Conference of ASEAN in July
1993 and consisting of eighteen countries in the Asian-Pacific region,[30] is a useful step in the right direction. It may be able to play
an important role in promoting a variety of confidence-building
measures, including exchanging views on military doctrine and
strategy, devising approaches to make real military expenditures
more transparent, and perhaps finding other ways to encourage
the peaceful settlement of territorial and other disputes. Actively
engaging China in these discussions is of paramount importance.
Getting China's military leaders and senior civilian officials to talk
the same security language as the United States, Japan, and other
countries in the region would be a major accomplishment for a
regional security forum. It is comparable to the role arms control
negotiations played in fostering better understanding and reducing dangers of miscalculation in U.S.–Soviet relations during the
cold war era.

However, a regional forum with members extending from
Russia to Papua New Guinea is hardly the venue for grappling
with serious regional security issues. The potential threats to peace
and security in Asia are diverse and require multiple mechanisms
to address them. Thought needs to be given particularly to establishing multilateral consultative mechanisms in Northeast Asia en-
compassing the six powers in the region (the United States, Japan,
South and North Korea, China, and Russia).

How Japan relates to these regional and subregional security
dialogues is a key and vexing question. Japanese leaders were
among the first to float the idea of a regional dialogue on security
matters. Yet the Japanese constitution, as currently interpreted,
prohibits Japanese participation in collective security. Even having
uniformed officials participate in regional security discussions is
bound to pose politically sensitive problems for the Japanese government. A more active Japanese security role, through participation in new U.N. sponsored peacekeeping operations, for example,

would be even more controversial. Over the long run, however, one of the positive benefits of creating regional fora, at both governmental and private levels, will be to engage Japanese more centrally in considering how to deal with the collective security problems of the region.

The conventional wisdom today is that we have entered an era in which geoeconomics rather than geopolitics dominates the international system. Yet providing for national security remains the primary obligation of governments in a world of independent states. It should not be necessary to denigrate the importance of economics, especially in the context of Asian policy, to draw the attention of policy makers to the dangers inherent in treating Asia's security situation with benign neglect. Rather, policy makers must grasp the need for new strategies to forestall the emergence of potentially serious security problems.

A Final Word

The challenge to U.S. policy in Asia is to continue to provide a leadership role in the region. In his Farewell Address, George Washington warned the nation about the dangers of getting involved in "entangling alliances." But in the Asia of the twenty-first century, U.S. policy should seek to weave just such a web of entangling relationships with Japan, China, and with other countries that encompass commercial, financial, political, and military issues. The United States can accomplish this only if it is an active player—in all these dimensions—in Asia.

Notes

[1] *The Economist*, July 31, 1993, p. 13.
[2] *The Economist*, July 31, 1993, p. 13.
[3] See Winston Lord, "A New Pacific Community: Ten Goals for American Policy" (opening statement at the confirmation hearings for Lord, assistant secretary of state-designate, Bureau of East Asian and Pacific Affairs), March 31, 1993.
[4] United States International Trade Commission (USITC) (1993), pp. 63ff.
[5] International Monetary Fund statistics cited in USITC (1993), pp. 64ff.
[6] APEC is discussed later in this chapter. Its members are Australia, Brunei, Canada, China, Hong Kong, Indonesia, Japan, Korea, Malaysia, New Zealand, the Philippines, Singapore, Taiwan, Thailand, and the United States.

[7] Figures on Japan's trade with Asia are drawn from the Ministry of International Trade and Industries annual White Papers (the *Tsusho Hakusho*).

[8] USITC (1993), p. 76.

[9] *The Economist,* June 12, 1993.

[10] Cited in *The Economist,* June 12, 1993.

[11] *The Economist,* May 8, 1993.

[12] *The Economist,* May 8, 1993, p. 72.

[13] See Courtis (1992), p. 47.

[14] On this point, see also Carnegie Endowment for International Peace (1993).

[15] See Curtis (1993a).

[16] For an excellent analysis of these enduring traits in Japanese foreign policy, see Baker (1993).

[17] See on this point Morley (1993).

[18] On the coming "clash of civilizations," see Huntington (1993).

[19] See the speech by President Clinton, "Building a New Pacific Community," to students and faculty at Waseda University, Tokyo, July 7, 1993.

[20] On U.S.–ASEAN relations, see Bresnan (1993).

[21] These figures are cited in Carnegie Endowment for International Peace (1993).

[22] See USITC (1993), p. 129.

[23] USITC (1993), p. 87.

[24] Analysis of U.S.–Japan economic frictions in terms of this kind of "game" is offered by Campbell (1993).

[25] See Chalmers Johnson, "Where's Clinton on Asia?" *New York Times,* February 8, 1993.

[26] See James Baker, "The U.S. and Japan: Global Partners in a Pacific Community," address before the Japan Institute for International Affairs, November 11, 1991.

[27] See USITC (1993), p. xvii.

[28] See Elek (1992).

[29] See Klare (1993), p. 140. I believe Klare is mistaken in viewing current military spending programs in Asia as representing a major arms race.

[30] The eighteen members of the Asia Regional Forum are the six ASEAN states, seven "dialogue partners" (the United States, Japan, Korea, Canada, Australia, New Zealand, and the European Community), China, Russia, Vietnam, Laos, and Papua New Guinea.

Bibliography

Allison, Roy. 1993. "Russian Defence Planning: Military Doctrine and Force Structures." In Wallin (1993).

Bergsten, C. Fred, and Marcus Noland. 1993. *Reconcilable Differences? United States–Japan Economic Conflict.* Washington, D.C.: Institute for International Economics.

Blaker, Michael. 1993. "Evaluating Japan's Diplomatic Performance." In Curtis 1993b.

Blair, Bruce. 1993. *The Logic of Accidental Nuclear War.* Washington, D.C.: The Brookings Institution.

Bosworth, Barry. 1993. *Saving and Investment in a Global Economy.* Washington, D.C.: The Brookings Institution.

Bresnan, Jack. 1993. *Beyond Subic Bay: Southeast Asia and the New American Agenda.* New York: Council on Foreign Relations.

Brown, Eugene. 1993. "The Debate Over Japan's Strategic Future." *Asian Survey,* June 33:6.

Campbell, John. 1993. "The United States and Japan: Games that Work." In Curtis 1993b.

Carnegie Endowment for International Peace. 1993. *Rethinking Japan Policy.* A report of the U.S.–Japan study group. Washington, D.C.: Carnegie Endowment.

Courtis, Kenneth. 1992. "Japan's Next Leap Forward." *Asia, Inc.,* December.

Curtis, Gerald L. 1993a. "Sino-Japanese Relations Through Chinese Eyes." *Institute Reports.* New York: East Asian Institute, Columbia University, June 1993.

———. ed. 1993b. *Japan's Foreign Policy After the Cold War: Coping With Change.* New York: Lexington Books.

Dobson, Wendy. 1993. *Japan in East Asia: Trading and Investment Strategies.* Singapore: Institute of Southeast Asian Studies.

Elek, Andrew. 1992. "Trade Policy Options for the Asia Pacific Region in the 1990's: The Potential of Open Regionalism." Paper presented at the joint session of the American Economic Association and the American Committee on Asian Economic Studies, annual conference, New Orleans, January 3, 1992. Mimeo.

Frankel, Jeffrey. April 1992. "Is Japan Creating a Yen Bloc in East Asia and the Pacific?" Cambridge: National Bureau of Economic Research, NBER Working Paper No. 4050.

Fung, Edmund S.K. 1991. *The Diplomacy of Imperial Retreat: Britain's South China Policy, 1924–1931.* Hong Kong: Oxford University Press.

Gilpin, Robert. 1981. *War and Change in World Politics.* Cambridge: Cambridge University Press.

Ginsburg, George. 1993. "The End of Sino-Russian Territorial Disputes?" *The Journal of East Asian Affairs,* Winter/Spring 7:1.

Glaser, Bonnie S. 1993. "China's Security Perceptions: Interests and Ambitions." *Asian Survey,* March 33:3.

Green, Michael J. 1993. *Arms, Technology and Alliance: Japan's Search for Autonomous Defense Production, 1945–1993.* Unpublished Ph.D. dissertation, Johns Hopkins School of International Studies.

Grieco, Joseph. 1988. "Anarchy and the Limits of Cooperation: A Realist Critique of the Newest Liberal Institutionalism." *International Organization* 42:485–507.

Harding, Harry. 1992. *A Fragile Relationship: The United States and China since 1972.* Washington, D.C.: The Brookings Institution.

Harrison, Selig S. 1991. "A Chance for Detente in Korea." *World Policy Journal,* Fall.

Huntington, Samuel. 1993. "The Clash of Civilizations?" *Foreign Affairs* 72:3.

Iriye, Akira. 1972. *Pacific Estrangement: Japanese and American Expansion, 1897–1911.* Cambridge: Harvard University Press.

———. 1990. "Chinese-Japanese Relations, 1945–1990." *The China Quarterly,* December.

———. 1993. *China and Japan in the Global Setting.* Cambridge: Harvard University Press.

Jencks, Harlan W. 1992. "Chinese Evaluations of 'Desert Storm': Implications for PRC Security." *The Journal of East Asian Affairs*, Summer/Fall 6:2.

Jeshurun, Chandran. ed. 1993. *China, India, Japan and the Security of Southeast Asia*. Singapore: Institute of Southeast Asian Studies.

Kaye, Lincoln. 1993. "Bordering on Peace: China and India Ease Tensions along Frontier." *Far Eastern Economic Review*, September 16.

Keohane, Robert, and Joseph Nye. 1989. *Power and Interdependence*. 2nd. ed. Boston: Scott, Foresman and Company.

Kissinger, Henry, and Cyrus Vance. 1988. "Bipartisan Objective for Foreign Policy," *Foreign Affairs*, Summer 66:5.

Klare, Michael. 1993. "The Next Great Arms Race." *Foreign Affairs*, Summer.

Krause, Lawrence. 1982. *U.S. Economic Policy Toward the Association of Southeast Asian Nations: Meeting the Japanese Challenge*. Washington, D.C.: The Brookings Institution.

Kristof, Nicholas D. 1993. "The Rise of China." *Foreign Affairs*, November/December.

Lawrence, Robert, and Charles Schultze. eds. *An American Trade Strategy: Options for the 1990s*. Washington, D.C.: The Brookings Institution.

Lincoln, Edward. 1990. *Japan's Unequal Trade*. Washington, D.C.: The Brookings Institution.

McNaugher, Thomas. 1993. "Reforging Northeast Asia's Dagger? U.S. Strategy and Korean Unification." *The Brookings Review*, Summer.

Mastanduno, Michael. 1991. "Do Relative Gains Matter? America's Responseto Japanese Industrial Policy." *International Security* 16: 73–113.

Mearsheimer, John. 1990. "Back to the Future: Instability in Europe after the Cold War." *International Security*, Summer 15:1.

Morley, James W. 1993. "Japan and the Asia-Pacific, Defining a New Role." *Asian Update*. New York: The Asia Society, May 1993.

Nishihara, Masashi. 1975. *The Japanese and Sukarno's Indonesia: Tokyo-Jakarta Relations*. Hawaii: University of Hawaii East-West Center.

Okazaki, Hisahiko. 1986. *A Grand Strategy for Japanese Defense*. New York: University Press of America.

Perkins, Dwight. 1986. *China: Asia's Next Economic Giant?* Seattle: University of Washington Press.

Pollack, Jonathan D. 1990. "The Sino-Japanese Relationship and East Asian Security: Patterns and Implications." *The China Quarterly*, December.

Richardson, Michael. 1991. "China Raises Spratly Fears." *Asia-Pacific Defence Review*, February.

————. 1992. "Deep Concern Over U.S.–Japan Relations." *Asia-Pacific Defence Reporter*, February–March.

Sait, Shiro. 1990. *Japan at the Summit: Japan's Role in the Western Alliance and Asian Pacific Co-operation.* London: Routledge for the Royal Institute of International Affairs.

Sakamoto, Masahiro. 1993. *Kokusai seiji keizai ron* [The international political economy]. Tokyo: Sekaishisosha.

Sandholtz, Wayne., et al. 1992. *The Highest Stakes: The Economic Foundations of the Next Security System.* New York: Oxford University Press.

Shambaugh, David. 1992. "China's Security Policy in the Post–Cold War Era." *Survival*, Summer.

Shibusawa, Masahide. 1984. *Japan and the Asian Pacific Region: Profile of Change.* Beckenham, Kent: Croom Helm for the Royal Institute of International Affairs.

Soeya, Yoshihide. 1993. "Japan's Policy towards Southeast Asia: Anatomy of 'Autonomous Diplomacy' and the American Factor." In Jeshurun 1993.

Sullivan, Roger W. 1992. "Discarding the China Card." *Foreign Policy*, Spring.

Tanino, Skutaro. 1988. *Ajia no Shooryuu: Gaikookan no mita Yakushin Kankoku.* Tokyo: Seikai no Ugoki Shakan.

Thom, Katarina, and Ian A. Macauley. 1992. *Crusaders of the Rising Sun: A Study of Japanese Managers in Asia.* Singapore: Longman Singapore Publishers.

Tokunaga, Shojiro. ed. 1992. *Japan's Foreign Investment and Asian Economic Interdependence: Production, Trade, and Financial Systems.* Tokyo: University of Tokyo Press.

Tyson, Laura D'Andrea. 1990. "Managed Trade: Making the Best of the Second Best." In Lawrence and Schultze 1990.

————. 1992. *Who's Bashing Whom? Trade Conflict in High-Technology Industries.* Washington, D.C.: Institute for International Economics.

United States International Trade Commission (USITC). 1993. *East Asia: Regional Economic Integration and Implications for the United States.* USITC publication 2621. Washington, D.C.: USITC.

Wallin, Lars B. ed. *Lectures and Contributions to East European Studies at FOA.* The Swedish National Defence Research Establishment, 30 July.

Waltz, Kenneth N. 1993. "The Emerging Structure of International Politics." *International Security*, Fall 18:2.

Wang, Qingxin Ken. 1993. "Recent Japanese Economic Diplomacy in China: Political Alignment in a Changing World Order." *Asian Survey*, June 33:6.

Whiting, Allen S., and Xin Jianfei. 1990–91. "Sino-Japanese Relations: Pragmatism and Passion." *World Policy Journal,* Winter 8:1.

Yu, Bin. 1993. "Sino-Russian Military Relations: Implications for Asian-Pacific Security." *Asian Survey,* March 33:3.

Zhang, Yongjin. 1991. *China in the International System: 1918–20.* New York: St. Martin's Press.

Final Report
of the
Eighty-Fourth American
Assembly

At the close of their discussions, the participants in the Eighty-fourth American Assembly, on "The United States and Japan in Asia: Challenges for U.S. Policy," at Arden House, Harriman, New York, November 11–14, 1993, reviewed as a group the following statement. This statement represents general agreement; however, it should be understood that not everyone agreed with all of it.

The leaders who will be crossing the Pacific to attend the Asia-Pacific meeting in Seattle later this week represent a region that is the most populous and economically fastest growing in the world. This region presents enormous economic opportunities for the United States, but also poses momentous political and economic challenges. The future economic well-being of the American people depends to a degree that many Americans do not yet realize on how well the United States takes advantage of these opportunities and how successful it is in meeting the challenges produced by economic dynamism and political change in the Asia-Pacific.

No region of the world is more important to U.S. vital interests than the Asia-Pacific. The region absorbs more American exports

($130 billion in 1992) each year than any other region in the world. Millions of American jobs depend directly or indirectly on commerce with Asia. The United States has fought three wars in Asia in fifty years. The American people have a vital stake in the prevention of future conflict in the region.

U.S. government attention to the Asia-Pacific region has accelerated in recent months with President Clinton's trip to Japan and Korea in July and his meeting with other leaders from the Asia-Pacific in Seattle. In this new post–cold war era and in an age when economic power has become more diffuse, the United States needs to rethink its policy toward Asia. There is a need to construct a more equally balanced partnership with Japan, establish a mutually beneficial relationship with China, respond to opportunities created by the dynamic economic growth of Southeast Asia, decide how to deal with current and potential threats to regional security, and develop a strategy to help shape an Asia-Pacific regional community. Asia welcomes continuous engagement of the United States in the region, especially within the context of regional, multilateral processes and institutions that provide mechanisms for regular trans-Pacific consultations.

For the past several days, sixty-two individuals from countries on both sides of the Pacific Ocean met at this American Assembly to consider these questions. The discussions revealed among most of the participants important areas of consensus, none more important than the belief that the United States has an important leadership role to play in the Asia-Pacific, and that a failure of the United States and Japan to successfully manage their bilateral relationship would have profoundly negative consequences for the entire region.

There also were important areas of disagreement. How the United States could most effectively pursue issues of human rights and democracy, what its military commitments should be in the region, and how it should balance unilateral, bilateral, and multilateral approaches in pursuing its economic interests in the region were some of the issues that divided not only participants from different countries, but in many cases people from the same country.

The following is a summary of major points of relevance to U.S. policy that were made in these extensive discussions.

The U.S. Context

Confusion and ambivalence within the American public about what roles the United States should play in the world generally are also evident in attitudes about Asia. Americans appear to be perplexed about what the United States should be doing in a world where they are deeply concerned about U.S. competitiveness and where the broader national interests cannot be described in stark ideological terms, as they could be during the cold war.

A startling note of pessimism runs through American public perceptions of Asia-Pacific economic growth. The general public tends to perceive such growth more as a threat than as an opportunity or as an engine for American prosperity.

Americans have yet to make the necessary adjustment to the new realities of the Asia-Pacific and of the United States. It is in U.S. interests to continue to play a leadership role in the Asia-Pacific, but now the United States has to do so in an environment in which its relative economic weight has been reduced. American political leaders have not yet convincingly articulated a policy that copes with this reality in a way that the American public can understand and support.

A new leadership role for the United States in the Asia-Pacific requires attention to several issues. Government leaders have to develop a more consultative style in dealing with Asian countries. How issues and people are approached takes on particular importance in cultures that appreciate both form and substance. Many Asian participants, especially from smaller countries in the region, stressed this matter of style and mutual respect.

The American people and their government need to commit to a broader engagement in Asia if they are to be successful there. American participants pointed to the perennial problem of the relative lack of Asian expertise in key policy-making positions in the U.S. government, and the small number of people with specialized knowledge of Asia handling trade and other issues with Japan in particular, and with Asia more generally. The private sector needs to give more sustained attention to the Asia-Pacific, and devote more resources, human and financial, if American business is going to be competitive in the region.

Discussion of the issue of human rights revealed sharp differences on the appropriateness of making human rights a high foreign policy priority for the United States. Many, though not all, Asian participants were critical of U.S. human rights policies. Some believed that they masked economic and other concerns; others felt that the way they have been pursued has proved to be counterproductive; and still others were of the view that they are simply inappropriate. American participants were by no means uniform in their views on this issue. Some believed that it should be a high priority, and most agreed that human rights constitute a legitimate foreign policy goal. Disagreements were more over tactics, and how to balance a concern about human rights with other important goals of U.S. policy in Asia.

Finally, in exercising its leadership role in the Asia-Pacific, the United States has to take into account the new level of self confidence and national assertiveness that characterizes Asian countries today. Several participants noted, in this regard, that the United States no longer can use the fear of other Asian countries about Japanese domination to gain leverage in its own dealings with Asia.

The Regional Economy

America's future relationship with the Asia-Pacific region has to contend with a different underlying economic context than in previous decades. The United States is experiencing a frustratingly modest economic recovery, with disappointing job growth. Japan is burdened by a deep recession, even as growing Japanese export surpluses heighten tensions with trading partners. Much of the rest of Asia, especially China, enjoys an economic boom. Thus, participants underscored the paradox of immense opportunity, combined with considerable concern over how existing and potential points of friction can be effectively dealt with.

The United States is Asia's best customer, and now exports more to Asia than to either Western Europe or Latin America. Economic relations with Asia go well beyond traditional merchandise trade, involving an array of business services, financial flows, and technology transfers. The participants stressed the mutual benefits of increasingly open and growing markets. There has been considerable continuity from one U.S. administration to the next in defining market access as an essential element of vital U.S. national interests in the Asian region. Protectionist policies do not serve the long-term interests of the Asia-Pacific region. Tariff and nontariff barriers, weak protection of intellectual property rights, restrictions on direct investment, and corrupt practices impede foreign access to markets. While reduction of these barriers is most appropriately negotiated gradually and in multilateral fora, lack of progress toward their resolution makes unilateral or bilateral approaches more likely.

In response to a combination of persistent macroeconomic, sectoral, and structural difficulties, the United States and Japan have launched a series of negotiations under the recently concluded Framework Agreement. While many saw this as merely the latest effort to cope with rather than resolve fundamental economic tensions, it was generally agreed that it offers a useful mechanism for identifying points of friction and addressing economic problems. Biannual meetings between the president and the prime minister will improve the possibility of sustained, continuing attention to these issues. But some participants were concerned that the process not be undermined by the apparent U.S. desire to set quantitative targets with implied threats of retaliation. Others argued that only by setting goals of some kind could real progress be expected.

There was agreement that trade imbalances are largely the product of a combination of U.S. and Japanese macroeconomic problems. Participants agreed that Japan should cut taxes to spur domestic demand. There was also a strong feeling that the U.S. budget deficit remains a fundamental cause of America's trade deficit, and that more deficit reduction measures may be needed to reduce the current account imbalance and improve the potential for U.S. long-term growth.

Sectoral disputes are particularly difficult to resolve. Many participants appreciate that U.S. efforts to open the Japanese market to both trade and investment can benefit everyone. Nevertheless, there was considerable concern that U.S. threats against Japan could get out of control and result in protectionist policies affecting the entire region.

Rapid Chinese growth offers enormous opportunities to U.S., Japanese, and other Asian exporters and investors. Most participants were confident that China would continue to achieve fast rates of growth despite domestic political uncertainties and the need to make fundamental structural changes. China's rapid economic growth and burgeoning exports also impose considerable adjustment costs on the rest of the Asia-Pacific region.

Many participants expressed concerns about U.S. policy linking economic and noneconomic issues such as human rights and missile exports. A number of Asian participants believed that this approach is counterproductive to efforts to incorporate China more fully into the region, and to develop constructive dialogues on political and human rights issues. While some Americans shared this perspective, others felt strongly that the U.S. threat of economic sanctions was directly responsible for changes in Chinese human rights and weapons export policies.

Cambodia, Laos, and Vietnam have also entered a reform period. Vietnam has expressed its willingness to join the Association of Southeast Asian Nations (ASEAN). The United States, Japan, and other Asian countries should work together to find ways to integrate Vietnam into the dynamic Asia-Pacific economy.

Participants agreed that the highest priority in managing the international economy is the completion of the General Agreement on Tariffs and Trade (GATT) Uruguay Round negotiations. The Asia-Pacific Economic Cooperation (APEC) organization can be a useful vehicle for promoting cooperative relations among Asia-Pacific economies supportive of regional and global economic liberalization. Many participants believed that a failure of the North American Free Trade Agreement (NAFTA) to pass the Congress would encourage protectionist pressures in the United States. No one supported an Asian economic bloc as a preferred option, although some Asian participants saw it as a possible fallback if the global and Asia-Pacific trading systems break down.

Regional Security

The collapse of the Soviet Union and the end of cold war tensions have created an opportunity to develop a new, constructive pattern of security relations in the Asia-Pacific region. At the same time, these structural changes have caused anxieties about the future roles of China, Japan, and Russia, and the relationship among them. There is also increased military spending in the region. Moreover, despite the end of the cold war, some real or potential security problems remain, including the rising tensions on the Korean Peninsula, uncertainty about the future of Taiwan, and unresolved territorial disputes.

There was broad agreement that a continued U.S. security presence in the region remains critical to maintaining regional stability, particularly in this time of uncertainty. U.S. political leadership will be challenged, however, to articulate the reasons for its post–cold war military commitments and presence in Asia and the Western Pacific to the American public in a clear and convincing manner. In view of Asia's growing economic importance, the United States has a vital stake in Asia-Pacific regional stability. Any abrupt major reduction in U.S. forces and commitments could aggravate anxieties, trigger a regional arms race, encourage proliferation of weapons of mass destruction in Asia, and contribute to tensions, possibly unleashing forces leading to conflict among major countries in the region seeking to establish a hegemonic position.

The U.S.–Japan and U.S.–South Korean security treaties are critical to the credibility of the U.S. presence and maintenance of the regional order. The U.S.–Japan treaty helps assure regional stability by ensuring that Japan remain secure in its current military posture, and providing forward based military facilities at moderate cost to the United States. Japanese and other Asian participants also acknowledged the value of these security relationships for the countries concerned, and recognized that increased burden sharing by U.S. allies is an essential element in their maintenance.

The most immediate security problem in the region lies on the Korean Peninsula, where North Korea's failure to accept full inspections by the International Atomic Energy Agency (IAEA) raises serious questions for the security of its neighbors and poses a wider global danger to the nonproliferation regime. All countries in the region have a strong and common stake in ensuring that

North Korea uphold its IAEA obligations, and develop peaceful relations with the South and other countries. Coordination among the United States, Japan, and South Korea and close consultations with China and Russia are especially critical in this situation. China has a vital role to play in defusing tensions and building contacts between North Korea and the rest of the international community.

A number of participants expressed concern that China's military modernization program, even if pursued largely for defensive reasons, will increase the sense of insecurity among China's neighbors and thus possibly spark a regional arms build-up. Other participants emphasized that China cannot afford confrontational policies toward other major Asia-Pacific countries, because these would jeopardize China's economic relations and its economic development, its highest priority. These participants felt China's military modernization programs and foreign policies are misunderstood in the region.

Bilateral and multilateral dialogues and other means of increasing transparency regarding military doctrines, budgets, and policies will reduce misunderstandings and ameliorate security concerns. It is especially important that countries with large military establishments maintain a high level of openness regarding their military programs, if they want to avoid tensions with each other and their neighbors. The resumption of high-level Sino-American contacts, including military ones, the initiation of a Sino-Japanese security dialogue, and multilateral security discussions can play a positive role in reducing anxieties and misunderstandings. The expansion of dialogue and economic contacts across the Taiwan Strait also facilitates regional peace.

The Cambodian settlement and the successful U.N. peacekeeping operation there demonstrate the utility of collaborative, multilateral means of addressing serious regional conflicts. Japan, China, ASEAN, the United States, and Australia all played important roles in helping the Khmer groups reach a settlement and in implementing the U.N. operation. The participants encouraged an expansion of such Japanese diplomatic and nonmilitary security roles, and Japan's continued involvement in U.N. peacekeeping activities.

The new security environment requires a combination of bilateral and multilateral security relationships and institutions. The participants encouraged multilateral security dialogue both at the official level and among nonofficial groups. The ASEAN Regional Forum can be especially useful as a new regional mechanism for political-security discussions among Asia-Pacific countries. For the foreseeable future, however, a strong network of U.S. bilateral security relations continues to be an essential underpinning for regional stability.

Several Asia-Pacific countries, as well as the United States, also face a number of problems that arise from rapid economic and population growth. They include environmental degradation, deforestation, inadequate water supply, toxic waste management, poor air quality, pollution of coastal waters, over-fishing, erosion of biodiversity, population growth and migration, and AIDS. Dealing with these issues will not be easy, but effective solutions will require cooperation that crosses national boundaries through regional and other multilateral fora. Failure to address these issues in a timely fashion will constrain economic growth.

Conclusion

The November 19–20 Asia-Pacific leaders meeting conference on an island in Puget Sound is a truly historic occasion. It will be the first meeting involving the leaders of the major Asia-Pacific nations. The occasion is important not only for developing greater personal rapport and contact among these leaders, but also because it symbolizes the importance to the United States as well as to other Asia-Pacific nations of the future development of an economic community of nations on both sides of the Pacific.

The leaders meeting, as well as the regular annual meeting of the economic and foreign ministers of the members of the APEC forum that precedes it, provides an opportunity for the nations of the region to review and strengthen their cooperation.

APEC is the only governmental forum for Asia-Pacific regional consultations. Its fifteen current members are major participants in Asia-Pacific economic relations. Initially conceived as an informal mechanism for regional dialogue on economic issues, APEC has created a small secretariat and a program of practical activities that can become the building blocks for sustainable development and cooperation. But it remains fragile. Participants agreed that the leaders should continue their efforts to strengthen APEC, while avoiding unrealistic expectations or forcing the pace. The participants also stressed that while the United States is expected to play a leadership role, this role will be in combination with other APEC members and should not be a dominant one.

APEC is also significant because it includes mainland China, Taiwan, and Hong Kong, and is thus a forum for discussion of the economic dimensions of the relationships of what some call "greater China" with the other Pacific economies. The economic dynamism of China and its economic integration are perhaps the greatest forces reshaping the economy of the Asia-Pacific today. The relationships among these Chinese communities, and the political evolution of each of them, are also of tremendous significance to the region as a whole. The United States and other Asia-Pacific countries need to be fully prepared to understand and develop appropriate policy processes for dealing with the multiple challenges presented by China.

Greater cooperation between the United States and Japan is essential to meeting this and other regional and global challenges. Since Japan and the United States are the world's two largest and technologically most sophisticated economies accounting for almost 40 percent of the world's production of goods and services, their cooperation is vital to addressing effectively many of the world's major problems. These include challenges in such areas as environment, health, population, arms control, and improved human rights. Both countries have a stake in demonstrating that they can work together. Such efforts at cooperation are not confined to the governments. Private sector and nongovernmental organizations have a vital role to play in identifying issues, developing feasible and imaginative modes of cooperation, and in developing broad linkages between their respective societies and bridging with other countries.

In the final analysis, a more effective U.S. policy toward the Asia-Pacific region requires a greater degree of American public understanding and appreciation for this region and the opportunities it provides. The United States needs individuals with the expertise, knowledge of languages, and other cultural skills to engage fully and effectively with the region. All participants believed that it is vital for the United States to invest in developing these skills in its young men and women.

Participants
The Eighty-Fourth American Assembly

C. MICHAEL AHO
Senior International
    Economist & Vice President
Prudential Securities, Inc.
New York, New York

P. BAI AKRIDGE
Academic Relations Manager
IBM Corporation
Norwalk, Connecticut

MICHAEL H. ARMACOST
Senior Fellow
Asia/Pacific Research Center
Stanford University
Stanford, California

LEE MICHAEL
    BERMINGHAM
Professional Staff
The Australian Labor Party
Brisbane

RICHARD BUSH
Professional Staff Member
Committee on Foreign Affairs
U.S. House of Representatives
Washington, DC

† GERALD L. CURTIS
Former Director, East Asian
    Institute
Professor of Political Science
Columbia University
New York, New York

DOUGLAS N. DAFT
President
Pacific Group
Coca-Cola International
Atlanta, Georgia

JING-PING DING
Deputy Director
Institute of Industrial
    Economics
Chinese Academy of Social
    Sciences
Beijing

PEGGY DULANY
President
The Synergos Institute
New York, New York

STEPHEN ECTON
Director
Office of Japanese Affairs
Bureau of East Asian & Pacific
    Affairs
U.S. Department of State
Washington, DC

ERIN M. ENDEAN
Director
Hills & Company,
    International Consultants
Washington, DC

JESUS P. ESTANISLAO
President
Southeast Asian Science
    Foundation, Inc.
Manila

PAUL M. EVANS
Director
Joint Centre for Asia Pacific
    Studies
University of Toronto-York
    University
Toronto, Ontario

GLEN S. FUKUSHIMA
Regional Director, Public
Policy & Business
Development
AT&T Japan Ltd.
Tokyo

FRANCIS FUKUYAMA
Resident Consultant
The RAND Corporation
Washington, DC

PETER F. GEITHNER
Director, Asia Programs
The Ford Foundation
New York, New York

JAMES O.
GOLDSBOROUGH
Foreign Affairs Columnist
San Diego Union-Tribune
San Diego, California

MAKOTO IOKIBE
Professor of History
Faculty of Law
Kobe University
Kobe

MERIT E. JANOW
Senior Research Associate
East Asian Institute
Columbia University
New York, New York

†GUOXING JI
Professor of Political Science
Director, Department of Asian
Pacific Studies
Shanghai Institute for
International Studies
Shanghai

DEXIANG JIN
Vice President
China Institute of
Contemporary International
Relations
Beijing

SIDNEY JONES
Director
Asia Watch
New York, New York

BILAHARI KAUSIKAN
Director of Directorate III
Ministry of Foreign Affairs
Singapore

ANDREW B. KIM
President
Sit-Kim International
Investment Associates, Inc.
New York, New York

TAKASHI KIUCHI
Chief Economist
The Long-Term Credit Bank
of Japan, Ltd.
Tokyo

AKIRA KOJIMA
Senior Editor & International
News Editor
Editorial Bureau
Nihon Keizai Shimbun, Inc.
Tokyo

**ROGER KUBARYCH
Manager
Henry Kaufman & Company,
Inc.
New York, New York

EDUARDO LACHICA
Editor
*The Asian Wall Street Journal
Weekly*
New York, New York

PAUL MAIDMENT
Senior Editor
Newsweek International
New York, New York

MARK MASON
Assistant Professor
School of Organization &
Management
Yale University
New Haven, Connecticut

THOMAS L. McNAUGHER
Senior Fellow
Foreign Policy Studies
Program
The Brookings Institution
Washington, DC

*CHARLES E. MORRISON
Director
Program on International
Economics & Politics
East-West Center
Honolulu, Hawaii

†DATO MUSA HITAM
Former Deputy Prime Minister
and currently Malaysian
Ambassador to U.N.
Commission on Human
Rights
Kuala Lumpur

RISABURO NEZU
Deputy Director-General for
Trade Negotiation
Ministry of International
Trade & Industry
Tokyo

KAZUO NUKAZAWA
Managing Director
Keidanren (Japan Federation
of Economic Organizations)
Tokyo

MICHEL OKSENBERG
President
East-West Center
Honolulu, Hawaii

††HISASHI OWADA
Advisor to the Minister of
Foreign Affairs
Tokyo

†CHOON-HO PARK
Director
Asiatic Research Center
Korea University
Seoul

**HUGH PATRICK
R. D. Calkins Professor of
International Business
Graduate School of Business
Columbia University
New York, New York

KIEN PHAM
Special Advisor to the
President
Tenneco Inc.
Houston, Texas

EDWARD POLLAK
Senior Vice President
Olin Corporation
Stamford, Connecticut

JONATHAN C. RAUCH
National Journal
Washington, DC

WILLIAM A. REINSCH
Legislative Assistant
Office of John D. Rockefeller
IV
United States Senate
Washington, DC

LINDA RICCI
Senior Producer
The MacNeil/Lehrer
Newshour
New York, New York

††JOHN D. ROCKEFELLER
IV
United States Senate
Washington, DC

YUKIO SATOH
Director-General
North American Affairs
Bureau
Ministry of Foreign Affairs
Tokyo

SICHAN SIV
Senior Vice President
Commonwealth Associates
New York, New York

HADI SOESASTRO
Executive Director
Centre for Strategic &
International Studies
Jakarta

YOSHIHIDE SOEYA
Associate Professor of Political
Science
Faculty of Law
Keio University
Tokyo

YOUNG-OH SONG
Senior Coordinator for Policy
Planning
Ministry of Foreign Affairs
Korean Mission to the United
Nations
New York, New York

BRUCE STOKES
International Economics
Correspondent
National Journal
Washington, DC

JOHN J. STREMLAU
Deputy Director
Policy Planning Staff
U.S. Department of State
Washington, DC

YUKO TANAKA
Professor
Hosei University
Tokyo

NORIHIKO TANIKAWA
Senior Managing Director
Fuji-Wolfensohn International
New York, New York

HUNG-MAO TIEN
President
Institute for National Policy
Research
Taipei

*KO-YUNG TUNG
Partner
O'Melveny & Meyers
New York, New York

*DANIEL UNGER
Assistant Professor
Department of Government
Georgetown University
Washington, DC

DAVID C. UNGER
Editorial Board
The New York Times
New York, New York

MARY
    WADSWORTH-DARBY
Executive Director
America-China Society
New York, New York

S. LINN WILLIAMS
Jones Day Reavis & Pogue
Washington, DC

ALAN WM. WOLFF
Managing Partner
Washington, DC office
Dewey, Ballantine
Washington, DC

CASIMIR YOST
Executive Director
Center for Asian Pacific Affairs
The Asia Foundation
San Francisco, California

**ALICE YOUNG
Partner
Milbank, Tweed, Hadley &
    McCloy
New York, New York

** Discussion Leader
 * Rapporteur
†† Delivered Formal Address
 † Panelist

The American Assembly

The American Assembly was established by Dwight D. Eisenhower at Columbia University in 1950. It holds nonpartisan meetings and publishes authoritative books to illuminate issues of United States policy. An affiliate of Columbia, the Assembly is a national, educational institution incorporated in the state of New York. The Assembly seeks to provide information, stimulate discussion, and evoke independent conclusions on matters of vital public interest.

American Assembly Sessions

At least two national programs are initiated each year. Authorities are retained to write background papers presenting essential data and defining the main issues of each subject.

A group of men and women representing a broad range of experience, competence, and leadership meets for several days to discuss the Assembly topic and consider alternatives for national policy.

All Assemblies follow the same procedure. The background papers are sent to participants in advance of the Assembly. The Assembly meets in small groups for four lengthy periods. All groups use the same agenda. At the close of these informal sessions participants adopt in plenary session a final report of findings and recommendations.

Regional, state, and local Assemblies are held following the national session at Arden House. Assemblies have also been held in England, Switzerland, Malaysia, Canada, the Caribbean, South America, Central America, the Philippines, and Japan. Over one hundred sixty institutions have cosponsored one or more Assemblies.

Arden House

The home of The American Assembly and the scene of the national sessions is Arden House, which was given to Columbia University in 1950 by W. Averell Harriman. E. Roland Harriman joined his brother in contributing toward adaptation of the property for conference purposes. The buildings and surrounding land, known as the Harriman Campus of Columbia University, are fifty miles north of New York City.

CLIFFORD M. HARDIN	Missouri
J. ERIK JONSSON	Texas
KATHLEEN H. MORTIMER	New York
CLARENCE C. WALTON	Pennsylvania

*On leave

Index